Fate Came Calling

by

Kurt Bryan

Other Books by Kurt Bryan

The Game Breaker

The Double Move

Fate Came Calling

Published by Fate Came Calling LLC, Fort Collins, Colorado

ISBN 978-1-7958-6365-0 (Paperback)

Also available in eBook format

Author – Kurt Bryan – kabteamwork@aol.com

Cover design by John Hamilton – John Hamilton Design

Book editing by Ron R. Lee – The Word Bureau, Inc.

Picture attributions are located at the end of the book.

Published and printed in the United States of America.

First paperback edition April 2019

Dedication

With great love and affection for my son, Parker, and stepdaughter, Roxanne. The world is a much better place with the two of you in it.   Kurt Bryan

Acknowledgments

Often, friends and family encourage one to write a book about one's life and adventures. Heaven only knows the number of people who have suggested that I do so. My deepest gratitude goes to my son Timothy, who accepted the challenge to make this book come to fruition. He collaborated with his author friend, Kurt Bryan, to have him transfer the memories of my life into book form. Kurt spent several months bringing the adventures of my life back together on the following pages.

My wife, Ingrid, and I have been living this story together for nearly sixty years, so her editing to verify that the written words match living memories was invaluable. My brother, Lendol, took on the many facets of publishing the book and my son, Brian, kept us energized with book cover design ideas. Cover design by John Hamilton and manuscript editing by Ron Lee was essential.

Like anyone reading this book, the story of one's life is woven from relationships with family, friends, and associates. Therefore, my final acknowledgment is to everyone who has been a part of my wonderful journey through life.   Warren K. Vest

FOREWORD

Author Kurt Bryan and my son Tim have hiked together for several years on the hilly trails east of the San Francisco Bay. Their conversations would often dwell on Kurt's great interest in Tim's flying career. It wasn't unusual for the discussions to gravitate to the years of Tim's youth and the adventures of his father. The two started urging me to write a book about my life. I was retired, playing golf three or four times a week, and serving as president of a large ranch corporation in Idaho. I had passed eighty years of age and had no time to write a book. So, Kurt agreed to apply his writing skills to author this book about many of the adventures of my life.

I thoroughly believe that if you work hard and have the desire, you can succeed. My journey in life, commencing at age eighteen, did not take shape because of hard work. It might have been called "good luck" or "being in the right place at the right time." But I prefer to look back on it as fate. It was *fate* of the best kind, which appears and reappears to this day. Thus, I chose the title *Fate Came Calling*, because fate has brought many positives throughout my life.

As you read my story, you will see where instances of fate guided my destiny in directions I had never anticipated. Although the words *fate* and *destiny* are often considered synonymous, I feel they are quite different. I believe fate puts opportunities in front of us, but our destiny is determined by the decisions we make and actions we take.

In January 1954, had I not noticed a Lloyd's of London letterhead on a sheet of paper lying on my college advisor's desk, or if he had not been called from his office for a few minutes, this journey would never have begun. Had a college student not answered a ringing pay phone in the dormitory hallway and left a note for me to call the Lloyd's office in Chicago, it is very unlikely that this journey would have gotten off the ground.

Without giving away too much, my decision to return the phone call resulted in my participation in a historic overseas advance in animal husbandry and, as it turned out, a trip around the world. This extended adventure at age eighteen exposed me to people, places, and ideas that I otherwise would never have encountered. Each dream that passed through my head seemed to lead to a career as a military pilot. In turn, fate again stepped in to hand me a job as a commercial airline captain. I can't overlook the fact that my job as a pilot flying international routes resulted in my meeting Ingrid Bakker in Germany. We were married thirty months later.

I have lived in Africa, Asia, Europe, and the Middle East, and I have spent wonderful times in Australia.

In our nearly six decades together, Ingrid and I have been blessed with a dear family. Tim brought his wife, Caroline, into the family, and they have given us three wonderful grandchildren, Gentry, Garrett, and Kinnon. Brian and his wife, Drue, have added two little wonders, Talia and Peyton. My hope is that fate will always be as kind to them as it has been to me.

I can't sit with each reader to bring life to my varied experiences. In my stead, Kurt, with his writing skills, will provide you with an enjoyable description of my journey. You are about to meet people in every country I visited, and you will have a chance to join in on adventures experienced around the world.

Bon Voyage,

Warren K. Vest

Dublin, California

April 2019

Dear Johnny & Jeanie,

So good to see you guys. Let us hope the reunions will get us together for years to come.

Hope you enjoy the book and it will remind you of good days from the past.

Warren

PROLOGUE
Present Day

WITHOUT A DOUBT, the greatest surprise of my life has been old age.

As I stand here watching members of my family enjoy themselves in my son Tim's back yard, I am reminded again how unique and remarkable my life has been.

More than eight decades have passed since I was born in Louisburg, Missouri, on April 28, 1935. Back then, many families like ours worked extremely long hours on farms or cattle ranches; it was a gritty lifestyle, yet rewarding in ways that form your life for the duration. Responsibility, dependability, perseverance, and a strong work ethic are a few of the traits I acquired working on the farm.

Even now, as I watch my family enjoy a summer afternoon, I see hints of the totality of my life. I am thankful for the lifespan I've been blessed with. Yes, I am humbled again.

I hear two of my grandchildren giggling and running up the broad staircase behind me. Then, much like life itself, their innocent sounds dissipate.

Most folks I know would describe me as determined, honest, fair, serious, and relatively fun. I have lived most of my days the best way possible, but my shortcomings and ornery stubbornness have always been present.

The primary reasons for my achievements have, at times, doubled as the anchors hitched to my failures. I'm guessing it might be that way for most good people, and I'm comfortable with it. I've never dwelled on my defeats too much.

How did I end up becoming a World Airways pilot and a successful airline executive? I have spent much of my life traversing the globe with teams of dedicated crewmembers and thousands upon thousands of trusting passengers on board my flights. I accrued twenty-seven thousand flight hours as a pilot, a significant number by any stretch.

"Granddad, are you busy right now?" It was my grandson Garrett.

I smiled and replied, "Not at all. What's going on?"

Garrett had a worried look. "Uh… I'm sort of at a crossroads in college right now, and I'm not sure what I want to do with my life. I'd like to ask you a few questions and get some advice."

I was moved beyond words. Here was a vibrant, handsome, bright young man brimming with untapped potential, and he wanted my input. Somehow, I was able to control my emotions. In my professional life, some people had described me as daring. But now, talking with my grandson, I had to work to prevent my eyes from welling up.

I placed my hand on his shoulder and replied, "Let's find a place to chat, and we'll share some stories about when I was in college a long time ago. It's amazing how fast time flies and how one unexpected event can change your life."

Warren and grandson Garrett

CHAPTER 1
1954

THE DRIZZLING RAIN did not bother me much as I strode across the University of Missouri campus in Columbia. The cold air reminded me that winter would be a nasty and bitter slugfest once again. Ice, sleet, and snow were inevitable.

At eighteen years of age, I was close to completing my first semester at Mizzou, majoring in agriculture with a specialty in animal husbandry.

Raising animals and growing food determined the respectable, linear track my life was traveling. I wasn't truly excited about it as a career; it was simply good enough.

The campus was quiet, with most students studying warmly indoors. I finally reached the majestic building where I would meet with my advisor to review my courses for the upcoming spring semester.

I entered the building, bounded up the stairs, and hustled down a long hallway into an empty waiting-room area. The receptionist appeared and soon thereafter I found myself sitting across a desk from my academic advisor.

He was a slight, balding fellow who wore glasses that appeared too big for his face. He said, "Warren, not a bad first semester that you're having. Everything seems to be on pace."

"Thank you," I replied, while understanding I had at least seven more semesters left.

A yellow rotary phone rang and before the second ring, my academic advisor snatched up the receiver. He nodded a couple of times and spoke into the phone, "Okay, I'll be right there."

"Sorry about this, Warren," he told me, "but I need to go downstairs and take care of an issue. I'll return in about ten minutes. Wait here for me, please."

After a few minutes of total boredom, I noticed a formal-looking letter on his desk. It was labeled Lloyd's of London in metallic gold lettering.

I read the notice upside-down from across the desk. Then I got so excited I picked up the stationary and read the letter much more closely. Lloyd's of London had contacted the School of Agriculture at the University of Missouri and at several other universities in search of a student to manage the shipment of livestock from the United States to Australia. The animals would travel on a Swedish freighter named the M.S. Stratus.

Now I was excited. Australia! What would *that* be like? I began to think about the possibilities.

I wrote down the contact information for the Missouri cattle rancher who was sending animals as part of the shipment, as well as information for the Chicago representative of Lloyd's of London. I folded the paper with my notes on it and stuffed it into my pocket, placing the letter back on my advisor's desk. Flushed with adrenaline, I sat back down.

A moment later my advisor walked into the office, closed the door behind him, and apologized for taking longer than expected. "Now we can get you registered for your classes this spring, not to worry."

"Alright, sounds good," I replied. But all I could think about was going to Australia.

After my registration was complete, I asked the advisor about the letter from Lloyd's. He said they wanted to hire a junior or senior to handle such a bigtime responsibility delivering livestock halfway around the world.

I practically skipped my way across campus back to my dormitory. I could not get the potential opportunity out of my mind. I was made for this, but I was only a freshman.

Back at the dorm, I stood in line waiting to use the only pay telephone located on my floor. When I finally got my turn, I dialed the number for the Missouri rancher. When he answered, I introduced myself and explained the reason for my inquiry. He was most friendly and suggested I prepare a short resume and send it directly to the Lloyd's representative in Chicago.

In short order, I had put together my first ever resume for a job.

A few days limped by and my hopes were beginning to fade. When I returned from class the following week, my roommate, David Croslin, handed me a note informing me that "someone from Chicago" had called and asked that I call him back. I collected as many quarters as I could for the pay telephone and dialed the number.

When the Lloyd's representative answered, I introduced myself. He said, "Oh, you're the kid that wants to go to Australia." Before I could reply, he continued with "Do you have a passport, and where can we send the train tickets for your travel to Columbus, Ohio? To be clear, young man, this is not a vacation, it's just a business trip to Australia and back. It's nothing fancy or glamorous. Alright, young man?"

It took a moment for my breathing to return to normal. I explained that I had a relative in Washington, D.C., who could rush the passport, and would the man in Chicago mind sending the train tickets to my home in Buffalo, Missouri?

The Lloyd's agent said five hundred dollars would be enclosed with the train tickets to Columbus. He explained more about the trip, then wished me a safe and good journey and ended the call. That was it! Done!

I was in a state of shock when I called my folks. My dad, Orville, answered the call by stating, "Vest residence, how may I help you?"

He was not a big talker. I replied, "Hi Dad, it's Warren."

When I told him about the livestock shipment headed to Australia and that I had been chosen to ride herd on it, he was speechless. He handed the phone to my mother, Martha. She listened as I told her about my opportunity, more excited than stunned. She couldn't wait to initiate the rapid processing of my passport. Not only was I buzzing with excitement, but now my parents and my six-year-old brother, Lendol, could join me in a state of disbelief.

During the next few days, I completed my final exams to end the semester. My roommate and I headed home to Buffalo for the winter break. The adventure that would change my life forever was about to commence.

Not long after I got home, I received a large envelope special delivery from Chicago. Inside were my train tickets, the promised five hundred dollars, and details about the trip. I was in awe of the level of responsibility I was about to take on.

My dad, as a young, unmarried man, had ventured from Missouri to California, where he joined the Adohr Dairy in Los Angeles. He began as a milker, later becoming a cattle buyer for the dairy traveling throughout the Northwest. He told me about his experiences and the level of maturity he acquired as a result, which helped ease my concerns.

The instructions from Lloyd's directed me to take a passenger train from Springfield, Missouri, to Columbus, Ohio. I was to be met there by an Ohio rancher who was shipping livestock to California, along with an additional two animals he was sending to Australia. A closed-in boxcar was cordoned off for livestock feed and for me in the front section, with the cattle in the rear. The door of the boxcar was kept open for ventilation, with a plank barrier installed across the lower part of the door opening. Our first stop out of Ohio would be in Missouri to pick up additional livestock. I was looking forward to meeting the Missouri rancher who had encouraged me to draft a resume and send it to Lloyd's.

The next destination after Missouri would be San Pedro, California. The cattle shipped from Ohio and Missouri would be Shorthorn beef cattle, along with two Guernsey dairy cows. Most of them would remain in California, but a few of the Shorthorns would be shipped to Australia. Joining the Shorthorns on the Swedish freighter would be eighteen head of pureblood Brahman cattle from the King Ranch in Texas.

CHAPTER 2
1954

WITH THIS LIMITED glimpse of what was to come, it was time for me to get underway. On an icy-cold day in January 1954, my father,

**Warren, Lendol,
Martha & Orville**

mother, and brother escorted me in the family car to the train station in Springfield. It was obvious that everyone in the vehicle wondered what lay ahead for me. At the train station, I hugged each member of my family for a very long time. We said our tearful goodbyes and wished each other well. I don't think any of us was one hundred percent certain that we would all see one another again.

I boarded a train in Springfield destined for Columbus, Ohio. In Columbus, I boarded a freight car with cattle bound for California via central Missouri. In my home state, I added more prized cattle destined for California or Australia. I shared space in a boxcar with the livestock and a few hobos as we moved westward. Between Cheyenne and Rock Springs, Wyoming, a blizzard and extremely cold weather forced me from the freight car into the caboose, which I shared with some of the train's hardworking crewmen. After chugging across the western states and California, we reached the port city of San Pedro. Arriving at the Pacific Ocean with a load of cattle completed the first leg of my journey. I knew then that things were rolling in the new direction of my life.

Having grown up in the landlocked Midwest, I was stunned by the immensity of the Pacific Ocean. And the beauty of the coastline was more impressive than any painting or photograph I had ever seen.

At the rail yard in sunny San Pedro, I met a twenty-five-year-old Texas cowboy who had transported the eighteen purebred Brahman cattle up from the King Ranch. He had been assigned to partner with me on the trip to Australia.

We would need to build cattle stalls and feeding troughs for the eighteen young Brahman cattle and five Shorthorns that we were prepping for overseas transport. From now on, the prized cattle were our responsibility. Lloyd's of London made it clear that we had to make sure the coveted shipment arrived in Australia unharmed.

I learned that the cowboy was "all hat and no cattle," as they say in Texas. But he did hail from the world-famous Texas ranch and, in his mind, that was all the qualifications he needed.

The cowboy was sitting atop a corral fence adjacent to our worksite. He was puffing a hand-rolled cigarette and staring at me with a pitiful look on his rugged face. He exhaled a plume of smoke and asked, "Warren, why do we have to ferry these dumb cattle all the way to Australia? Makes no sense at all, none!"

I replied, "It's our job, and those Brahmans are very special to the ranchers of tropical Australia. They want to crossbreed them with the Shorthorns and further develop the Santa Gertrudis stock that has sweat glands and are highly resistant to the nasty ticks in the infested areas of northern Australia." I gave the cowboy my sternest look.

He rolled his eyes. "Shucks, beef is beef."

Truth be told, the cowboy was arrogant and lazy. After a few days of hard work, he walked off the worksite without even saying goodbye. He hightailed it back to Texas to enjoy his much cushier and familiar routine lifestyle.

Now I was on my own in the care and upkeep of twenty-three animals. Before the ship left port, I had to build twenty-three livestock stalls to contain the cattle on the ship's aft open deck.

Brahman cattle

I set up an account at a nearby lumber yard that was willing to bill the Lloyd's office in Chicago. The shopkeeper helped me find two local carpenters and added the cost of their labor to the invoicing. Having to singlehandedly do all the prioritizing, itemizing and planning, I realized this endeavor had quickly become my business. The success or failure of the mission rested on my shoulders. Lloyd's of London was writing the checks, but I was the only person who would be held accountable for everything that transpired from here on out. And I was a teenager.

It took a great deal of backbreaking work to construct stalls for each of the animals—with every stall equipped with a trough for feed and water. My hands were covered with thick calluses and stinging blisters. My skin was tanned by the California sun. I was constantly dusty and worn down to the bone. However, I met the challenge of getting each animal into its stall so the cattle could be loaded onto the ship one at a time. My real tussle came in working with the Brahmans, a breed I had no prior experience with.

I worked with a crane operator and members of a freight crew to load the bellowing animals onto the Swedish freighter. The loading of the cattle was keenly observed by my fellow first-class passengers, several of whom unabashedly watched me work as they lingered with drinks in hand.

The Swedish cargo ship, M.S. Stratus, would be carrying twelve passengers, ranging from a rookie eighteen-year-old cattle wrangler to a retired eighty-two-year-old judge from San Francisco. Unbeknownst to any of us, my fellow passengers would gain an education in feeding cattle and shoveling mounds of wet manure

M.S. Stratus

overboard to drive the trailing sharks crazy. During a seventeen-day cruise, the first-class passengers learned more animal husbandry than most folks learn in a lifetime.

We set sail on February 5. I located my stateroom, where I shaved, showered, and dressed. I realized I was feeling like the best-ever version of myself. I still had trouble believing that I was standing onboard a Swedish freighter embarking on a voyage to Australia.

It had taken ten hours to securely load the Brahmans into their stalls and slot them safely onto the ship's aft deck. I had to secure the cattle in their individual stalls to prevent them from slipping and sliding overboard during the intermittent rough seas that awaited us. I had loaded enough hay, grain, and salt onboard to sustain my twenty-three animals during the seventeen-day trip to Sydney.

I had passed the first major test of my young life while far from home. I was no stranger to hard work on our Missouri farm. Every day I had hammered through a list of chores for my dad. But never had I worked as hard as I had over the past several days, and I did it all without my dad's firm guidance.

I joined the other passengers on the foredeck of the massive ship, where we enjoyed a cool dusk breeze. I stood on tiptoes and looked over the port side of the huge vessel. Down below, a crowd standing on the wharf bid us bon voyage.

The ship pulled away from the port of San Pedro. I stayed above deck until the orange and reddish hues of the setting sun eventually disappeared over the horizon. The twinkling lights of Catalina Island provided the last glimpse of land I would have for the next seventeen days.

A warm and comfortable feeling came over me. For the first time in my life, I understood that I was living a life I was intended to live. I sensed fate had called upon me that day when I read the letter on my advisor's desk, and subsequently was chosen by Lloyd's of London and the Missouri cattle rancher for this job.

The booming and crackling call for dinner rang out through the loudspeakers. I worked my way back toward the dining room in the main cabin to gather with the passengers and the ship's captain, the first mate, and the chief engineer. Each dining table was headed by one of the ship's three senior officers and accompanied by place settings for four passengers. Everyone introduced themselves and briefly described their backgrounds as we enjoyed a fabulous meal of broiled salmon, roasted potatoes, and a medley of vegetables.

An attractive Australian woman named Audrey, with olive skin and wavy brunette hair caught my eye. She was elegant, a secretary by trade, and she appeared to be in her early forties. When she smiled, her teeth shone brightly. Her glittering hazel eyes were seductive and alluring. Each time she laughed I was drawn to her wit and natural sensuality. I was smitten, but as my buddies back home used to say, "She's out of your league."

Amidst the dinner conversations, I'd be bombarded with questions about the cattle that occupied the aft deck. When my shipmates learned that the Brahman cattle—nine males and nine females—were among the first-ever Brahmans to be imported to Australia, their interest spiked.

Many of the passengers asked about the Brahmans and the hybrid Santa Gertrudis developed by the King Ranch in Texas around the year 1910. The cattle had been bred from foundation stocks of about five-eighths Shorthorn and three-eighths Brahman ancestry. Due to their uncommon sweat glands, they were not as susceptible to debilitating tick infestations and were highly adaptable to the semi-tropical U.S. Gulf Coast region. Australian cattle ranchers hoped the hybrid would adapt well to similar conditions in the tropical states of Queensland and the Northern Territory of Australia. The cattle we were hauling were headed to Queensland.

After dinner, we drifted toward our staterooms. I was exhausted, but still, I had trouble falling asleep. Crossing the Pacific would be a great journey, but I hoped the seventeen-day voyage to Australia would only be the first journey of a lifetime of adventure.

CHAPTER 3
1954

LIVING ABOARD THE M.S. Stratus freighter and caring for my stable of floppy-eared Brahmans gave me time to reminisce about my family back home in Missouri.

My father, Orville, was not a tall man, about average height, with a face that reminded me of a bit-part movie actor I recognized from several films, but I could never recall the actor's name.

On the other hand, my mother, Martha Bennett Vest, was statuesque—taller than my father. She had prematurely gray hair. I always thought she was similar in looks to a more chiseled version of the late Princess Diana.

My birth on April 28, 1935, occurred during the Great  Depression in a tiny home outside Louisburg, Missouri. My mother had a hard time bringing me into this world. She was twenty-five years old and began having intense labor pains during the afternoon of April 27.

My father had contacted her doctor, Dr. Gammond, who arrived on horseback around five that evening. After examining my mother, he explained to her that she would not give birth for another twelve hours. Rather than have the doctor ride back home on horseback, only to return the next day, my father decided it was best for him to spend the night at our place.

After ensuring that my mother was feeling alright, he unpacked the supplies from his horse. Then he grabbed a fishing pole and walked to the creek behind our house. He caught some grasshoppers for bait and was able to catch seven perch. He returned to the house, cleaned the fish, and cooked up a fried-fish dinner for himself and my father. Meanwhile, my mother grappled with labor pains.

The next morning, Dr. Gammond checked on my mother. She still was not ready to give birth, so he made breakfast for my soon-to-be parents, cleaned up the kitchen, and sterilized the surrounding areas.

At eleven that morning, my mother was ready, and my life on earth officially began. My first clear memory of growing up on our farm dates back to when I was about three years old. The families that lived nearest to our house had children a bit older than me and we often played together, even before I learned to walk.

A couple of the kids owned a small red wagon. They would remove the front wheels and hitch up their dog, using a jerry-rigged harness.

The kids would prop me up in the wagon, and the dog would tote me gently around the farmhouse front yard. But this time was different. A rabbit came leaping across the yard and sprinted down the lane. The black dog went berserk and took off in hot pursuit of the zigzagging rabbit. The dog's explosion into a run from a dead stop caused my little neck and head to snap backward and my feet to fly into the air.

The bumpy ride seemed like it was never going to end. I could hear some of the concerned shouts and cries of my friends trying to catch up to me and save me from the wild ride, but they were too far behind. I was on my own, and it appeared the determined dog was not going to stop until he caught the rabbit.

I looked up to see the rabbit diving under the fence and scurrying beyond it. The black dog never slowed down as we bulleted into the brush-covered, chicken-wire mesh. The dog tore through everything in its path and continued to pursue the rabbit unimpeded. The red wagon tore loose from the dog's harness and lodged in the fence.

The next thing I remember is looking up at the worried faces of my friends and the concerned looks from my mother and father. My parents rushed me back to the house and quickly checked me for serious wounds. I was scratched up and dirty, but no permanent injuries were sustained to my eyes or face. From that day onward, my friends and I were no longer allowed to hook up their black dog to that red wagon.

Another early memory dates to a few years later in Buffalo, Missouri. I was six years old, and a thin layer of snow covered the ground. A covey of quail was skirting the edge of the farm we now called home.

My mother created a makeshift box cage from scraps of wood and a window screen. She tied a long piece of thick string to a small stick. She sprinkled seeds and breadcrumbs underneath the cage and used the stick to prop up one side of the cage. She stretched out the length of string—still tied to the stick—away from the trap. A few hours later, my mother and I watched from our kitchen window, hoping the quail would take the bait.

Our patience was rewarded when six unknowing quail started pecking away at the bait my mother had left in the trap. She quietly went outside and tugged on the string. The stick pulled loose, and the cage crashed down around the quail.

My mother was thrilled. "We did it! We caught them!"

I was surprised by her ingenuity and impressed by her innovative bird-trapping methods. I helped my mother pluck and clean the small birds and watched her cook the game hens until the smell was irresistible.

Later that night, my father got home from working as a member of the highway development crew. It was a dangerous job. Every time he returned home, I saw my mother's face relax a bit. That evening, the three of us had one of the best dinners I can recall. I happily retold every detail of our trapping escapade, as my father delighted in my storytelling ability and praised my mother for her smartly planned accomplishment.

In some ways, my mother and father had reversed the typical gender roles of their era. My mother loved to fish in the nearby creeks, rivers, and ponds, and she was not opposed to hunting for small game. Our dinner table was rich with fresh, delicious food.

My father, on the other hand, was more task-oriented and industrious. He did not go out of his way to fish or hunt, but he enjoyed the resulting meals. Instead, he handled the major upkeep of the farm, with its daunting requirements and its strict timelines needing to be met.

CHAPTER 4
1954

MY MOTHER WAS a teacher, and most years she taught in one-room or two-room schools. For a good part of her career, she taught students in first through eighth grade in a single room and all at the same time. On average, she earned thirty dollars per month. From that amount, and out of her own pocket, she would pay one of the older boys two dollars a month to bring in chopped wood to fuel the heating stove. She paid another kid one dollar a month to haul well water into the school in a bucket.

I never had my mother as a classroom teacher. She thought it best that I learn from a different set of teachers. Looking back, it was a smart move on her part. It kept me interested in schooling and it was better for our mother-son rapport.

She had been "blessed" with prematurely gray hair that contrasted well with her blue eyes. Standing five feet eight inches tall, she could become an imposing figure to most kids. My mother was a loving woman, but she had a streak of stubbornness, which she developed as a defense mechanism against bullying students and rude parents.

My father had a slighter build but was very strong. He had dark, thinning hair, green eyes, and a lived-in face. I marveled at the fact that my father married a woman much taller than he was. My mother possessed a much higher level of formal education, but to my father, it made no difference. They were different but equal and loving.

My father's education came to an end after the eighth grade. That's when my Grandfather Vest purchased a large herd of cattle and needed my father to help manage the herd. At the age of thirteen, my father was forced to become a young man with considerable farming responsibilities. When he was seventeen, his mother passed away and my father had to help raise his three junior siblings. When other teenagers were attending high school, my father was farming and tending cattle full time. His education was crafted in the form of being held accountable for every task and chore getting done on time, without any excuses.

My father told me about the time he took a bus from Missouri to California to get work. Along the way, the bus had thirty-seven flat tires. Thirty-seven flats on the same trip. Unbelievable!

Farming is far from a safe or comfortable occupation. The dangers are inherent to farm life, ranging from insect bites, critters, wild or domesticated animals freaking out, exposure to raw materials, and the potential for injury associated with working with machinery.

A memory comes to mind, this one dating to the summer when I was four years old. I was playing on the front porch with our little dog, a mutt named Skippy. He had a black spot on his left ear. I was wrestling with Skippy; then I popped up and ran to leap off the front of the porch. Skippy charged into my legs and knocked me off balance, and I fell to the side. Skippy then started growling and fiercely bit down on the mid-section of a venomous copperhead snake. Under different circumstances, the snake could easily have struck at me and potentially ended my young life.

I heard Skippy whimper when the copperhead's fangs sunk deep into his neck. I screamed for my mother. Tears were pouring down my face. My mother ran onto the porch. I thought Skippy was a goner. Soon, my parents and I and the dying Skippy were in our car speeding toward the veterinarian office in town. When we arrived, my father scooped Skippy from my arms and darted inside.

My father shouted to the vet, "Charlie! Skip got bit by a copperhead. Help him, please!"

The vet used a scalpel to lance the wound before suctioning out as much of the venom as possible. I stood there transfixed and watched Skippy, thinking he was going to die. Fortunately, the surgical procedure worked, and our dog managed to survive. But for the rest of his life, Skippy had an uncomfortable crimp in his neck and his head was slightly tilted to one side, an ever-present reminder of that awful day when my brave little dog saved my life.

Even though my parents worked hard, it took them years to put together enough money to purchase a home. My father would labor on the land that we rented. Our family was responsible for taking care of animals, crops, pastures, fences, and waterways. Beyond that, we had to repair and maintain the residence provided by the landowner while we tried to save enough money to buy a house of our own.

When I was six, my parents purchased a home in the country near Buffalo. Our new house was small, but it was ours. To me, it was a castle. I loved it, even though we had no indoor plumbing and we heated with wood.

In 1941, my mother was hired to teach in a two-room schoolhouse at Plad, Missouri. Together, she and I drove to the schoolhouse for two years. My mother taught fifth grade through eighth grade, while I was in the younger class taught by a Ms. Poole. Eventually, I transferred to the school in Buffalo, Missouri, for my third-grade through sixth-grade years. Then, during my seventh- and eighth-grade years, I attended a two-room school named Cowden, which was just down the hill from where we were living.

Later, during my time at Buffalo High School, my friends and I enjoyed messing with slingshots and playing baseball, softball, and basketball. We loved basketball, and a buddy's dad had an old, cast-iron basketball hoop. He secured it to one side of our barn so we could shoot baskets after school and in the summer. Not one of us kids had the money to buy a net for the hoop, so the bare circular rim was our target. If we missed  badly with a shot, the ball would ricochet back to us after hitting the side of the barn. Years later, several high school kids played on that old barnyard court with my younger brother. Some of them became collegiate basketball stars and one was drafted by an NBA team. My hometown Buffalo Bisons won Missouri state basketball championships in 1949, 1964, and 1965. My brother, Lendol, was on the 1964 and 1965 teams.

My family raised chickens for meat and fresh eggs, hogs for meat, cows for milk, and horses as draft animals for farming. We grew tons of hay, and harvesting the crops was difficult work for a youngster like me. I didn't mind the work most of the time, and I enjoyed knowing I was helping my family.

One spring, a mare of ours gave birth to a pair of mules, which I named Jack and Jill. Mules are unlike any other animals I've been around. For starters, they are more intelligent than horses, and most of the time they are relentless workers. Mules are the offspring of a male donkey and a female horse and, due

Jack and Jill

to their quirky genetic makeup, mules can't reproduce. They seem to have an innate sense of self-preservation and usually respond well to smooth talk and an understanding voice. But they won't tolerate abusive behavior.

I enjoyed revisiting my growing-up years, but I had things to do onboard the M.S. Stratus. I put on a pair of swim trunks and hustled to the topside of the ship. The ocean air was warm and salty, and my breath caught in my throat as I stared at the pinkish hues of the sky as the sun receded below the horizon.

The ship's captain deserved credit for his ingenious response to his passengers' desire to go swimming. A few days earlier, the captain had commissioned his crew to construct a large, wood-frame skeleton for a makeshift pool. Once built, they covered the six-feet-deep opening with a thick tarpaulin, which was fastened securely on all sides. It was fun as hell to take a dip in that makeshift swimming hole with my new friends.

Duane Skari, a twenty-three-year-old shipmate, was traveling to Melbourne to attend the university on a Rotary Scholarship. He flashed a devilish grin as he stood on the edge of the pool. Then he jumped high into the air before executing a cannonball that covered me in its wash. I gladly joined the frolicking passengers in our last swimming session before arriving in Australia the next day.

Duane Skari

After dinner, I returned to the pool and found myself to be more relaxed and at peace than I could remember. A couple of hours passed by leisurely. Nighttime settled over the ship with its utter blackness, broken only by the twinkling lights from the blanket of stars dotting the velvet sky. I had never seen the quadrant constellation of stars known as the Crux with its five brightest stars famously known as the Southern Cross. Its gleaming boldness captivated me and, as my legs and feet dangled in the pool water, I felt myself drifting into slumber.

"Warren…Warren." A woman's voice cooed at me. "It's me, Audrey."

I gazed across the pool as Audrey breast-stroked toward me under the glow of the rising moon. Her mane of dark hair was slicked back, and she dipped and rose with each stroke.

"Hello, Audrey," I whispered.

I swam toward her. I was a tad nervous but confident of myself, even though she was far more experienced.

On Audrey's last arm stroke above the waterline, I realized she had removed her bikini top.

We came together in the middle of the dark pool, where we embraced and kissed. Audrey teased me with her mouth, luring me into pressing forward as we swirled together in the water.

The next morning, I was yanked out of a deep sleep when a series of hard knocks crashed on my cabin door.

"Wake up, Warren! Get up. Come on. We're almost there!" One of the deckhands was shouting at me through the closed door.

Startled, I sat up in my bed. "Of course, Australia!" I whispered.

I turned to my left and realized Audrey was nowhere to be found. I pulled back the curtain covering the cabin window and watched as our ship cruised across the swells of the South Pacific, but I didn't see any telltale signs of land.

I scrambled out of my berth, quickly donned a pair of pants, and slipped on my shoes. I bolted out of the cabin door and hurried down to the main deck as fast as I could go.

CHAPTER 5
1954

ATOP THE FOREDECK on February 22, I found myself basking in the sunlight with many of my fellow passengers. We were thankful that our seventeen-day crossing was coming to its end below the equator, as planned.

We celebrated and hugged one another. Kisses were exchanged while chilled bottles of champagne were uncorked. We made a few toasts, sipped at the bubbly, and clapped our hands while jumping with excitement. Our freighter blasted its horn three times as we passed under the famous Sydney Harbor Bridge. For a fleeting moment, I found myself a tad bit lightheaded.

Quickly, though, I refocused on my primary duty: attending to the twenty-three cattle in my care.

After the ship docked at Circular Quay, we said our goodbyes

Peter Norrie

and disembarked. My legs felt rubbery from being at sea for so long. I hit the wharf doing a wobble-walk. In the midst of trying to regain my land legs, I was greeted by a wiry, energetic, dark-haired Australian who would become a lifelong friend.

"Welcome to bloody Australia! And the name's Peter Norrie!" he said while shaking my hand vigorously and displaying his broad smile. "Warren," I replied. "It's nice to finally be here." Peter said, "Let's get you cleared through customs so you can show me these special cattle you've brought from America."

After getting my passport and papers officially cleared, Peter and I oversaw the offloading of the cattle. The herd was moved to a quarantine area operated by the Ports of Australia.

On February 26, Peter and I met with his superiors. I was told that I would not immediately be heading back to America as I had expected. I learned that livestock was required to be held in quarantine for thirty days in New South Wales before being transported to the State of Queensland. Peter's boss at New Zealand Loan and Mercantile helped with the communication between me and the agent for Lloyd's of London in Australia. Lloyd's offered to extend my employment with a bump in my pay during the unanticipated quarantine period and the subsequent delivery of the Brahman cattle from Sydney to Brisbane by railroad.

Peter's boss, a portly gentleman, advised me to "Enjoy the beauty of Australia."

I sent a telegram to my parents informing them of my change of schedule. After ensuring the cattle would be secure and well fed during their month-long quarantine, Peter and I took off to do some sightseeing around Sydney. We penciled in my activities for the next thirty days.

Peter could effortlessly spin an entertaining tale. In addition to describing himself as a jack-of-all-trades for his company, he served as an outstanding auctioneer for his employer's impressive animal trade. Peter prided himself on raising the stakes of any purchase, landing a higher sale price for any beast that went up for bid.

I sat on the left side of Peter's vehicle—a passenger occupying what my instincts told me should have been the driver's seat. His car was a light green, bulbous-nosed Holden. He drove on the left side of the roadway and chattered away in his unique accent, with his voice coming from my right. We zoomed around a tight, blind, bend to the left. I gripped the armrest and flinched with my eyes closed. I expected us to get obliterated by an oncoming vehicle and finally let my breath out when we cleared the bend unharmed.

It took several minutes of riding in the Holden for me to get used to riding on the "wrong" side of the road. Eventually, I calmed down and began to enjoy the journey.

Peter was a bundle of energy and very proficient in the use of Australian slang. We drove beyond the city limits toward a remote region and he noticed a gaggle of Australian ladies about our age. He pointed them out with a quick nod of his head and said, "Take a look at those lovely Sheilas!"

He tooted the horn and the women smiled at us as we drove by.

The baking heat of thirty-two degrees Celsius in Australia's February summer was stifling. We drove onward and I spotted a disturbing sight coming up on the left.

"Good Lord, is that what I think it is?" I asked Peter.

He replied, "Yep! That's a boomer, a big roo, and there's a joey behind the bush, too."

An enormous, heavily muscled male kangaroo was squaring off, trying to kickbox an angry rancher. The rancher was pointing a shotgun at the intimidating beast. The behemoth marsupial was feinting, circling the rancher, angling for an opportunity to clasp its forepaws around the rancher's head so it could deliver a double-kick with its powerful hindquarter paws. The small joey hiding nearby was its offspring. The protective adult male bounced on its springy feet and used its massive tail as a pivoting third leg to stabilize its shifting position. The kangaroo unleashed a few snapping kicks at the rancher, but the man was keeping the beast at bay, at least for the time being.

As we rapidly approached the dueling combatants, I exclaimed, "Peter, we need to stop and help that man!"

"Bloody hell not," he retorted. "That bloke has got the jack under control." Peter laughed. "If that roo makes one wrong move he'll end up on the butcher block. And their meat is quite tasty, actually."

Seconds later, I heard the booming echo of two shotgun blasts. I looked behind us and saw the mortally wounded kangaroo cartwheeling backward.

"Told ya, mate!" Peter shook his head while driving. "He's supper now."

I wondered aloud, "What's next?"

CHAPTER 6
1954

PETER SERVED AS a jolly tour guide around Sydney. We visited the zoo, several clubs and parks, and Bondi Beach, where we flirted with some of the local ladies. When we stopped for lunch, Peter suggested mutton. I knew that mutton was cuts of meat from sheep at least two years of age, and it wasn't my favorite thing to eat. It had a stronger taste than a rack of lamb and was decidedly chewier.

I stayed at Peter's home, but never far from my mind was the status of the Brahman cattle spending time in quarantine.

In Australia, the cattle I had brought from America were nicknamed Zebu, and it took less than a week for Peter to tag me with that moniker. I started answering to Zebu.

A few days later, Peter and I flew from Sydney to Melbourne aboard an Australian National Airlines DC-4. We had accepted an invitation to visit my new pal Duane, the Rotary Scholar I met aboard the M.S. Stratus. The flight over the green, mountainous peaks of  Kosciuszko and Alpine National Parks gave me a greater appreciation for the gigantic size of the continent. I recalled my brief stint as a member of the Air Force ROTC during my first semester at the University of Missouri. As we flew to Melbourne, for the second time in my life I seriously entertained the prospect of becoming a pilot (the first being during my first semester ROTC classes). I was visiting Australia in the South Pacific and being halfway around the world made the prospect of being able to fly worldwide even more appealing.

After landing in Melbourne, we attended a Rotary Club luncheon as the guests of Duane's sponsor. I was seated next to a cheery gentleman who served as head of the Australian Postal Service. He chattered away at light speed, never once appearing to pause to take a breath.

The postmaster explained, "Australia is so vast, but it's not that developed in terms of its infrastructure. So, the best way of getting around our country is by Royal Mail aircraft. How does that sound to you, Warren?"

Before I could answer, the postmaster general said, "Listen here, young bloke. You should take advantage of your time down here and tour as many of our villages and towns as possible. Trust me, you won't regret it."

I told him I would like that very much. The postmaster took me around the meeting hall and introduced me to his peers at the club, who were celebrating and congratulating Duane for his academic success.

A couple of days later, the postmaster arranged for Peter, Duane, and me to fly to the Northern Territory into a beautiful area, Alice Springs. During our flight, we sat behind the pilots and I listened intently to the seriousness in their voices and carefully clipped words. These Royal Mail pilots were worried about a looming dust and sand storm. They were able to steer us around it and land the airplane in a remote, tiny hamlet by the name of Birdsville. It had a population of only fifty inhabitants.

Eventually, the weather broke in our favor and we took flight again, this time landing in Alice Springs. I had never seen anything so otherworldly and lovely in my life. The turquoise rivers and emerald-green pools sparkled like liquid jewels. The waterfalls slicing through the reddish-black canyon walls and deep gorges were inspiring. The three of us took off on foot with backpacks, exploring caves and trails, climbing funky trees, and sloshing through creek beds. We ate our lunches on a sandy beach next to the largest boulders I had ever seen. Our meal included kiwifruit. It was the first time I had eaten this delicious fruit.

It was late in the afternoon on that hot and dry day when Peter and Duane ventured to the edge of a forty-foot drop overlooking an

aquamarine swimming hole. Across the waterway and coming down the bluffs from the other side were a couple of male Aborigines. I gave them a slight nod of my head and a smile. It was the first time I had

Alice Springs

seen Aborigines in person. Their mahogany-colored skin looked like chocolate, and each young man had a wide, flat nose and long, kinky, jet-black hair. They took a lofty position across the lagoon from us and waited.

The shorter Aborigine grinned at me, then pointed toward Peter and Duane. He said, "You three go first. We vegemites come here often. No problem, go ahead."

The taller Aborigine had a leather lanyard draped across his chest with a trio of colorful boomerangs dangling from it. He plucked one of his boomerangs from its cord and casually flung the curved piece of wood in my direction. Before I realized what was happening, the whirring projectile flew past my left ear about three feet away. It came zinging back around the right side of my head before it returned to the smiling Aborigine. Its flight took ten seconds.

Peter shouted at me. "Zebu! Get a move on up here, mate, so we can tackle this jump together!"

I scrambled up the rocks. Near the top, I lost my footing and cut a gash in my left knee. After a few minutes, I reached my friends.

Peter glanced at my injured leg and cracked, "Should we cut off the whole bloody leg, mate?"

"Sure," I replied sarcastically, "cut them both off."

Duane looked down at the huge swimming hole and quipped, "Gravity always wins, and we're going to hit that water at approximately forty-miles-per-hour, give or take."

"Yep" was the only retort I could muster.

Peter called to the Aborigines, "Tell ya' what, you dust eaters. Watch how we do this and, if your aerials are better than ours, I'll buy the first pints for us all!"

The Aborigines cackled and gave a thumbs-up sign.

Peter and Duane sprinted toward the lip of the cliff and launched themselves into the air. Awestruck, I watched them plummet for a few seconds toward the immense watering hole.

My friends hit the water hard, feet first, and torpedoed beneath the surface before finally bobbing up for air. Their adrenalized shouts and celebratory screams echoed throughout the gorge.

Peter shouted up to me, "Wahoo, mate! What a rush. Come on, Zebu, jump!" They swam out of the way to give me the clearance I needed to land.

The ledge rose higher into the air than anything from which I had jumped before. I hustled forward and sprang from the precipice. Then gravity sucked me down toward the water at an alarming rate of descent.

"Crap!" I shrieked right before striking deep into the basin. Surging water and air bubbles filled my nostrils following the impact, and I continued to speed downward for what seemed like forever before my feet touched the sandy bottom. I gladly pushed myself up to the surface.

I pumped my fist into the air and let out a guttural yell. "That was amazing! Yes, holy crap!"

The Aborigines mimicked our passionate celebration with cries of their own. This was just before they blew our minds by diving from atop the cliff, headfirst, with no hint of fear or hesitation. Their streamlined dual dive made hardly a splash.

Both men casually swam over to us with knowing grins. Without a question, Peter, Duane, and I had been bested by our competitors.

Peter introduced us to the Aborigines, smiled, and said, "Well, mates, I bloody guess that I'm buying those pints after all."

A couple of hours later, Peter bought the first round of pints, and two more rounds followed to celebrate Peter's twenty-third birthday a few days earlier on March 1, and Duane's twenty-third while onboard the M.S. Stratus on February 17. Alice Springs was a long way from Buffalo, Missouri, but I was really liking Australia.

CHAPTER 7
1954

AFTER OUR EXHILARATING adventure at Alice Springs and return to Melbourne, Peter and I bid farewell to Duane and returned to Sydney. I needed to check on my eighteen animals still in New South Wales quarantine. We found they had been well cared for and would be in good condition for travel when the quarantine period ended. I could see that—even at eighteen to twenty months—the cattle were properly on their way to becoming full-grown adults. The males would eventually tip the scales at fifteen hundred to two thousand pounds each.

The colonial railway system of Australia consisted of mismatched track gauges from one state to another. My trip from Sydney to Brisbane would cover about four hundred twenty miles, but due to track-gauge changes at the New South Wales and Queensland border, we would have to change to a Queensland train at Grafton. This would require an overnight stay in Grafton.

Peter and I had arranged for two railway cattle cars and one passenger car for me. The three cars would be connected to a freight train in Sydney about dawn on March 26. Everything went well and Peter and I met the train's engineer and his small crew. The engineer mentioned that they occasionally stop to pick up locals along the way. He asked if I had a problem with local pickups joining me in my personal car. I told him it was no problem at all.

I told Peter goodbye knowing I would see him again upon my return to Sydney. Peter hugged me and quipped, "If ya' bloody get lost along the way, just give me a holler and I'll come to the rescue!" I sheepishly replied, "Will do, and thanks for everything, Peter."

The powerful steam-engine train chugged to life and pulled away from the wooden platform with a series of squealing lurches before the wheels caught hold. The two-day ride northeast to Brisbane would parallel the eastern coast of Australia. It was going to be sublime.

It was hard to believe, but I had met with my academic advisor at Mizzou only a few weeks earlier. My desire to review all that had happened since was interrupted by the train's slowing down and then stopping to pick up additional passengers. Four locals were standing just off the track. I opened the door to the passenger car, and they boarded. The quartet consisted of a couple and their young son, plus a lady in her twenties who looked like she was part of a wild west show based in Cheyenne, Wyoming.

The family didn't say anything as they found a seat near the forward door. However, the young lady took a seat next to me. She was dressed in a pair of denim shorts and a white sleeveless shirt, and her long legs were tucked into a pair of tall, weathered cowpoke boots that stopped below her knees.

She shook my hand with a rigid grip. "They call me Bluey, for this long and curly red mane of mine." She pulled at her red locks and waited for my response. I cocked my head, grinned, and replied, "Bluey? Hmm, that's funny. I'm, Warren."

Bluey appeared to be about my height, but given the lift of her boot heels, she stood three inches taller than me. Her moderately freckled skin was faintly bronzed by the sun. When she smiled, I was taken aback because she was missing her front left upper incisor.

Bluey noticed my reaction. She chuckled and said, "My pony gave me a swift kick last week. I'm lucky I only lost one chopper and she didn't break my jaw."

I spent the next few hours being entertained by Bluey's colorful storytelling. She had grown up with ten brothers on a horse ranch. I told her I was transporting a herd of Brahman cattle in the two cars just behind my passenger car. She wanted to see the herd and, when the train stopped in Port Macquarie, I was able to oblige her.

Bluey was extremely comfortable around the Brahmans and the stench of cow dung didn't bother her. She inspected the cattle and said, "These are magnificent specimens, remarkably well kept." I told her I was feeling pretty good about them myself.

The train's loud steam whistle signaled it was time to go. We were more than one hundred miles from Grafton, where I would have to switch from the New South Wales gauged rail to a Queensland gauged railway.

I enjoyed Bluey's innate playfulness and refreshing curiosity about the bizarre nature of people and the world around her. Once she had boarded the train, I had not had a chance to see much of the scenery. Fortunately, between Nambucca Heads and Woolgoolga, the tracks were laid within one hundred yards of the beach, and the scenery was breathtaking. Agile surfers rode their surfboards on surging waves and jockeyed for the best position. One of the surfers raced ahead of the pack and zoomed down the face of a huge crest at a terrifying speed before wiping out headfirst and being consumed by the crashing flood that swallowed him. Momentarily worried, I poked my head through the open window and peered back to the right. The lucky surfer had bobbed back to the surface.

As we approached Grafton, I asked Bluey if she had intended to get off the train somewhere along the way. She replied, "Oh no, I'm just starting my trip. I have a long way to go to Darwin, on the northern coast, where I'll join seven of my brothers for a month-long boating adventure. We'll sail to the Indonesian islands, Banda Arc, and Papua New Guinea."

All I could manage was "Wow!"

The train pulled into the South Grafton rail station and we said our goodbyes. I wished her a safe journey.

The train's engineer dropped my three cars at the stockyard area, where I could offload the Brahmans into a holding corral. News of the Brahmans had preceded our arrival. It seemed half the population of Grafton was there to view the animals.

The locals had dozens of questions and kept me busy for a couple of hours trying to answer every inquiry. When the crowd began to thin out, a family came up to introduce themselves. The man was an American GI who had remained in Australia after World War II. He had married an Australian lady, and their sons were eight and six. His name was Charles Nelson, and he had been born and raised within one hundred miles of Buffalo, my hometown.

The transfer of the cattle to Queensland-gauged rail cars was going to be delayed until the following morning. So, the Nelsons invited me to spend the night at their home. I enjoyed a great dinner at their modest home, followed by a wonderful conversation with my fellow Missourian and his family.

We were up early the next morning. The Nelsons drove me to the stockyard, where I loaded the Brahmans onto the new train. The Nelson family stayed for the loading before we hugged and said our goodbyes. I had spent about fifteen hours with this lovely family, and it felt like a lifelong friendship.

I met the new train's engineer and he estimated the final leg of the trip would take three hours, depending on how many stops we'd make to pick up locals. Then he added, "You'll find some crazy cowgirl in your car bumming a ride to Brisbane if you don't mind."

Sure enough, I climbed aboard and there was Bluey. From Brisbane, she planned to hitchhike nearly two thousand miles to Darwin. She unfolded a map of Australia and we explored the best routes. Highways were limited and railroads nonexistent in the last half of her route to Darwin. It occurred to me that I could help her get six hundred miles closer to Darwin.

Once we arrived in Brisbane, the Brahmans would continue by truck for another six hundred sixty miles to a 15,000-acre ranch known as a cattle station. If Bluey could catch rides on the cattle trucks, one of the drivers could drop her off in Townsville, getting her six hundred miles closer to Darwin. From Townsville, there was a highway and a railway that ran west to Cloncurry. This would leave her only eight hundred miles by road from Darwin.

We were so wrapped up with getting Bluey to Darwin that we hadn't realized the train was slowing for its arrival in Brisbane. At the depot, men from the Cattle Stations ranch were hooting, laughing, and clapping their hands. They were thrilled that their expensive and prized Brahman cattle had been delivered unharmed, on time, and in good health. I found myself standing in the Brisbane train station surrounded by well-wishers and the two owners of the safely delivered Brahman cattle. The ranchers, Leo Tuft and George Bryant, had deeply lined, leathery but pleasant faces battered by years of labor under a pounding sun. Their ranch lay outside Ingham in Northern Queensland.

The people in the group introduced themselves. One stocky fellow relieved me of my bag and playfully teased at my hair. "Good job, lad!" he boomed. "We didn't know if you would pull it off!"

Leo Tuft joined in. "Warren Vest, all the way from Missouri and California! It's wonderful to finally meet you in person."

I realized my duties had been completed. "I am so glad to hear that, Mr. Tuft. Thank you."

Leo issued some orders, and crew members hustled to begin off-loading the eighteen Brahman cattle into large cattle trucks. Bluey had been standing off to the side, and George Bryant said, "Is this young lady with the nice boots your assistant?" I explained that we had met on the train and that Bluey was making her way to Darwin for a family reunion. I mentioned that she was hoping to catch a ride on one of the cattle trucks as far as Townsville.

George said, "Certainly, if she's good company."

I chuckled. "You won't get drowsy with Bluey."

The ranch's foreman appeared and said the cattle were loaded and the trucks were ready to pull out.

Leo Tuft mentioned that he would see me back in Sydney at the Royal Easter Show. He added, "We'll have a big surprise for Easter and your upcoming birthday when we see you."

With the trucks running and the drivers ready to leave, I hugged Bluey and gave her a kiss. I checked into a hotel and later contacted a distant relative of my father who had married an Australian and lived in Brisbane. They invited me to stay at their home for two days. We did some sightseeing and I had a wonderful time before I flew back to Sydney. Once there, Peter and I would need to prepare for the Royal Easter Show.

CHAPTER 8
1954

IN SYDNEY ON April 10, 1954, I began working with Peter at his employer's large tented booth at the Royal Easter Show. Peter's company, New Zealand Loan and Mercantile, had become a significant merchant throughout Australia and New Zealand. The Royal Easter Show was an excellent venue for attracting new patrons and showing appreciation for longtime customers.

The Royal Easter Show was a two-week extravaganza, unlike anything I had ever seen. The show began in 1823 and developed into a gargantuan affair celebrating Christianity and the unique aspects of life in Australia. It consisted of nearly one thousand equestrian acts, livestock judging, art exhibits, horticulture, sporting contests, live music, dancing, food, and the most important event of all, the Grand Parade.

Peter and I worked together in the booth and interacted with Aussies throughout the fairgrounds. We chatted with hundreds of new business prospects. Many of the folks I communicated with were surprised when they heard my American accent. Australians and New Zealanders surrounded me day and night, and I reveled in their distinctive way of talking. I was thriving, happy, and fulfilled. Truthfully, even though I was slightly homesick, I was not yet ready to return home.

Hundreds of thousands of people attend the Royal Easter Show every year, where the Grand Parade is the highlight experience. The top contenders for the Best in Show class proudly exhibit their prized

Sydney Royal Easter Show

beef cattle, horses, sheep, and bulls. It was a special honor for me to be strategically positioned on the turf with hundreds of large animals and their caretakers. I was reminded that human beings are rather weak and puny in comparison to these majestic creatures.

The circular arena surrounded by giant grandstands held more than two hundred animals and trainers walking on the green. The venue was packed with jovial spectators. Peter and I had been asked to help guide a pair of horses from the Stallion Brigade of show horses. We walked side-by-side while holding the short reins.

Peter poked me in the shoulder, nodded his head to the right, and said, "Hey, Zebu! Look in the bleachers about ten rows up. Do you see that cute Sheila in the yellow hat and big sunglasses?"

I spotted the lady in a lemon-colored outfit. "Yes, but who is she?"

Peter said, "She's a bloody rich widow and only twenty-six years old. Her name is Vanya. She's an Eastie from the suburbs. Her beau was devoured by a Great White Shark last summer while he was spearfishing in the Coral Sea."

We continued walking with our steeds while thousands of onlookers took in the spectacle. Within the inner circle of the green pitch were twenty male judges wearing white blazers and four female scorekeepers wearing ivory-colored dresses. All of the two dozen experts were taking notes on a clipboard, expertly tracking the finest traits and slightest flaws of the animal contestants parading around them.

My horse raised its head and impatiently shook it from side to side. The stallion whinnied, obviously tired of his prancing charade.

"Easy boy," I said while gently brushing my hand down its long face and nose. Peter mentioned he was getting "bloody hungry."

I agreed and said, "Let's put these big boys back in the stables and have lunch."

After returning the stallions to the stables, Peter and I meandered through the bustling crowd toward the open-air food courts. I smelled barbequed racks of lamb cooking over charcoal pits, as well as the sweet aroma of caramel corn.

"This way, Zebu," Peter exclaimed. "Come on."

I shook my head. "No, our favorite place is *that* way." I stopped walking and aimed my fully extended arm in another direction.

"Bloody trust me," Peter said. "I found a new spot, and everybody says it's top notch. You'll love it, mate. Not to worry."

We walked for a few minutes, eventually moving through an entryway welcoming us into a lofty tented area. I had to pause to allow my eyes to adjust to the dimly lit confines.

"Surprise!" boomed the large party concealed in the enclave.

I was speechless. I stared blankly at the throng of people while trying to process what was happening.

"Zebu, are you alright, mate?" Peter put his arm around my shoulders and laughed. Finally, I gathered my senses and gushed, "Oh my God!" Partygoers began to filter toward me. Familiar faces from my time in Australia emerged. I was amazed to see so many of them there. Peter's superiors from New Zealand Loan and Mercantile had shown up, as well as most of our peers from working the booth. My friend from the M.S. Stratus, Rotary Scholar Duane Skari, was also in attendance. And would you believe it? There was the amiable head of the Australian Postal Service. Peter's mother was in the crowd, as were the two ranchers who now owned the Brahman cattle, Leo Tuft and George Bryant.

Finally, I managed to ask: "What's the special occasion?"

"You bloody are, mate!" Peter replied. "And we've got something for ya!"

The men who owned the Brahmans pushed their way through a seam in the crowd. They joined me, and we shook hands.

George Bryant spoke loudly so everyone could hear him. "Warren, it was no small feat for you to uproot your life from the University of Missouri and venture to California to manage the shipment of livestock all the way down here. It shall never go unnoticed that your unyielding work to transport and successfully bring a new species of cattle to our country was accomplished with great expertise."

Several people in the crowd shouted encouragement. George Bryant continued, "To demonstrate our appreciation for a job exceptionally well done, my business partners and I pooled some resources and bought your tickets on the beautiful cruise ships the Orsova and Queen Elizabeth. Congratulations, Warren! Now you'll get the chance to visit other parts of the world on your way home to America!"

CHAPTER 9
Present Day

A FLURRY OF quick knocks sounded from the study door at Tim and Caroline's home in Livermore, California. I turned to see the door opening and my eldest son, Tim, entering the room.

"What're you guys doing?" Tim asked me and my grandson, Garrett. His salt-and-pepper hair had been trimmed recently and he was toting a mug of beer. I saw the quizzical look on Tim's face vanish when he realized Garrett and I were simply relaxing in the overstuffed chairs.

I told him, "I was telling Garrett about the time I went to Australia when I was only a couple of years younger than he is now."

Garrett added, "It's all good, Dad. Granddad and I are just chilling. We're good."

Tim sipped his beer. "Australia is awesome. That was one of the best trips ever when our family went there a few years ago and we got to meet Peter."

"Yes, it was," I agreed. I winked at Garrett and said, "It's intriguing how a single turn of events or a simple action can completely change the course of your life forever. Quite remarkable, actually. I call it fate."

Garrett nodded in agreement but remained silent.

Tim turned his left palm upward and asked, "Do you guys need anything? Mom has all kinds of food out back."

"No thanks," I said, and Garrett shook his head signaling no for him as well.

Tim shrugged and said, "Okay, but there's a great party going on outside. You guys should come join the fun."

Both Garrett and I nodded our heads appreciatively. Tim left the study, closing the door behind him. I rubbed my chin, trying to recall the latest point of my storytelling. "Where did I leave off?"

Garrett replied, "You were about to tell me about taking a cruise to other parts of the world on your way home from Australia."

"That's right...." My thoughts began searching for fond recollections from a long time ago.

CHAPTER 10
1954

TWO DAYS AFTER my nineteenth birthday, I said goodbye to Peter in Sydney. It was an emotional time for both of us, but especially for me. A tear rolled down my cheek. The successful delivery of a new species of Brahman cattle would benefit generations of Aussies for years to come.

"Cheer up, Zebu," Peter said after giving me a farewell hug. "Next time, I'm bloody coming to Missouri to see ya!"

I grinned and replied, "I'd like that, Peter. Thanks for everything, mate. You've been an incredible host and a true friend. I never dreamed that this cattle assignment would turn out like this. I honestly thought I was just going to bring the Brahmans down here and then turn around and go back home.

SS Orsova

A few hours later, I boarded the massive British ocean liner the SS Orsova. The ship was bound for London with ports of call to Melbourne, Adelaide, and Perth, Australia. From Australia, we would head northwest up the vast Indian Ocean to Colombo, Ceylon (present-day Sri Lanka). From there it would steam into the Gulf of Aden and the Suez Canal to enter the Mediterranean Sea heading for

Naples, Italy; Marseille, France; and Gibraltar on the Iberian Peninsula. Then on to our final stop in England.

Eventually, I located my own cabin. I opened the door only to be greeted by two men a bit older than I. They introduced themselves as Richard and Jason, my triple-occupancy roommates for the duration of the month-long journey. We exchanged pleasantries before each of us claimed a bunk and unpacked our belongings. Richard was tall and pale-skinned with wavy blonde hair, while Jason was stocky and dark-skinned, with a shock of carrot-colored locks.

After settling in, Richard suggested we grab a drink and scout the ship.

We took turns washing up at the bathroom sink and I changed into a fresh shirt and khaki pants. It was interesting to observe the way Richard navigated his exceptional height beneath the cramped ceiling. He moved cautiously, mindful not to bump his forehead on a doorframe or unforeseen pointy object.

Richard pulled open the cabin door, stating, "After you, gents. And please be advised there are hundreds of pretty ladies awaiting our arrival."

CHAPTER 11
1954

AFTER SEVERAL DAYS at sea, with stops in Melbourne and Adelaide, the SS Orsova anchored its hulking mass in the vibrant harbor of the southwestern Australia city of Perth. Richard, Jason, and I met up with our new group of friends. Our posse of ten walked down the gangway and into the sun-splashed city's bustling port.

Our troop moved through Perth's warm and welcoming seaside air and, after exploring shops and trinket stores, the normally quiet Jason stopped our group at a forking coastal road. He pointed to the left. "Listen up, people. Our deck's butler, Clancy, told me about a secluded little restaurant on the beach over there. How about we try it?"

We walked in that direction and soon found ourselves moving over rocky outcroppings and craggy dunes overlooking a stunning white sand beach that stretched up the coast for at least two miles. The beautiful beach was bordered by the blue-green waters of the southeastern Indian Ocean. The rest of the group veered off to the right on a sandy path that cut behind the grassy mounds above the beach, which would lead them to the restaurant's more discrete seafront location.

But I felt restless and unsettled and decided to head directly for the beach. I removed my sneakers and socks and rolled up my pant legs. I tucked my socks into my shoes, tied the laces together, and tethered the pair over my shoulder as I ran down the powdery embankment toward the sea.

A young woman's Australian voice beckoned from above. "Warren! Where ya going? Aren't ya coming with us for lunch?"

I stopped and peered above me. Betty was standing alone on the crest. Her tall, lithe body, dazzling smile, and short, curly hair had attracted my attention on the trip. Not only was she pretty, but she also was witty and fun. Betty's hands shielded her eyes from the glaring sunlight while she gazed down on me.

I shouted up to her: "I want to check out the beach first. I'll meet you there in a little while!"

Betty nodded and scurried off to catch up with the group. I continued into the balmy waters of the ocean's gentle tide. It felt so damn good to have my feet submerged in the water. I just stood there, staring at the infinite expanse in front of me. I closed my eyes, tilted my head back, and allowed the shallows to soak my lower legs and pant cuffs. For a few precious moments, I totally lost track of time.

I had no idea how long I'd been daydreaming, but shrieks of laughter brought me back to the present. Down the beachfront, an exceptionally attractive couple caught my attention. Physically, they were a marvelous and riveting sight to behold.

Just then, echoing from down the beach on my right, came a shout. "There's a whopper!"

About fifty yards away, I spotted a burly, tanned man wearing black shorts, a wicker pith helmet, and sunglasses. He was surf fishing with a long pole, and it was evident that he had hooked a big fish. While battling the sea creature at the end of the line, the man whistled sharply at me two times and jerked his head for me to come to join him.

I skedaddled up the shoreline and noticed a colony of small, kangaroo-like animals flitting around and chirping. Caught off-guard, I finally uttered the name of these creatures. "Quokkas!" The friendly creatures were a surreal sight to behold in person, and their one-foot height added to the fascination. They were cute, furry,

Quokka

and popping up and down across the dunes.

I continued to make my way up the beach when I saw a small, rustic-looking hut and a few palm-shaded picnic benches in the distance. As I drew closer to the angler, I caught the enticing aroma of grilled meats cooking on a barbeque. I saw my friends filter through the grounds and take seats at the beachfront tables.

Short of breath, I walked up to the robust fisherman and gasped, "What do you have on the line?"

He kept reeling in the line and then yanked back on the bending pole, doing his best to wear out the big fish. Then he grunted and answered my question with "Dinner!"

"It's a big Mulloway, probably twenty-five pounds." He cranked several more turns on the reel and blurted, "I'm Jake. Watch this and stand back. I've got to land this Mully!"

Jake dashed toward the surf while reeling furiously with his fishing rod held high. Once he was thigh-deep in the saltwater, he whirled around and yanked back on the pole to erase any slack in the line. In a matter of seconds, he backpedaled out of the water and onto the damp beach. He bent down and grabbed the fat Mulloway before hoisting it up for me to admire.

The brassy, silver fish undulated defiantly in Jake's grasp. "That was fantastic!" I exclaimed.

Jake and I trudged up to dry sand and once we were far enough away to ensure the fish could not get back into the ocean, Jake set it down on the beach and shook my hand. "Great timing, young man. What's your name?" "Warren," I responded.

We chatted for a moment as the fish twitched. Jake asked, "So, Warren, when are you going to join your friends over there at my canteen?" "That's yours?", I replied.

Jake shrugged. "I moved my wife and kids here from Boston six years ago. World War II had ended, and I retired from the Navy as a pilot. We love it here. Our front porch is the ocean and our back yard is Australia."

I started telling Jake about bringing the Brahman cattle from California to Australia, but he held up his hands. "Wait a minute. Are you telling me you're him? You *are* the Zebu man?"

"Zebu man? That's funny. Do you mean you've heard of me all the way out here in Perth?"

"Heard of you? Hell yes!" Jake gushed. "In fact, once those ranchers breed the new cattle, I'm going to buy a few of the stock for my family."

We discussed the attributes of the Brahman cattle that made them ideal for thriving in the extremities of Australia's environment.

Jake scooped up the hefty fish and asked me to bring his rod and tackle box. "My wife and I will cook up a free lunch for you and your friends that you'll never forget."

As we walked to his picturesque beachside diner, I asked, "Can you tell me more about your time as a Navy pilot?"

"Sure," he said, "but how much time do you have tonight?"

"Plenty," I told him.

CHAPTER 12
1954

LIVING ABOARD THE SS Orsova, with nearly fifteen hundred passengers, made for an outstanding first leg of the London cruise. On a mild evening before we arrived in Colombo, Ceylon, the travelers, including myself, were in high spirits.

I had been doing a lot more thinking about a career in aviation. My lengthy conversation with Jake—the Perth beachfront-café owner from Boston—served a dual purpose. On the one hand, I learned a lot about the day-to-day life of a pilot on a pragmatic level. On the other, I gained insight into what it takes on a philosophical level. Jake had developed himself into a fearless man of action. He achieved that persona by confronting his demons and anxieties head-on and without hesitation. "There is a clear difference between thought and action," Jake had said. He added, "Only become a pilot if you have a passion for it, and never forget the lives of the passengers who are in your hands." He even gave me sage nuptial advice. "Marry a woman that is already happy."

The captain of the ocean liner apparently was feeling positive about our upcoming rest stop in Ceylon the following morning. He had the crew doll up the forward lookout deck below the bridge. Once nightfall arrived, the colorful festivities revved up in earnest. The floor-to-ceiling windows enclosing the spacious arena allowed for a panoramic view of the dark ocean, and the strings of amber lights that dangled from above were angelic. Hordes of jovial, sharply dressed passengers were sipping cocktails and sampling appetizers at the perimeter buffets, and a big-band orchestra was about to begin playing.

I arrived with Richard and Jason, and our group of friends corralled us. Betty was teeming with energy and raring to go. She and I stood about the same height at five feet ten inches. But dressed in her red pumps and indigo cocktail dress, she was slightly taller. She resembled the American ice skater Frances Dorsey. Betty flashed her brilliant Australian smile and the soft lighting gave a warm hue to her skin. She tasted her icy rum and cola, smacked her lips, and set her tumbler on the roundtable.

Members of the Orsova's ten-member band took their places on the stage, and the scene erupted into a full-blown musical extravaganza. Gyrating patrons spilled onto the dance floor and a swing-pop frolic ensued. It was a wild display of unbridled joy and frantic jitterbugging. Betty couldn't stand still any longer. She leaned toward me and planted a kiss on my lips. Then she backed away, wiggled her hips, and sashayed while urging me to join her. "Come on, Warren. It's been two weeks and we've not yet danced. Let's go!" Her personality sparkled.

I couldn't resist and told her, "It won't be pretty, trust me. My Lindy Hop is a bit rusty."

Betty grabbed my hands and tugged me into the bustling crowd of dancers. We blended ourselves together into the raucous celebration.

I heard Richard chime in from afar. "Warren! Now you're a swinging cat!"

CHAPTER 13
1954

I WAS BLEARY-EYED, foggy-headed, and severely sleep-deprived. But I joined most of our group as we disembarked via ferry boat tender to the westerly shores of the humid port city of Colombo, Ceylon. I stepped foot onto the teardrop-shaped island that lies southeast of India and found it to be a foreign world, unlike anything I had seen before. The majority of the colorfully dressed, multi-ethnic people had mahogany skin and black hair. According to what I'd learned about their culture prior to our arrival, most of the people were of devout Sinhala Buddhist faith.

I found the culture's hierarchical structure, which owes much to the caste system, to be unappealing. I was curious to see how that preordained way of life would reveal itself. I remained hopeful that in the future, every person on earth would simply be allowed to fulfill his or her unique potential, regardless of social status, wealth, or which social class the person was born into.

I saw some people who appeared to be well enough off, but more often than not the Ceylonese were barefoot. It was easy to see which individuals had access to money and which did not. It was lunchtime, and street vendors lined the street for several blocks. They were selling aromatic rice bowls accompanied by cups of spiced meats and sautéed vegetables.

My cluster of friends was strolling down the busy walkway when Jason wrapped his arm around my shoulders and whispered, "I had far too much rum last night, and my noggin is absolutely killing me. How about you?"

I told him, "You know I'm not a big drinker. I only had two beers. But Betty and I stayed up talking until sunrise, so I'm tired."

Jason wagged a finger at me and said, "Just talking, eh Warren?"

"Yep," I said. "It's hard to find any privacy on the ship, and Betty and I each have two roommates. It makes things difficult at best."

"True, my good pal." Jason released me and our posse worked its way through the crowd. We came to a stop underneath a shady awning in front of a delicious-smelling eatery that specialized in curry and coconut milk dishes.

Jason spoke up as the *de facto* leader of the group. "Okay, ladies and gentlemen, we don't have a lot of time before our shuttle van picks us up about three blocks from here. So, let's grab a bite to eat in this cozy little spot right here."

It was a small, open-front diner. We enjoyed a tasty lunch featuring chunks of meat and vegetables swathed in red, yellow, and green, curry-based broths. We also had some outstanding, spicy, deep-fried fish and tender jumbo prawns. The couple that owned the eatery came to our table to make sure we were satisfied. The cheerful woman explained that the succulent surf perch had been caught by acrobatic stilt fishermen who set up and often reset their lofty pole positions as the tides change along the southern coast of Ceylon.

About two hours later, our group of ten was packed into four rows of tattered seats inside a faded beige van. The semi-toothless driver spoke little English as he transported us to the centrally located city of Kandy in the hill country. We were about to see the renowned Temple of the Tooth. Betty was riding in the first row of seats, but I was being careful not to crowd too much into her vacation lifestyle. I was heeding a bit of wisdom from café owner, Jake, the man from Boston via Perth: "Don't turn a great situation into a bad one."

Intermittent rain pelted the van's windows and its tinny rooftop as we ascended into a lush inland range. The muddy roads concerned me, but our diver raced onward without a care in the world.

To my right, seated in the back row with me, Richard stuck his head out the window. "Hey, what's that big green field over there with all those people spread all over it? Is that a game or something?"

The portliest member of our group piped up in his British accent. "Cricket!"

I peered down the hillside overlooking the broad stadium field as we zoomed past. I took in the view, and my memories kicked in. I recalled my sports career as a trusty and above-average third baseman for the Buffalo High School baseball team. I had relished the camaraderie amongst my teammates and the day-to-day grind of batting practice, fielding drills, and preparation for situational gamesmanship. Even then, I understood my playing days would be over before I knew it. I never allowed myself to take that wonderful experience for granted.

I heard Betty squeal from the front of the van as we crossed a bridge above a vast brownish river. Betty exclaimed, "Oh God, look at the elephants down there, a bunch of them!"

The herd of elephants, from big to relatively small, was wading, relaxing, and bathing in the river. Their trumpeting sounds reverberated loudly up and down the bluffs. Our van driver hooked a dangerously sharp right-hand turn down the embankment toward the river and, after nearly toppling the vehicle, brought it to a sliding halt. His maneuver sprayed a rooster tail of muddy water over the smiling tour guide who awaited our arrival.

Our driver turned to face us. He pointed at the elephants and shouted, "Go, go! You ride, you ride!"

We exited the van as the dripping-wet tour guide and our driver exchanged heated words and a charade of angry glares. Then the well-spoken tour guide explained the ground rules and elephant-riding instructions. Then he clapped his hands thrice and a quintet of assistants came over to pair us up. Betty and I skipped off together to join our teenage Ceylonese host.

The shoeless young man wore a gauzy red shirt and yellow shorts and carried a long bamboo cane in his right hand. He introduced himself as Kosala.

Kosala motioned for us to follow him down to the riverbank toward a large elephant standing in ankle-deep water. Green lily pads swirled around the animal's legs, and Kosala bent down to adjust a wooden step ladder stuck in a sandbar. He stood up and tapped the elephant on the rump with his bamboo cane.

Kosala turned to me with a smile and a quick wag of his fingers. "Come! Up!"

I winked at Betty as I climbed the step ladder, which was leaning against the side of the giant pachyderm. I leaned forward with my hands touching the elephant's tough, leathery hide.

Kosala grew impatient with all my admiration of the elephant, and he smacked me on the buttocks twice with his bamboo cane. "Up! Up! Up!"

"Ouch! Okay!" I said with a chuckle. I grabbed the rope harness looped behind the elephant's head and drooping ears and pulled myself onto its back before settling into a comfortable position in the crook of its forequarters. Once I was properly aligned, Kosala and I helped Betty onto the beast. She saddled up behind me with a giggle and wrapped her arms around my waist. Kosala rapped the elephant on the left rear flank and barked stern commands.

Gently, the elephant moved forward into the rising waters of the slow-flowing river until the waterline crested its thighs. Kosala followed us on the left and watched closely while using his exceptionally long cane to tap and steer the elephant away from dangerously deep pools in the middle of the river. The elephant roamed farther out into the waterway than I was expecting it to go, and instinctively I gripped the reins more tightly while our feet became momentarily submerged. The gigantic beast carried us effortlessly while bobbing downstream, utilizing its natural buoyancy.

Betty extended her arm and pointed downriver, "That-away!"

I scanned the gorgeous scenery and turned to Betty. "Now this is really incredible. What a ride!"

Betty pecked me on the cheek and gave my tummy a squeeze. "It's amazing!"

The elephant seemed to be enjoying the situation, and as we continued downstream the rotund animal filled its long trunk with water and curved its snout toward the sky. Then it blasted hard and the downpour covered us in a deluge of pleasant spray. Kosala, the elephant, and Betty made excellent companions for the river adventure. But of course, I much preferred Betty.

CHAPTER 14
1954

WE TOURED GILDED rooms in the Buddhist Temple of the Tooth in the city of Kandy before we resumed the cruise. Upcoming ports of call included Port Said, Egypt; Naples, Italy; Marseilles, France; and Gibraltar, Spain. Finally, we would arrive in London.

After showering and shaving, I looked at my reflection in the steamy mirror. I leaned close to the glass and asked myself, "Do you really want to be a farmer?"

Before I could answer, my two cabin mates barged into the room accompanied by two carefree, suntanned ladies.

Richard said, "Get your fanny in gear! Betty is looking for you. Come on, man, don't keep a lady waiting."

Less than an hour later, my friends and I, along with hundreds of other passengers, stood on the starboard side of the Orsova's aft deck, taking our first look at the arid Arabian Peninsula. The ship moved through the warm, sapphire waters of the Gulf of Aden and skirted between the shores of Yemen on our right, and Djibouti in northeast Africa to our left. After navigating the channel and jockeying for position among an armada of oil tankers, freighters, and other cruise ships, the Orsova entered the southern end of the Red Sea. We were headed to the Suez Canal.

The oppressive heat caused my eyesight to play tricks on me. I tried but failed, to get a clear look at the wide, light-brown horizon. I knew it was there, but it seemed to undulate in the hazy light. Meanwhile, Betty and I agreed to pursue a secret, two-day agenda upon our arrival in Port Tewfik at Suez City, Egypt.

Betty's light-pink blouse, ivory-colored skirt, and Middle-Eastern sandals were a pleasant distraction. Her alabaster skin had gained a light tan, and her hair moved in the breeze. She asked, "Have we thought of everything? I want to be sure that we have everything we need for our excursion and we won't be late getting back to our ship in Port Said."

I nodded. "We're good to go." She gave me a devilish grin. "I'm so excited to see the Pyramids and to get the chance to be alone with you!"

I couldn't have agreed more.

After rejoining our group, we spent the next several hours playing shuffleboard and ping-pong, having lunch, and exchanging stories while the Orsova glided northward up the Red Sea past the Muslim Holy City of Mecca, Saudi Arabia. Our route took us parallel to the east coast of Egypt. As dusk arrived and cooled down the air temperature, the Orsova docked at the port city of Suez. Betty and I began preparations for our covert getaway off the ship.

At midnight in Suez City, we hailed a cab to take us to the train station. By three o'clock that morning, we were snuggled together in a sleeping car on the nearly empty train headed for Cairo. Even though Betty and I were dazed from lack of sleep, our excitement at being together supplied the energy needed for us to share our affection. The next thing I knew, we were startled awake by the porter's loud knocks on our door as the train pulled into the gloriously designed Ramses Station in Cairo.

After making ourselves presentable, Betty and I emerged from the train, strode through the brilliantly painted depot, and located a tour-guide service. We chartered a driver to take us to the Giza Plateau. Our Egyptian driver pocketed the five-dollar advance I gave him to transport us in his battered coupe. Soon we were careening down dusty paved roads jammed with tourists from around the world. About an hour later, we reached the awe-inspiring Sphinx and the Great Pyramids of Egypt.

In short order, Betty and I joined waves of bewildered tourists and were quickly surrounded by beggars and self-declared tour guides. Most of the males had wrapped their heads in vivid, cotton keffiyehs to protect against the searing sunshine. We pushed through the crowd until we spotted a middle-aged man sitting on a large cornerstone while smoking a cigarette.

Betty was getting a bit nervous in the heat, the crowds, and the chaos. I grabbed her hand and said, "Don't worry. Follow me."

Eventually, we reached the smoking gentlemen and I negotiated a fee for the man to give us a private tour. Within fifteen minutes we were standing near the huge body and expressionless face of the strangely beautiful Sphinx. I asked our guide, "Is it true that Napoleon's army shot off its nose with a flurry of cannonballs?"

He took a drag off his cigarette and replied, "No, it's a mystery, sir."

 We toured some of the sacred underground tombs and shared a loaf of Aish Baladi bread with yogurt dip and beans. By noon, we had worked our way to the base of the pyramids while managing to evade spit wads from a pissed-off camel that was tethered to a palm tree and taking aim at the passing tourists.

I backed away to gain a better perspective of the Great Pyramid's height of more than four hundred feet and stood there in wonder of its mind-blowing construction. The guide ran off to get us bottles of fresh water, and I saw that Betty was walking like Cleopatra, the legendary Egyptian Queen of the Nile. She crooked her arms and hands at opposite angles and playfully walked like an Egyptian character. Then she said, "Meet me over there behind that shady corner of the pyramid, Warren. I've got a little surprise for ya!"

"Yes, my Empress." I hustled across the sandy grounds to join Betty in the welcoming shadows. Sure enough, dwarfed by the ancient, towering pyramids, she stood there in her most exotic, Cleopatra-like pose beckoning me to join her, which I eagerly did.

CHAPTER 15
1954

TWO DAYS EARLIER, Betty and I had explored antiquity. Then we took a dusty, uncomfortable train ride from Cairo to the northern end of the Suez Canal, where we rejoined our friends aboard the Orsova in Port Said. I had purchased some small gifts for my mother, father, and brother. Now that I was back aboard the ship, I had time to read a stack of thoughtful letters from my family and to drop off letters I was sending to them.

As the Orsova cruised northwest across the sparkling waters of the Mediterranean Sea toward the southwestern coastline of Italy and the island of Sicily, I felt myself growing more mature and a bit worldly. I sensed that my future would not involve growing crops or breeding livestock. That night I joined my friends relaxing beside the swimming pool atop the sun deck. Twinkling stars cast a blanket of glittering darkness over us as we sailed near the southeast beaches of Sicily toward the Straits of Messina.

Richard stood up and stretched, then exclaimed, "Look at that!" Everyone followed the direction of his gaze and gasps of amazement rang out.

I dashed to the ship's port side and witnessed an eruption of Europe's largest volcano, Mount Etna. It was releasing a fiery mixture of orange and red molten lava in a spewing-fireworks display at eleven thousand feet above sea level. I stood transfixed by the spray of neon colors spouting from the horn of Mount Etna. If

Mother Nature were about to unleash the wrath of Mount Etna's burning magma upon us, this would undoubtedly be my last night on earth.

Mt Etna erupting at night

A short, bespectacled, bearded man wedged himself next to me as the crowd pressed in around us. I was sardined against the rail and unable to move more than an inch or two. I was shaken by Etna's volcanic display and at the same time feeling claustrophobic.

Just then, the short man said, "Mount Etna is merely releasing some of its refuse in a Strombolian-type eruption. There's nothing to fear at this point, ladies and gentlemen. This seems to be normal, so far."

I glared at the man. "What do you mean *at this point*?"

Other people in the crowd seconded my question. I can only assume that they, like me, sought greater assurance of our collective well-being. The man explained, "I was a professor of geothermal dynamics at Cambridge for twenty years before I retired with the highest honors. These little hiccups from Mount Etna are nothing like the cataclysmic annihilation she released over the town of Catania in 122 B.C. That mega-explosion devastated the region for a decade and the stricken citizens did not have to pay financial homage to Rome during their city's long and painstaking recovery."

I heard Jason's voice rise above the sound made by the nervous throng. "If we're going to die tonight," he shouted, "then it's time to party!"

The skittish spectators cut loose with laughter and shouts of celebration. I joined the impromptu spree with my reassured shipmates.

By noontime the next day, my group was touring Pompeii, the buried Roman city near the Bay of Naples. Our guide led us through the haunting ruins of the ancient city that had been buried under tons of toxic ash from the eruption of Mount Vesuvius nearly two thousand years earlier. Dario, the Italian guide, had captured the ladies' attention with his charm and rugged good looks.

Betty held onto my hand, and silently we meandered through the walled enclave, stopping to marvel at the spooky, statue-like human remains that lay where they had taken their last breath. The corpses were covered with hardened ash casings that had formed around them like individual tombs. One heartbreaking scene revealed brave parents who perished under the deadly downpour of volcanic cinder while cradling their doomed infant child.

Tears ran down my face. I crouched down to touch the encrusted profiles of the family that had met its end two millennia in the past. Dario caught me in the act and gently stopped my hand before it reached the brow of the entombed baby.

Slightly ashamed of myself, I looked up at him. He kindly reminded me of the visitation rules: "Please, no can touch, Signore."

I rose to my full height and wiped the stream of tears from my face. Only then did I realize that Betty had also been overwhelmed by the macabre scene. She struggled to regain her composure with a blushing hue of anguish casting a pall on her face.

"Oh, Warren," she said. "These poor souls. How tragic." She caught her breath and added, "That could have been us last night."

CHAPTER 16
1954

"ARE YOU SURE it's okay that I join you, Dudley? Won't the captain mind?" I was looking for an excuse to use, in case that became necessary.

Dudley, the Orsova's British cartographer, shook his brown-haired head and responded, "Bollocks, we're fine, Warren. The captain allows me a certain amount of leeway, and he's got us heading along at twenty-two knots on the Alboran Sea. We'll be pulling into port at Gibraltar in a few hours, so let's get cracking."

I followed the navigation officer over the windy deck and traced my fingers across the bulky, cast-iron anchor latched astern of an outer wall. We ducked into a narrow bulkhead and descended a dark, spiraling companionway. Carefully, we moved through the stifling chambers of the boiler room and I spied grease-covered laborers tending to the byzantine assortment of pipes, gauges, valves, and latches. Finally, we reached the main engine room where a trio of engineers went about their work. My eyesight adjusted to the dimness of the room, but the rumbling from the tireless machines and growl of the industrial setting overwhelmed my hearing.

Dudley explained that, in addition to the captain, rotating shifts of crew members work in harmony from the bridge to the hull to safely steer the Orsova around the world. "Don't get me wrong," he continued, "the captain is a good man and probably understands the nuances of the Orsova better than that of his wife. He must, otherwise, we would never complete our voyage."

We entered a small annex and sat at a round table with a color map of the world spread over it. There were markings and pinpoint notations written on the diagram, detailing the route of my trip from San Pedro, California, to Sydney, Australia, and then from Sydney to London, and London to New York City.

"Dudley, did you do all this for me?" I asked.

"Yes, it was fun," he said. "After learning more about your journey, I thought you would appreciate this type of unique perspective from a mapmaker's point of view."

He pulled a pencil from his jacket pocket, tapped it on the graphics, and began a nautical lesson. "As you can see, by the time you return to the States in New York, you will have been at sea for fifty-one days and traveled over thirty-three thousand miles around the world. That's not too shabby for your first time venturing abroad."

Amazed at the fine-tuned calculations and the precise marking of my route, I said, "I can't thank you enough for doing this. How remarkable of you."

He smiled, shook my hand, and said, "My pleasure. This is all yours to keep."

CHAPTER 17
1954

I NEEDED TO be alone for a while to think about my life. I extracted myself from my troupe's exploration of the British territory of Gibraltar on the Iberian Peninsula at Spain's southern tip.

I walked alone toward the looming, split-faced Rock of Gibraltar and picked up a fistful of slim stones to skip across the surf. My windbreaker flapped non-stop, shielding my body from the whirlwind that attacked the coastline. A few hundred yards down the beach I spotted my friends waiting for me to catch up. I gripped a perfectly shaped stone and whipped it at the sea. I watched the projectile skip across the water and carom into the surf, and I looked up at the cloudy sky to witness a Pelican dive-bombing face-first into the water after its concealed prey.

"Are you doing alright, son?" A voice beckoned to me and I turned around. The gentleman was not wearing his official uniform, and it took me a moment to recognize him in his casual attire.

"Hi, captain. What are you doing here?" I asked.

"Same as you," the ship's captain answered. "I love this spot, and I try to sneak away each time we're here." He continued, "I see your shipmates biding their time for you down there, but do you mind if we walk that way together?"

The captain of the Orsova joined me on a saunter toward the base of The Rock, where my friends were raring to get going.

I enjoyed listening to the captain tell about the lessons he had learned in pursuit of his passion to command a cruise ship. When we walked up to my friends, the captain greeted them and then bade me farewell.

"Sorry for being late," I said to my friends. "But it's not too often that I get the opportunity to linger down the beach with the captain of a ship."

Betty had set off ahead of us and, when we caught up with her, she handed me a bottle of water. Then we began the long climb up the winding road of the monolithic, thirteen-hundred-foot slope toward a green canopy.

At two o'clock that afternoon, our group arrived at the entrance of St. Michael's Cave. Our chaperone, Ava, was wearing a miner's helmet and holding a lamp. She had a placard that displayed Richard's playful name for our group: Misfits.

Ava issued us our own miner's helmets and banded lanterns. She decreed in her unique accent, "Misfits, please follow me. And if you get lost within St. Michael's Cave, look for this sign above my head or work back up toward the light. But don't keep going into the bottom of the cavern because we will never find you. Some unlucky people have been lost forever in the abyss."

We appreciated the cool air in the chambers of the cave, and Ava's pleasant-sounding oration became angel-like. Her descriptions and anecdotes were bolstered by the acoustics of the cave's arched ceilings. We marveled at the thousands of hanging stalactites and yawning enclaves. Suddenly, Jason shrieked wickedly, his vocal projection silencing the rest of us. Ava spun around and roundly scolded the mischievous culprit.

"No mas, Misfit," she warned. "No mas!"

We all knew Jason's outburst was meant as a joke, and we couldn't help but burst out laughing. Our snorting guffaws even had Ava chuckling. And even better, our bellowing chorus of merriment set off a concert of giggling echoes throughout St. Michael's Cave.

I moved close to Betty and told her I was getting hungry. Her lamplight twitched up and down. "Me too," she said. "I can't wait to eat dinner in town."

But before we could eat dinner, we had to take a picture at the top of The Rock. We would enjoy the weather in the company of Europe's tiny, flirtatious troops of monkeys perched on the cliffs overlooking the seas below. And that's how the Misfits happened to frolic with the Barbary

Gibraltar Monkey

Macaques that live atop the summit of Gibraltar.

CHAPTER 18
1954

OUR CRUISE ACROSS the northeast Atlantic Ocean proved to be blustery and wet. So, we welcomed the less-hostile waters of the English Channel. The Orsova docked inland at the industrial Port of Tilbury, twenty-six miles from downtown London.

It's difficult to describe my turbulent, melancholy feelings as I checked to make sure I wasn't leaving anything behind in the cabin. The captain of the Orsova and his crew were standing at the top of the gangplank, shaking hands with departing passengers. I was about to leave my Orsova friends after doing almost everything with them over the past month. Fortunately, my time with Betty would carry on for ten more days in London. With a few thousand people ambling around us on the bustling docks, my collection of friends exchanged long embraces and fond wishes.

Richard looked down at me, hugged me twice, then pulled back and stated, "You give Americans a good name. And if you ever find yourself in Northern Ireland, please look me up and I'll show you around my country."

"Will do, Richard. And the same holds if you ever come to Missouri."

Suddenly, Jason was beside me. He jabbed playfully at my shoulder and blurted, "Going to miss you, mate! Don't be a stranger, and good luck in the States!"

I shook Jason's hand and replied, "You too. It has been an eye-opening trip."

Betty had planned our stay in London in advance. After locating the prearranged taxi, the driver loaded our suitcases into the trunk of his FX-3, and soon we were headed for the capital of the United Kingdom. Once again, as had been the case in Australia, the driver seemed to be positioned on the wrong side. Even if he had steered from the left side of the cab, I still would have felt uncomfortable weaving through oncoming traffic.

"Relax," Betty said. "We're fine."

"Yep," I replied. "Hey, I'm looking forward to meeting your Aunt Clare."

The cabbie puffed away at his cigarette, sending billows of smoke through the taxi. The driver glanced over his shoulder and said, "Young lady, your Auntie gave me a nice stack of pounds to deliver you safely after a quick tour. Is there any place special you'd like to see before I drop you both off?"

Betty said, "Please take us by the Houses of Parliament, the Tower, Buckingham Palace, and then to my Aunt Clare's. We should get the lay of the land before we go exploring later this week."

The cabbie veered aggressively into the Tuesday traffic and about twenty minutes later we drove past the expansive Palace of Westminster, with the Thames River running behind it. The narrow windows and doors, and the high pinnacles and spires jutting into the sky were fantastic. The famous four-faced clock tower, home to Big Ben, stood tall at the north end of the palace.

"Rebuilt after the fires over a hundred years ago," said the taxi driver, "and beautiful again."

Betty kept the cabbie engaged in polite conversation, but I had trouble paying close attention. That is until one of his queries yanked me out of tourist mode. The driver asked, "What are your plans for the future? Do you have things all set?"

Betty replied, "I'll be starting my teaching career back in Australia." She scooted closer to me and I cranked down the side window. The added ventilation cleared the smoky air and refreshed my foggy thoughts. Betty whispered, "I'm so glad you're with me, before you go home, and I leave for Scotland, Europe, and Australia."

"Me too, Betty, very happy," I said. "You're going to make a great teacher, and the kids will be lucky to have you. They're going to love you, trust me."

I admired the simple fact that she had settled on a profession and the probability of a lifelong career.

The driver kept at me until I answered his question. By then, we had reached the impressive, gated grounds of Buckingham Palace with its golden statue, the Victoria Memorial, towering over the gawking tourists. I thought about the monarchies that had reigned supreme over the residents of England. I reminded myself to respectfully disagree with the U.K.'s outdated system of honoring its royalty, which only symbolically ruled Great Britain.

"How about it, lad?" It was the cabbie again. "What do you do back in the States?"

I didn't want to answer, so I kept quiet. I recalled a brilliant statement made by the captain of the Orsova: "Silence can never be misquoted."

Betty gave me a withering look and I finally answered the driver. "I'm not sure yet. I just want to enjoy the last part of my trip. Thank you, though."

The taxi driver resumed his patter as we moved past Buckingham Palace. "Did you know that our beloved Queen Elizabeth visited The Rock of Gibraltar a couple of weeks before the two of you were there?"

"Yeah," Betty replied. "In fact, we stood in the same spot as she did with the monkeys."

Finally, I warmed up to the driver, who kept doing his best to keep us entertained. I said, "One of those little rascals stole a deli sandwich out of my hands and the monkey was halfway down the face of the cliff before I realized what happened."

"You're lucky it was only a sandwich," the driver said. "The last time the wife and I were there, we saw a monkey swipe the engagement ring from an unlucky, nervous bloke who was kneeling and proposing to his beautiful fiancé. Everybody was stunned when the monkey tossed that big diamond ring over the cliffs and into the sea. It was funny as clowns, but the distressed bride-to-be ran down the mountainside bawling. Her boyfriend was running in hot pursuit."

The story was hilarious. The taxi driver winked at us and pointed at a medieval walled castle with a moat. "The Tower of London."

I looked at the ominous structure and tried to imagine the legendary kings, queens, dilettantes, and prisoners who had lived or died within its concentric grounds. Sir Walter Raleigh, King Henry III, Queen Elizabeth I, and other notables lived and perished there. Betty and I were set to visit the Tower later in the week, and I was eager to get a firsthand look at its dungeons and torture chambers. I also looked forward to seeing the Crown Jewels on display within its guarded walls.

Thirty minutes later, the driver took us through an attractive neighborhood, Dulwich Village. We pulled into the circular driveway of a three-hundred-year-old home.

"We're here!" Betty exclaimed. "This is my Aunt Clare's."

CHAPTER 19
1954

ON A FOGGY Friday morning, Betty and I sipped at cups of Aunt Clare's bitterly strong coffee. We enjoyed her homemade quince scones and scrambled eggs in a kitchen that had been in her family for three centuries. Betty's rotund aunt shuffled merrily around the galley without stopping her soft whistling, except when we resumed our pleasant conversations.

Aunt Clare asked me, "Warren, have you enjoyed your initial days in London? It sounds like the two of you have visited many of our best sights, but I'm sorry to see you off so quickly."

Betty gave me a knowing look and I responded, "I loved it, Aunt Clare. And your hospitality is first-class. We're excited to spend this week headquartered at the youth hostel downtown before I go home."

Aunt Clare grinned. "Is there *any* chance you'll follow my dear Beatrice back to Australia? It would be lovely."

I had been ready for any question from Aunt Clare, except that one. Thankfully, Betty saved me by saying, "No, Auntie, we're fine."

Aunt Clare said, "Oh well, I tried."

I winked at Betty. After breakfast, we helped Aunt Clare tidy up the kitchen and then packed our bags. We cleaned our separate guest rooms and the loo and finished by moving heavy boxes and antiques into the garage for Aunt Clare. At four o'clock, Betty and I said goodbye to her aunt and took a taxi to London. We checked into a quaint youth hostel on the outskirts of downtown. We were pleased that our room contained a tiny bathroom and a queen-sized bed. Most other niches were outfitted with two, three, or four mattresses.

Betty showered, then unpacked her bags. After venturing around the block for an hour, I returned to the hostel, but Betty was gone. She left a note in our room that read, "At the grocer, back by eight."

I emptied my suitcase into the bottom drawer of the dresser, leaving Betty the narrow closet. I lay down on the bed and took a nap, needing some rest before my last week of sightseeing commenced. My dreams returned to facial images of my father, mother, and brother. I was curious about their well-being on our farm. I awoke at dusk, but Betty had not returned. I shaved and showered. When I finished and returned to the dim bedroom, I was thrilled by the sexy, *au naturel* figure of Betty lying across the bed with her womanly curves in full view.

All I could think to say was "Oh yes, God save the queen!"

Betty and I intertwined our bodies and forgot about everything else.

CHAPTER 20
1954

THE OVERCAST SKY that shrouded the docks of Port South Hampton, England, failed to dampen my spirits. I was ready to depart for home aboard the famous, one-thousand-foot-long ocean liner, the RMS Queen Elizabeth. Betty and I embraced for a very long time during our tearful goodbye.

"I doubt that we will ever see each other again," Betty whispered during our extended hug. We both were overwhelmed by the onrush of youthful emotion. Her slight trembling and her uneven breathing let me know she was silently crying. Even though I tried to steel myself, my eyes dammed up with impending tears.

"I truly hope not, Betty. But if so, please know I will *always* remember you and I've had a wonderful journey with you."

A short while later, with a heavy heart, I walked up the gangway onto the stately Queen Elizabeth. I was honest with myself as I worked through the corridors of the huge ship toward my shared cabin on L deck. I was in turmoil over leaving Betty, but my greater desire now was to arrive safely in New York City in five days.

When I reached my room, I noticed three gray-haired men sitting on separate bunks, clad in boxer shorts, dress socks, and white undershirts with suspenders.

When the fattest one of the three stood to greet me, he accidentally farted. "Please excuse that, my dear boy," he said. "I have an ongoing war with my innards, especially when I eat seafood. I'm Victor."

I shook hands with Victor and introduced myself. One of the other men spoke up. "Seafood, ha! Victor, the only time you *don't* pass gas is when you consume fresh shrimp or soft-shell clams. Otherwise, your awful fumes could power this ship halfway across the Atlantic Ocean!"

Victor replied, "At least you can sleep through my odorous exhaust at night, but your beastly snoring could wake King Tut. So, pipe down, Henry."

They chuckled, and Henry greeted me as if nothing unusual had occurred. My third roommate, a black fellow, shook my hand and said, "George, good to meet you, Warren. Between these two geezers, you won't get much sleep. Every time we travel together throughout the world, I return home grumpier than when I left. It's a dilemma, but I cherish it."

We sat on our individual bunks and talked for two hours while going about our business within our cramped quarters. Victor, Henry, and George eventually got dressed and stood by the door waiting for me.

"Would you like to join us for a late lunch on the private deck, courtesy of the captain?" Victor asked. "We've got four VIP passes, and I've heard the poached Orange Ruffy with hollandaise sauce and the garlic-infused deviled eggs are superb."

I replied, "Thanks, but I'm not hungry. I think I'll take a walk around the ship. I need the exercise."

I spent hours exploring the multitude of decks, nooks, and crannies of the impossibly large Queen Elizabeth. As we steamed across the North Atlantic, I kept on the move in a futile attempt to work myself to exhaustion. As I hiked the length and breadth of the ocean liner, walking one deck and then another and then another, I barely spoke to another person. I arrived back at my cabin at nine that night and was dismayed to discover my shipmates sound asleep. I crawled into my bunk and did my best to sleep, but it was hopeless. Henry's God-awful snoring kept me awake. And the intermittent doomsday gas exploding from Victor's backside was devastating. I was stunned by George's ability to sleep soundly throughout the ferocious assault on our auditory and olfactory senses.

At seven the following morning, my elderly cabin mates arose as if on cue and began joking around. However, I had not slept during the night and I was edgy and bleary-eyed. I pulled the sheets over my head and ignored the senior citizens until they left for breakfast. I promised myself I would never suffer through that type of night again. I stayed in my bunk until noon, then showered and dressed in my warmest clothes. I took my heaviest jacket with me for another exploration of the ship. Hours later, I ate a light supper in the ship's deli and then got slaughtered by a twelve-year-old genius from Newfoundland in two straight chess matches. His overbearing parents applauded his expert moves in the calculated decimation of my fleeing chess pieces. Nearing midnight, I found myself sitting alone beside a small bar table, sipping on a flat soda while thinking, wishing, and praying the ship would reach the shores of America as soon as possible.

That's when I noticed an enticing woman with flowing, strawberry-red hair. She was perched on a barstool and looked bored beyond words. I rallied the courage to walk over and introduce myself. I found out she was Marlene, from Denver, Colorado.

She was direct. "You look like you're battling food poison."

I said, "Nope, it's the effects of severe sleep deprivation."

She replied, "Me too. Oh my God! I have three roommates from hell, and I dread going back to my room. That's why I'm here, by myself, in a bar…. alone."

Marlene and I shared some laughs, and we talked for the next few hours. I listened to her engaging tale of inheriting a twenty-thousand-acre cattle ranch in Colorado's Vail Valley. We made a pact that regardless of what happened during the day, for the next three nights we would meet at the bar at seven o'clock. So, for the next three evenings, Marlene and I flirted and grew fond of each other. We established an innocent midnight routine that involved snuggling on lounge chairs on the aft deck, underneath wool blankets. Our nightly rendezvous under the shimmering stars made certain aspects of our journey to America rather pleasant after all.

CHAPTER 21
1954

THE AFTERNOON SUNSHINE felt good as I took one last look at the Queen Elizabeth docked along the harbor in New York City. As thousands of people hugged one another in happy reunions all around me, I was alone and lacking sleep. But I felt wonderful and glad to be on American soil. I would be back in Missouri in less than a week.

Queen Elizabeth arriving in NYC

The previous day onboard the ship, I had traded my suitcase to a witty, post-graduate student from England for his small duffel bag. I strode through the busy streets of the Big Apple with the satchel strapped across my shoulder. I needed to find a hotel that would serve as my base for the next two nights. Compared to London, a greater percentage of pedestrians were tourist types. In addition to well-dressed businessmen and women, other locals were wearing Yankees caps and New York Giants and Knicks shirts. In the shadows of impossibly tall skyscrapers, I meandered for an entire afternoon. The sidewalks and streets were crowded. In the endless stream of vehicles, many of the exasperated drivers loudly encouraged their peers to get the hell out of the way.

I arrived in the heart of Times Square. I bought a hot dog covered with mustard and onions and a soda at Nathan's walkup window.

While devouring my snack, a modestly dressed man puffing a cigarette approached me. In his raw Brooklyn accent, he said, "Hey, buddy. My wife and I can't make the hit Broadway show *Lunatics and Lovers* tonight because she's not feeling well. But if you want a great deal on the tickets, they're only ten bucks. How about it?"

I was still chewing on my last bite of the hot dog, and before I could reply, a gentleman nearby rebuked the solicitor. The second man flipped open his wallet to display a law-enforcement badge. "Those are fake vouchers," the plainclothes cop told me. "That show is not open on Broadway yet." To the Brooklyn con man, he said, "Scram pal, before I take you into the precinct for booking. Beat it!"

The scam artist didn't take time to debate the undercover officer. He just slithered away into the masses. The officer shook my hand and said, "Miller's the name. Sorry, these crooks are everywhere. Don't ever buy anything from them. Anyhow, is this your first time in New York, young man?"

"How could you tell?" I joked. I introduced myself and mentioned that I was looking for a hotel. Miller motioned for me to follow him. We chatted as we walked. The cop expertly weaved through hordes of people, and I followed as we discussed Yankees superstar Mikey Mantle. I was disappointed to learn I had no chance of seeing him play because the Bronx Bombers were on the road during my stint in New York.

A few minutes later he pointed out a modest-looking hotel just off Times Square. Miller extended his hand and said, "Good luck, Warren. Sounds like tomorrow will be a fun day for you to enjoy the best New York has to offer. It's been a treat."

Fatigued, I checked in and found my room. I dropped my duffel bag on the bed and fell fast asleep.

I woke up well-rested early the following morning. I showered and readied myself for a day of exploration. Breakfast was a mug of coffee, a bagel with cream cheese, and a bowl of fruit at the diner across the street. I hailed a taxi in Times Square and asked to go to the Statue of Liberty. We cruised through surprisingly moderate rush-hour traffic, and the driver pointed out Wall Street and the New York Stock Exchange.

The driver pulled into Battery Park, at the confluence of the Hudson and East Rivers. The taxi deposited me at the end of a long double line of people waiting to board a boat to Liberty Island. I purchased my ticket and waited in the slow-moving progression behind a sweet, elderly couple and their chattering, four-year-old, twin grandsons.

The antsier of the two boys tugged on my right pinky and gazed up at me with an innocent smile. He wanted to whisper something to me, so I bent down. He quietly uttered, "We're going to see the Big Green Lady."

I grinned and replied, "Me too." The boy nodded enthusiastically, and his grandmother asked, "Have you been to our Lady of Liberty before?"

"It's my first time," I responded. "I've only seen her in pictures and on a postcard."

The woman said, "We try to return each year to give thanks and remember how lucky we are to have created such a beautiful life after coming to America fifty years ago with nothing."

"That's amazing," I said. "Congratulations! And your grandsons are adorable."

The line of passengers began moving toward the double-decker ferryboats. By 9 a.m. I was cruising toward the world's most recognizable symbol of freedom and democracy. I rested my elbows on the boat's railing, inhaled the fresh air, and scanned the harbor. To my right was Ellis Island and the greenery of Liberty State Park. The ferry sailed across the harbor toward the Statue of Liberty.

In my worldly travels since leaving Missouri, I had seen incredible sights. However, as the boat drew closer to the majestic and proud Statue of Liberty, perched high on an enormous pedestal, I was left speechless. The ferry docked and soon I was standing on

Liberty Island. I looked up from the circular path in front of Lady Liberty. She stood more than the length of a football field high.

"Magnificent," I said.

CHAPTER 22
1954

AFTER A FOUR-HOUR train ride south from Grand Central Station in New York City, the train pulled into the depot in our nation's capital. I walked into Union Station in the political epicenter of the world, Washington, D. C.

Even though World War II general Dwight D. Eisenhower had been elected president of the United States nearly two years earlier, fading *Eisenhower for President* and *I Like Ike* stickers remained in a few discreet places throughout the station. I walked outside, into the slightly humid air, and was rewarded with a pink-colored sunset. Almost immediately I was rewarded again, this time by greetings from my delightful "Uncle Bus," Wilburn

Uncle Wilburn "Bus" Vest

Vest, and his wife, Aunt Edie. They were standing by their red, 1951 Chevy convertible, with the top folded down.

"Warren!" Aunt Edie called. She was scurrying my way with her arms stretched out.

I had not seen any members of my family for five months, and the surge of emotion choked me up. Right then, I was unable to speak. I embraced my aunt and uncle warmly.

My husky Uncle Bus relieved me of my duffel bag, tossed it into the trunk, and asked, "Hungry, kiddo?" "Yes indeed," I replied, and we piled into the immaculately detailed vehicle.

Uncle Bus got behind the wheel, and my beaming Aunt Edie turned to face me in the back seat. She peppered me with questions from the front passenger seat.

"So, Warren, now that you're a world traveler, tell us about your trip. What were your favorite highlights? Did you see some amazing things and meet lots of interesting people?"

In his good-natured, southern drawl, Uncle Bus interrupted. "For goodness sakes, Edie, leave the young man alone for a few minutes. Let the kiddo get his bearings first. He's been around the world and he just got here from New York five minutes ago."

Aunt Edie shook her head and grinned. She said, "Tonight we're having a special dinner at our home in Virginia, and then you will *have* to tell me absolutely everything."

I nodded and said, "Deal."

Uncle Bus cruised down Constitution Avenue and we rolled past the U.S. Capitol's domed complex.

"That's where those money-drunk politicians spend our tax dollars," Uncle Bus declared.

I chuckled and gazed up at the bronze statue rising from atop the Capitol's dome. The Statue of Freedom's helmeted female figure holding a sword and shield was a silent warning against an oppressive government. Uncle Bus steered us onto Madison Drive and along the National Mall.

Aunt Edie pointed out the Smithsonian Castle and the Washington Monument. "Tomorrow and the next day we'll tour many of these wonderful sights," she said. Just then, four police cars raced past with lights flashing and sirens blaring. Aunt Edie said, "People are still a little bit edgy after those misguided Puerto Rican nationalists opened fire from the Ladies' Gallery in the Capitol building a few months ago. Luckily, nobody was killed. But it was spooky."

"I read about that when I was in Australia," I said. "I thought about you two, and the little ones, Beverly and Ron."

"We've come a long way from our days in Missouri," Uncle Bus said. "Remember when I taught you how to help bale hay for a penny a bale and ride your dad's horses, Rex and Barney? Those were the days, right?"

"Uncle Bus, I'll never forget the time when you got blindsided by the neighbor's big, angry, buck sheep," I said. "It rammed you silly and almost killed you. You went flying!"

We started laughing, and Uncle Bus drove us past the White House, the temporary home of President Eisenhower. Tourists were taking photographs, and a few picketers were marching as the sun was setting. Uncle Bus made a left turn and we continued by

President's Park and the dark-green Ellipse before returning to Constitution Avenue.

Nighttime had arrived by the time we approached the stunning Lincoln Memorial glowing in the darkness. I surprised myself by making a request.

"Can we please stop for a few minutes?" I asked. "I want to check out the Lincoln Memorial."

Uncle Bus stopped the Chevy. I hopped out of the car and hiked up the impressive staircase. At the top, I stared up at the marble carving of Abraham Lincoln seated in his chair and eternally resting in peace.

CHAPTER 23
1954

THE SATURDAY-MORNING flight from Washington, D.C., to Kansas City, Missouri, further piqued my interest in becoming a pilot. I spent most of the somewhat-turbulent trip observing the flight attendants, and I snuck a peek into the cockpit to glimpse the pilots.

Back on the ground in Missouri, I enjoyed a four-hour, celebratory drive home in my parents' car. I was in my home state again, with my mother, my father, and my six-year-old brother. My father pulled the vehicle into the gravel driveway at the farm. Before he could turn off the engine, a crowd of happy Vest and Bennett family members poured out of the house. I forced myself to postpone all thoughts about my future hopes and plans so I could fully enjoy being welcomed home. Coming at me from every angle—front and back, low to high—were cousins, aunts, uncles, and other relatives. My name was called out as various people met me with energetic hugs and extended greetings.

I worked my way into the house and continued greeting relatives in the living room as my brother, Lendol, held onto my hand.

"Warren, tell us about your trip, and let us know if you made the acquaintance of any ladies!" my cousin Deryl "Tuff" Hamlet shouted. People laughed and a few whistled and playfully catcalled.

Before I could answer, my father shocked me by speaking to the group. "My oldest boy came home safely to us," he said, "and that's what matters. He had an amazing journey, but now he's back in Missouri for a long time. At least we hope so. Right, Martha?" Surprisingly, tears were welling in my father's eyes.

Everyone in the room looked at my mother and awaited her reply. Caught off-guard, she sipped at her iced tea, held up her left hand, and spoke in her most professional teacher's voice. "Yes, that would be wonderful. But we will just have to wait and see what transpires."

My Uncle Fred Bennett raised his glass and made a toast. "Here's to Warren being back home. Cheers!"

I raised my glass of Coca-Cola® and replied, "Thank you all very much for being here tonight. I am humbled and honored. Let's have a great time together! Cheers!"

I spent the next few hours visiting with my extended family and some good buddies I had not seen for quite some time. At some point, I walked into the softly lit back yard where my father and Uncle Bert Hamlet tended to the hamburgers and hot dogs on the barbeque. A few people were icing down watermelons in small tubs, while others were cranking away at the freezer to make homemade ice cream. The sun was about to disappear over the western horizon, and I spied a few of the horses fidgeting in the field adjacent to our vegetable garden. My two favorites, Rex and Barney, trotted over to the fence near me as if to say, "Welcome home."

My father motioned for me to join him near the fence line. We stood there quietly until my mother joined us.

Not a single word was spoken among the three of us. We remained there, tranquil, gazing out over the darkening countryside. I draped an arm over each of my parents' shoulders, and we swayed gently in silence.

Finally, my mother said, "We want you to live your life, Warren. Please understand, we'll always be here for you, no matter what. We love you."

My father was having difficulty speaking. He gave me a firm squeeze around my lower back, and I pulled my parents closer.

A warm and loving, spiritual feeling filled my soul. My skin broke out in goosebumps.

I gave each of my parents a kiss on the cheek and whispered, "It's good to be home."

CHAPTER 24
1954

AFTER A FEW days of contemplation, while working on the farm with my dad, I realized that I would need money to move forward with my life. So, I moved to Kansas City to live with my Aunt Mary and Uncle Glenn and took a job at a downtown bookstore.

On Thursday morning in downtown Kansas City, the day's sweltering humidity was arriving as I strode past the famous Katz Drug Store with its huge neon sign featuring a black cat's face with gleaming eyes. A cherry-red Hudson Commodore convertible parked in front of the bookstore at 30th and Main streets where I was headed to begin my second day of employment. A sharply dressed gentleman emerged from the vehicle and marched into the store. His female companion remained in the passenger seat with the car's canvas top folded down. She applied lipstick and examined herself in the visor's backside mirror.

As I neared the bookstore, the well-dressed man was leaving the store while shaking his head. He slid behind the wheel of his Hudson, driving off with his lady friend attempting to console him.

I entered the bookstore ready to begin the day.

"Warren! Thank God you're early. I need to speak with you!" exclaimed the store manager.

My new boss was stacking books in the store's gardening section.

He stood up and said, "Warren, our assistant manager, Shirley, has called in sick. I need you to handle something for me today at lunchtime."

"Sure, Paul, what is it?"

He pulled out a handkerchief and wiped some sweat from his face. "You just missed it before you walked in. A few minutes ago, I got both sides of my fanny verbally tattooed by one of the top company executives. It was a humiliating experience."

"What did you do?"

"Nothing," Paul said. "But it appears that our sales volume of sympathy cards has fallen below the company's forecasted projections for the first two quarters. Executives at our parent company are cracking the whip on distributors and bookstores."

"I had no idea about any of that stuff," I told him.

"Just give it a couple of years and you'll know the ins and outs of the bookstore and greeting-card business."

I had no intention of making a career out of selling books or greeting cards, either one. But I recalled the mantra I had learned from the captain of the Orsova. "Silence can never be misquoted."

Paul took me to the front of the store and pointed at the bulky cash register. "Have you ever used one of these before?" he asked.

I replied, "Nope, but I'm a quick study."

Paul spent fifteen minutes showing me how to handle transactions and keep a written record of each sale in a logbook.

We opened the store at 9 a.m., and I was sent to the warehouse to resume my regular duties until noon.

I began to slash open and unpack cartons of novels, magazines, and trinkets that had been dropped at the store's loading dock overnight. I grouped the books in rows by category for Paul and Shirley to sort out later.

At fifteen minutes to noon, Paul stuck his head into the warehouse and called, "Warren, ten minutes, up front, please!"

I hustled into the locker room to change into clean clothes. I washed my head and upper body in cold, soapy water. Feeling presentable, I hurried back into the bookstore, said hello to a couple of customers, and went to the front counter.

"Are you sure you can handle such a huge responsibility like this for the next hour or so?"

I replied, "I'll do my best to make you proud."

Paul left for his afternoon meal. I stood at the counter while three customers browsed. A man in his mid-twenties was examining books farthest from the street-side store entrance. He selected three volumes and brought them to the front.

He had a book on auto repair and a hefty edition regarding world travel. But his third choice is the one that caught my attention. It was a booklet titled *How to Become a Pilot.*

I totaled up his order and completed the transaction. He paid, took his books, and left the store. I stood behind the counter feeling inadequate, wondering about the trajectory of my life. Shortly, the other customers, a duo of elderly women, came to the counter. Both of the women were red-eyed, but the older of the two was far more distraught than the other.

I asked, "Is something wrong, ladies?"

They stood there and wept. One of them said, "Our best friend, Edith.... Well, her husband died three days ago, just after they moved to California."

"I'm so sorry," I said. "Please accept my sincere condolences."

The women nodded and placed two sympathy cards on the counter. I rang up their purchase and wished them the best of luck during their difficult time. During the next half hour, a few people entered the store but left without buying anything. Just after one o'clock, Paul walked in carrying a sandwich wrapped in white butcher paper. He put the roast beef sandwich next to the cash register and asked, "How did it go?"

"Good," I said. "I sold three books and a pair of sympathy cards for thirty cents."

Paul clapped his hands and exclaimed, "Outstanding, Warren. I have a good feeling about you. You have a bright future in this business!"

CHAPTER 25
1954

EVEN THOUGH I had known Aunt Mary my entire life, every time I looked at her, I couldn't help but see my mother. She and Aunt Mary were twins. But unlike my mother, Aunt Mary had no interest in fishing or hunting.

Aunt Mary and Uncle Glenn

Uncle Glenn and Aunt Mary's quaint, single-story home was decorated in red, white, and blue streamers and balloons in preparation for the celebration of our country's birthday. Uncle Glenn was a slim man with slick, jet-black hair. He worked as a pharmacist in downtown Kansas City.

At two o'clock in the afternoon, he had finished his party prep with my help, and he was relaxing in his rocking chair on the shady front porch. He wore a straw hat with a patriotic ribbon wrapped around the crown, and beige shorts tethered by red, white, and blue suspenders. He sipped at a cold bottle of Falstaff beer and rocked slowly in his chair while reading the *Kansas City Star*.

I sat on the porch next to Uncle Glenn and gazed at the decorated homes on 29th Street. Children were running around on the cordoned-off street. I heard a scream followed by a toddler crying. I saw a little boy rubbing his scraped-up knees. Some of the neighbors had rolled barbecue grills onto driveways and front-yard walkways and were grilling meat and vegetables.

From behind his newspaper, Uncle Glenn said, "Tell me, Warren, how much longer are you going to squander your time selling Hallmark® cards and cookbooks?"

His question caught me off guard. I chuckled and said, "Hopefully, not too much longer. But I need to save up more money."

Uncle Glenn smiled with a wise look in his eyes. He asked, "If you had more money right now, what would you do with it? How would things be different?"

He patiently awaited my response. Eventually, I answered. "Well...I sold three of my prized Shorthorn steers before I moved here to work. Between that money and anything I earn at the bookstore, I should have enough to go back to college in the fall."

Aunt Mary walked onto the porch and said, "Warren, I spoke to your mother. They will be here around six o'clock. Would you fellas like a cold drink or anything to snack on?"

I said, "That lemonade looked good."

After Aunt Mary went inside to get me a drink, Uncle Glenn said, "Warren, is going back to college what you really want to do? Because you could have fooled me."

"How so, Uncle Glenn?"

He replied, "You have three different books about airplanes, piloting, and navigation on the nightstand in the guest bedroom. I know for a fact that my penny-pinching buddy, Paul, who runs the bookstore, did *not* give you the books for free. Those big manuals cost you a fair amount of cash, am I right?"

Aunt Mary returned with a glass of lemonade and a bowl of homemade macaroni salad and a platter of potato chips. We thanked her, and she left the porch to visit with the family across the street.

Uncle Glenn had more to say. "I've had two conversations with your father, and even though he wants you to be close to home and work on the farm, he knows that's not what you want to do for the rest of your life."

Finally, I said, "I *want* to fly."

Uncle Glenn winked at me. "We've been waiting for you to say it out loud."

He picked up the newspaper and found the page he'd been searching for.

He tapped his finger on a Help Wanted ad and said, "You missed it." He had been holding the paper up in front of his face, wanting me to pay attention to the classifieds' subliminal clue.

"The Ford aircraft factory northeast of here is hiring guys to buck rivets while building the wings of B-47 bombers for the Air Force," Uncle Glenn said. "This is how you get in."

CHAPTER 26
1954

TEN DAYS AFTER my front-porch conversation with Uncle Glenn, I edged my way into the arc of my life's potential.

With a gray lunch pail in hand, I stood on a corner waiting for my ride to the Ford Motor Company's assembly plant in Claycomo, Missouri. I had been lucky to find out about their ride-share program at my employment interview.

At seven o'clock, I slid into Jameson's rumbling Oldsmobile Super 88 and forked over fifty cents for gas money. "Thanks, Buffalo," he said. "since you are from Buffalo, I will call you that if you don't mind." I replied, "No problem". Then he punched his foot down on the gas pedal and my head snapped back. Jameson cackled and puffed on a cigarette. His heavily muscled and tattooed right arm lazily guided the sedan as we surged above the speed limit.

"I'll tell you what. If you're dead serious about flying airplanes for a living, then you're off to a decent start by learning how to buck rivets!" He whooped.

I glanced at my beaten and bruised hands and forearms. My first two days of tough labor inside the dark confines and narrow skeleton of the B-47's pre-attached wings had taken a toll.

As we neared the vast industrial compound, Jameson said, "Buffalo, if you don't want to do my rough job for the rest of your life, learn how to fly the damn airplanes instead of building them!"

I replied exactly as I had done both days before. "Got it, agreed."

Jameson veered into his unofficially reserved parking spot adjacent to the plant supervisor's space. Then we walked together into the expansive facility of Ford's military manufacturing complex. By 7:30 I had changed into navy-blue coveralls and was climbing a ladder toward the yawning mouth of the wing of a B-47 bomber.

From behind me, Jameson barked, "Remember to put your earplugs in unless you want to be deaf by noon!"

I stuffed the spongy, orange earplugs into my earholes. They were effective in deadening the pounding sounds made by the pneumatic rivet gun that I would buck all day.

Jameson flashed me a thumbs-up and yelled, "Hey Buffalo, just keep dreaming about soaring above the earth at thirty thousand feet."

I nodded before easing headfirst into the dark inner wing of the B-47 jet bomber.

CHAPTER 27
1954

AT LUNCHTIME IN the pleasantly cool, shady confines of a corner area in the manufacturing facility, my co-workers and I enjoyed homemade meals. A transistor radio was broadcasting blues music. I reflected on the unique characters I'd gotten to know during my first month on the job.

We were a mixed bunch of white and black men of various ages, and I was the youngest member of a nine-person group that had lunch together every day. Jameson was our unofficial leader, and his warm personality and worldly wit kept everybody's spirits upbeat. Benjamin, a black man two years older than me, would trade parts of his lunch for parts of mine.

"What did your auntie put in your lunch box today?" Benjamin would ask. He twitched his eyebrows while awaiting my response during what had become our customary negotiating repartee.

I opened my lunch pail. "A big turkey sandwich, an apple, two cubes of cheddar cheese, and three chocolate chip cookies. How about you?"

"Cookies, eh?" Benjamin mumbled. He pulled out a barbequed beef rib covered in seasoning. "I'll trade you one of my mama's home-cooked ribs for two of those cookies and half that sandwich."

"Don't do it!" Jameson said from across the table. "Ask for two ribs. Benny's got five of them today!" Benjamin waved a rib and traded goods with me.

After a few minutes of eating in silence, Benjamin asked me his daily question. "Any word yet from that Air Force major in Waco, Texas?"

I shook my head. "Nope, not a peep."

Benjamin frowned. "Don't get too discouraged. I have a feeling that something good will happen."

I nibbled on a square of cheddar cheese. "By now, the Air Force Cadet Training Center should have received the results of my pre-flight aptitude testing from my freshmen year in ROTC."

Benjamin said, "Be patient."

"Yea, but the deadline for registering at Mizzou is right around the corner, and I have to make a decision. I'm running out of time."

Guys were passing around a magazine. Jameson held it up for everybody to see. "Check it out, fellas. It's the first issue of a new magazine called *Sports Illustrated.* They put a picture of Braves third baseman Eddie Mathews on the cover swinging for the fences."

I looked at the beautifully shot image of the lefty batter taking a cut at the plate versus the New York Giants. "Mathews is great," I said, "but Stan the Man is still the best player in baseball, even though the Cardinals are having a bad season. Musial hit five home runs during a doubleheader in May. Unbelievable feat!"

My coworkers and I bantered about our favorite players and the best teams in baseball, and then it was time to get back to work. We cleaned off the table and headed off to our workstations.

My hands, arms, back, and neck had been punished by weeks of twisting work within the narrow B-47 wings. The drudgery of the repetitive work caused me to daydream about flying around the country and seeing the world.

Three hours later, I thought I heard my name being called out. I lifted my head but heard nothing. I re-inserted the earplug and went back to work. Less than a minute later, I felt a rapid tapping on the aircraft's aluminum skin.

I pulled out both earplugs and heard the excited voices of Jameson and Benjamin. "Warren! Warren! Warren!"

I descended the ladder and my two friends were there to greet me. "What's going on?" I asked.

Jameson exclaimed, "Buffalo, that major from the Air Force called. He wants to speak with you, ASAP!"

Benjamin patted me on the shoulder. "Now, Warren! He's on hold, on the phone in the break room. Hurry up!"

I sprinted to the break room, praying for great news!

CHAPTER 28
1954

I ENLISTED IN the United States Air Force on November 14, 1954. I was now five weeks into my eleven-week stint of basic military training at Lackland Air Force Base outside San Antonio, Texas.

I slogged my way through muddy terrain during the second awful night of our bivouac field exercise that simulated battlefield conditions. Live ammunition zinged and hummed overhead to keep us alert and to prepare us for the evils of a wartime environment.

"Holy crap," a voice cried out. "That was a little too close, don't you think, guys?"

I witnessed a couple of glowing orange tracers scream through the blackened night sky. I moved forward with the left side of my face slurping through dirty puddles and mucky ground. As rain poured over the brim of my cap, I squinted back at four wet trainees who were trailing in my lowdown wake.

Our motley quintet slithered ahead on elbows and bellies toward an unseen enemy target. I pondered how radically my life had changed since I had set sail for Australia early that same year. I grinned at the irony of life's unpredictability as a few more rounds whizzed above our heads.

"Hell, with this!" a trainee nicknamed Porter exclaimed. "I enlisted in the Air Force to meet pretty girls and see the world, courtesy of Uncle Sam – not to get shot!"

"Pipe down!" I replied. But it took every ounce of composure for me not to laugh at his candor under monumental stress.

Our tiny platoon finally reached the mound we had been seeking. We took a position behind its sloping backside, remaining six feet apart to reduce the likelihood of more than one of us being injured by a hand grenade. Remember, this was simulated combat.

The rain began to lighten up. The five of us were worn out after two full days of the brutal mobile encampment and tactical-survival training. Years of hard work on a Missouri farm had hardened my body into a lean and respectfully fit instrument. But this type of unrelenting physical punishment was far different from anything I had done before.

Porter asked me, "Now what do we do, Vest? Stay put or what?"

I wiped the rain out of my eyes. "Listen up, guys. We have seven hours until sunrise. Then this bivouac trial will be over."

"Jeezuz!" Porter squawked.

"We should rest here for a couple of hours and then work our way toward the extraction point," I said. "I need a break, and from the looks of it, so do you guys."

We settled in against the comforting slope of the embankment, which concealed our position from the makeshift enemy's line of sight. The rain stopped and, for a couple of minutes, things became exceptionally peaceful and quiet.

But the silence was broken by Porter's commentary. "I can't wait to get back to our barracks tomorrow morning to shower up and dry off. Then I'm going to eat about ten pounds of bacon, eggs, and grits, and wash it down with a few mugs of hot coffee."

Every member of the group was starving and cold. We were wet and incredibly tired, but for once I agreed with every word Porter said.

CHAPTER 29
1955

LESS THAN ONE week before I was to complete Basic Military Training, I was scrubbing and mopping the barrack's latrines, showers, sinks, mirrors, and floors with two of my peers. Suddenly, a chorus of shrieks, giggles, and weird calls filled the relatively quiet afternoon.

I looked at the other trainees and asked, "Any idea where that came from?"

They shook their heads, and the sounds rang out again louder this time.

"That's Porter!" I exclaimed.

We ran toward the rear exit of the housing complex. "Oh my God!" a trainee said.

I gawked in disbelief at Porter's attempt to put on his pants while stumbling around in a drunken stupor. He was shirtless and shoeless and wearing only underwear and a tattered sock. Each time he lifted a leg to put on his pants, he listed to the side or tumbled onto his ass. For now, at least, we remained unnoticed.

I hissed, "Porter! Get over here!"

I received no response from Porter. The three of us crouched down and crept toward Porter.

When I was less than five yards away, he looked up and his glassy, bloodshot eyes took a moment to recognize me. Then he shouted, "Vest, what are you doing here? Wanna go to a cool party?"

I replied, "Quiet, Porter. Somebody will hear us."

The three of us held him upright as we assisted Porter into his pants. He had not vomited yet, which gave me hope. We probably could scoot away unnoticed.

With help from the other two trainees, we slowly spun around to work our way back to the rear entrance of the barracks.

But no sooner than we could turn, we were met by the barking, angry voice of our company's staff sergeant. His face was turning redder by the split second. He stepped closer to me, clutching his hands behind his back. I was petrified.

The pissed-off sergeant blistered me and the others with his bellowing. "What in the mighty mother of our Lord Jesus H. Christ is going on back here? Vest, I gave your four-person group one small task, to clean up the bathroom area. And you turn this place into a damn wild west whiskey saloon! As far as I can tell, the only thing missing is some naked ladies."

Before I could gather myself to speak, Porter weighed in. "Not so fast, sarge. I was with some nice gals all afternoon, and two of them happened to be nude."

The staff sergeant whipped his eyes at Porter for a millisecond, then directed the full force of his ire back at me. He roared even louder, "Vest, good Lord almighty! You have been an absolute beacon of professional diligence since day one. And for the life of me, I cannot understand why on God's green earth you pulled this type of foolish garbage."

The sergeant took a breath, then continued. "Vest, you are so damn lucky that the major gave you a sterling recommendation after reviewing your pre-flight aviation scores. In fact, right now that is the *only* thing keeping me from shipping your sorry butt back to that cow pasture in Missouri."

I dared not say a word, but I noticed that a regiment that had been marching on the parade grounds had stepped in unison toward our location. The regiment was twenty yards away and standing transfixed, watching everything unfold.

"Are you ignoring me, Vest?" the sergeant hollered! He was fuming because he had caught me glimpsing at the crowd that now encircled our sorry group.

"You and your pitiful little team are going to finish wiping down those bathrooms! And then, you will personally get young Porter showered, shaved, and shined crystal clean before chowtime. Is that clear, Vest?"

Respectfully, but loudly I said, "Yes, staff sergeant!"

He did not blink while giving the four of us his most withering glare. Then he stomped back to lead his formation of men.

Without spelling it out, the sergeant had given me the priceless lesson that you never let a member of your military family down. If we had been caught in battle and Porter had gone missing, it would have been partly my responsibility for not looking out for my teammates. It was a stinging reminder that many events in life do not go as planned, so I was always to remain vigilant.

CHAPTER 30
1955

IT HAD BEEN just over twelve months since I had voyaged across the South Pacific from California to Australia. The most recent development was that I had processed out of Basic Military Training at Lackland Air Force Base and now had the status of pre-cadet at Reese Air Force Base in Lubbock, Texas.

Six days after being assigned duties as a pre-cadet, I had already grown accustomed to military life. I was deep into my work as a mechanic's assistant on the B-25 medium bomber.

On an overcast Valentine's Day, my work clothes, face, arms, and hands were covered with grease and grit. My working superior, Sergeant McGee, was showing me the ropes step-by-step on how to repair the B-25. McGee's appearance reminded me of legendary New York Yankees slugger Babe Ruth, with his pudgy but strong body and welcoming smile.

One of Elvis' songs was playing from a transistor radio, and the stocky B-25 in our care was raised up on heavy wing jacks. McGee was halfway upside-down in the aircraft's glassy nose, where at one time a machine gun had been mounted.

McGee stuck out a hand behind his back and wiggled his fingers. He shouted, "Vest! Hand me that old socket wrench with the red tape wrapped around the handle."

I located the red-handled wrench and gently slapped it into McGee's hand. He slid smoothly into the glass-domed enclosure of the bomber's nose cone and signaled that it was my time to take a break. I snatched up my water bottle and circled the suspended bomber's fuselage and wingspan.

I ran my fingertips along the fuselage of the B-25. This is the bomber that became famous following the Doolittle Raid in April 1942. Lt. Col. Jimmy Doolittle led sixteen bombers on an aerial assault of the Japanese mainland in retaliation for Japan's attack on Pearl Harbor the previous December.

An athletic looking, dark-haired man strode toward me, but bright sunlight behind him prevented me from seeing his face. He had a relaxed stride, even though he walked with a sense of purpose. He was looking for McGee, or me, or both of us.

He walked up to me and we shook hands. He introduced himself as Doug Peterson, pre-cadet officer.

I introduced myself. "Warren Vest. I'm a mechanic's helper in the maintenance squadron."

Peterson's next statement caught me off-guard. "I've been asked to deliver some very good news."

"What is it, sir?"

"Your folks just got off the telephone with our commanding officer, and a good friend of yours from Australia is coming to visit you and your family in Missouri. Our commanding officer would like to speak with you, after your shift ends, to see if a short leave can be worked out so you can go home."

"Wow!" I said. "Thanks for bringing me this great news."

McGee flashed me a winning smile, winked, and said, "Get out of here for the rest of the afternoon, Vest. You've done a good job, and you don't want to keep the C.O. waiting."

I saluted McGee before shaking hands with Doug Peterson and leaving the hangar to go meet with the commanding officer.

CHAPTER 31
1955

THE WARM, SUNDAY-AFTERNOON sunshine greeted our pre-cadet, fast-pitch softball game. During pre-game warmups, I got into a smooth, underhand, fast-pitch rhythm. My team's catcher called out, "Coming down!" He snatched up my last fastball and fired a laser to second base to begin the routine, around-the-horn session before I would throw the game's opening pitch. I had a softball game to play, but my memory skipped back to the reunion with my Australian buddy, Peter, and his pipe-smoking friend, Charles Lock.

Charles, Warren, and Peter - March 1955

I was given a one-week leave, and I returned to our farm near Buffalo, Missouri. Peter and Charles met me there, and I turned into a Missouri tour guide.

We ventured to Springfield, where the Australian visitors were honored guests on a radio show. The show's producer, Lloyd Evans, had learned about my adventure with the Brahman cattle. We moved on to Columbia, home to the University of Missouri, where we enjoyed a raucous house party. Then we drove to St. Louis before circling back to the southwest through the boldly beautiful Mark Twain National Forest. Peter's bubbly personality won over most of my family and friends. My father formed an alliance with him as if he were kin.

"Batter up!" the softball umpire shouted, and my thoughts snapped back to the present. I spun to look at my teammates poised across the field of play. I glanced at the first baseman, Doug Peterson, who had become a close friend.

Doug quipped, "You got this! Just throw strikes and we'll handle the rest. Let's make it ten in a row and bring home the trophy!"

Brimming with confidence from our team's nine-game winning streak, I whipped a blazing fastball toward the left-handed batter. This was the championship game, and he was crowding the plate.

The hitter uncoiled his body and exploded with bat-swinging energy. He smashed my first pitch, sending it directly over my head.

I hit the deck, then popped back up to dust off my tattered blue jeans and T-shirt.

Several jovial and slightly inebriated onlookers barked out some teasing calls. "Batting practice is over, Vest!" "Vest is no longer the best, he needs a rest, we don't jest!"

The crowd roared with laughter as the cocky little batter crossed first base and settled onto the bag next to Doug. I caught the relay throw from our shortstop and shielded my lower face and mouth with my ball glove while quietly cursing. I gathered my wits, took a few deep breaths, and smoked my next offering to a husky, right-handed batter.

Boom! He crushed the rising fastball and sent it sailing high into the sky and far over the head of the backpedaling left fielder. The husky hitter scored, as did the base runner who had been on first. We were down two to nothing.

Two of the good-natured hecklers relaxing in beach chairs down the left-field foul line egged me on, but I ignored them.

Doug signaled the umpire and shouted above the din, "Time out, ump! Time, please!"

He walked up to me with a grin. "Hey, at least it's not *three* to zip." Then he got serious. "Think about the big picture."

"How so?" I asked.

"Both of us are kicking butt in our classes, and we are neck-and-neck for the top few slots in the pre-cadet rankings. Overall, we're looking pretty good."

"That's true. And?"

Pete shrugged. "Next weekend, our drill team gets to perform at the Lubbock Rodeo in front of thousands of people. We're going to have a blast, so relax."

The umpire said, "Time's up, fellas."

While moving back toward first base, Doug said, "Remember a few weeks ago when you told me about the time you tried out for third base in the St. Louis Cardinals' organization? You could've played minor league pro baseball, so this game is a walk in the park."

Doug's comments relieved my nerves. I took to the rubber again, wound up, and whirled my third pitch of the championship game. The batter just looked at the curveball as it swerved across home plate.

"Strike one!" the umpire bellowed.

I pitched out of the first-inning jam. We entered the top of the seventh inning leading by a score of 4–2. I retired the first two batters. The hecklers along the left-field foul line had been relatively silent since the first inning. But now the estimable left-handed batter who had opened the game by hammering my first pitch stepped into the batter's box. The season was on the line.

I threw my fastball lower than usual, then immediately shuffled backward into a defensive position. The southpaw took the bait and smacked a wicked line drive that hissed toward my knees. I arched left and backhanded the liner with my glove. It was the third out. We won it all!

Warren holding softball

CHAPTER 32
1955

IT HAD BEEN seventeen months since my front-porch chat with Uncle Glenn. I had to smile when I remembered him holding up the *Kansas City Star*, thinking I would notice a tiny help-wanted ad for the Ford Aircraft Company.

Doug Peterson and I were still pre-cadets at Reese Air Force Base. Doug received orders assigning him to Aviation Cadet Class 57A. A few weeks later, I received my orders to commence the next stage of my training as a member of Class 57J. Our friendship meant a great deal to each of us. We said our goodbyes before going our separate ways, sincerely hoping to rekindle our accord in the future.

I put the finishing touches on my routine tasks at Reese and prepared for my transfer to San Antonio, Texas, for my aviation cadet pre-flight training. The first day after arrival, we were expected to be smartly dressed in full uniform and adapting to the confines of our busy aviation cadets' pre-flight barracks in preparation for a formal inspection. I re-examined the crisp folds, corners, and edges of my bunk's sheets. Just then the thundering voice of our brutally demanding upper-classman cadet filled the barracks. *"Attention!"*

I stopped what I was doing, turned, and snapped to attention. Chin up, shoulders back, chest out, arms at my side, my feet pointing forward. That's when I realized that a first lieutenant accompanied the upper-classman cadet. The upperclassman had pulled on his dreaded pair of white gloves for an unscheduled inspection. All the trainees hated white-glove inspections.

I forced myself to inhale through my nose even though I had been battling a cold. Very slowly, the lieutenant and the upper-classman cadet walked down the center lane of the barracks. I dared not turn my head even the slightest bit to monitor their progress.

Cadet Williams murmured, "Here they come, and they have touched nothing yet with those whitees! Crap!"

The upper-classman cadet and the lieutenant were less than six feet from me on my left, but instead of zeroing in on my position, the upperclassman turned in the opposite direction and focused his wrath on Cadet Jones. His ear-splitting shouts reduced Jones to a withering mass. Much to my dismay, Cadet Williams let out a minuscule burp of a chuckle.

Immediately, the upper classman's fury was centered squarely on me. He took three strides and began unloading on me. "Vest! What in the world is so funny? Tell me right now!"

I kept my eyes focused high on a daddy-longlegs hiding in the corner rafter. I replied loudly to the cadet upperclassman: "Nothing, sir!"

"Do you think I'm running a comedy club down here in Texas, Vest?" Spittle was flying from his mouth.

"No sir!" I said.

The upperclassman rolled on. "Do you know how many fine young men have flunked out of the Air Force's Aviation Pre-Flight Training Program during the past ninety days?"

"No sir!" I barked.

"Several of them who did not take this part of the program seriously," the upperclassman answered.

"Vest! Your instructors have informed me that you've earned some of the top marks and scores in the altitude chamber tests. Plus, mission planning, navigation, aeronautics, *and* mathematics. But for some damn reason, you think it is damn kiddy playtime right now. Is that right, Vest?"

I sharply answered, "No sir!"

He raised his white-gloved hands into view. "Let's see how clean and tight your bunk area is."

I stepped aside but remained at attention.

The upperclassman bent forward like a curious egret and angled his face next to my exceptionally well-made bed. He whipped out his white-gloved right hand, extended his fingers, and traced them along my bunk framework. After a few quick swipes, he flipped over his hand to see if he could find any dust on his spotless mitt. But he saw nothing.

After another minute of insanely detailed scoping of my area, the upperclassman spun around to face me.

"Vest, this is the cleanest bunk I have inspected in Class 57J!"

"Thank you, sir!"

Then he added, "I have a good feeling about you, and I believe you will make an outstanding officer one day. Understand me, Vest?"

"Yes sir! Thank you, sir." For the first time, I realized that my life as a pilot was about to lift off.

CHAPTER 33
1956

AFTER SURVIVING NINETY days of pure hell during my second assignment to Lackland Air Force Base outside San Antonio, I entered primary flight training at Graham Air Base in Marianna, Florida. This interactive military compound is tucked away in the northwest panhandle of the state, just south of Alabama and southwest of Georgia.

On the morning of my twenty-first birthday, I was sitting in the flight room along with forty-three other cadets.

Our civilian chief flight instructor was about to commence his daily briefing to review key points about the day's flight-line schedule. But he bowed out of the room momentarily to speak with his superior. My mind drifted back nearly two years to the day I had said goodbye to my Australian buddy, Peter, on the docks in Sydney. In terms of my emotional maturity and professional perspective, and my vastly improved physical training, it seemed like my Australia trip had taken place a lifetime ago.

I now knew without a doubt that I would spend my career as a pilot, either with jet fighters or transport aircraft.

The chief flight instructor returned to the room and took his position behind the podium. A massive blackboard behind him was covered with his sprawling notes in white chalk detailing vital factors and memos for the day. We were being trained in weather trends, landing-pattern inclinations, pre-flight checks and protocols, and emergency procedures. We would cover urgent planning measures during intense oral questioning prior to our training flights.

From the moment I arrived at Graham Air Base, I realized the value of my past training experiences, which allowed me entry into this more refined and professional learning environment. Gone were the relentless screaming and shouting from our superiors. Instead, the tactful teaching ambiance at Graham reinforced the truth that I now was living an efficient life while overcoming all fears and flying challenges. This was the only life to live if I really wanted to become an outstanding pilot.

The chief flight instructor spoke quietly. "Cadet Vest, since today is your twenty-first birthday and given the fact you scored so well yesterday during oral emergency procedures, I'll give you a choice. You can either select a fellow cadet to undergo a round of EP (emergency procedures) questioning, or you can single-handedly vote for the entire class to skip today's three-part questioning. If you choose the second option, some cadets will take you out on the town to celebrate your milestone birthday tonight."

Most of the cadets turned their attention toward me, while sounds of "Happy birthday, Warren" and "Give us a break, Vest!" echoed around the room.

I feigned indecisiveness between the two options.

"Come on, Vest!" said Cadet Miller. "Let's hit the town tonight and I'll buy the first few pitchers!"

The chief flight instructor called for the question. "Okay, Cadet Vest, what shall it be?"

I merrily replied, "Sold! And Miller is picking up the first round!"

After finishing his pinpoint analysis of the finer issues listed on the chalkboard, the chief flight instructor dismissed us. I filed out of the room escorted by eager cadets.

We still had the day's flight training ahead of us. In the locker room, I donned my flight suit and Air Force cadet ball cap. Then I headed onto the tarmac to locate my T-34 piston-engine Beechcraft.

CHAPTER 34
1956

I SLIPPED MY sunglasses on and walked across the active tarmac beside my flight instructor, Joe Turner.

The noise of the soft wind rolling across the runways and the sounds of buzzing aircraft motors from a multitude of trainees taxiing their planes felt normal to me.

Here at Graham Air Base in Marianna, Florida, I had executed six flights while accompanied by my flight instructor. I felt different today because soon I would take a T-34 on a flight without the presence of my flight instructor. That is, so long as Joe Turner decided to set me free after evaluating my performance during one flight together.

"Warren," he said, "you're ready and I'm sure of it. But let's get through this flight and, if it goes well, I'll sign off on your first solo."

Throughout my pre-cadet Air Force training, I had heard frightening stories about prospective pilots suffering panic events, heart attacks, nervous breakdowns, and even, at times, terrifying hallucinations rendering them incapable of taking control of their own aircraft. One of the most haunting tales had to do with a trainee pilot speeding down the runway during his first solo takeoff attempt. His nerves went haywire and he freaked out, causing his T-34 to buck wildly down the runway before he lost control. The airplane burst into flames, and he was burned alive as he desperately struggled to get free.

To help prevent the buildup of anxiety or debilitating panic, a flight instructor accompanied modestly experienced students through pre-flight preparation and the first takeoff and landing on an expected soloing day. If the instructor was confident of the student's calm demeanor and overall behavior during that takeoff and landing, the instructor would have the student drop him off at a location adjacent to the runway. Then the instructor would observe the student performing three takeoffs and landings to complete a solo flight initiation.

I approached the T-34 that I had been scheduled to fly for my solo mission. I checked the number 796 and the exterior features of the twenty-six-foot-long aircraft. The propeller affixed to the nosecone was clean. The U.S. AIR FORCE logo embellishing the mid-sections above the inner wings. An oversized tempered-glass dome canopy protected the  tandem cockpit, and the innards had been spacious enough for my flight instructor to sit four feet behind me during my training flights.

I put my left foot onto the retractable step, pulled myself up, and eased into the cockpit to review the maintenance logbook and begin my preflight checklist. Meanwhile, Joe Turner and Keith, a member of the ground crew, stood by. I sensed that Joe was working to create a relaxed environment while keeping a sharp eye on me.

Inside the cockpit, I checked the flight controls, trim tabs neutral, landing-gear handle secure, and that the canopy emergency-release handle seal was good. I moved back into the rear cockpit and inspected the safety belt, shoulder harness, and directional indicator, among other checks, to complete that phase.

I extracted the pre-flight checklist from the left breast pocket of my flight suit, exited the aft cockpit, and dropped back onto the tarmac. It was time to conduct the exterior inspection of the T-34. I silently quizzed myself and intermittently answered aloud: "Wing flap, check." Then I examined the aileron to ensure lateral balance, and said, "Check." "Wingtip and Navigation lights, check."

I checked the wheel chocks, tires, and brakes and saw that the wheel wells were unobstructed. I advanced to the nose section and Joe gave me an approving look and a quick lift of his head. I checked the left augmenter tube and propeller and the air intake. "Check." After completing the nose inspection, I walked to the right wing and checked the fuel quantity and ensured the cap was secure. I examined the right side of the fuselage and the fuel tank vent, checking that it was set at a twelve-degree forward pitch. "Check." The antenna was secured, and the static air vent was clear. I moved back to the empennage to examine the tail section and checked the right and left horizontal stabilizers, elevator and trim tabs, and vertical tail fin. I walked to the left side and checked the tail skid and modest baggage compartment.

Finally, I stepped to my left and extended my right hand to greet Keith. "It's good to see you this morning. How does she look?"

He smiled and replied in his southern Alabama accent, "She's ready to fly, Warren, as smooth as my mama's gravy sandwich."

"Thanks, Keith." Then I stepped up the left flank of the T-34 and eased down into the cockpit.

I continued through my checks and locked my seat into place before fastening my seatbelt and harness. The flight controls were responding nicely. I looked at the flap and trim controls, the pump and valve switches, and the settings for the fuel-mixture levels. I examined gauges, lights, and instruments, and mumbled, "Clock and altimeter, set. Vertical velocity indicator at zero, check. Primer, starter and battery switches off, check. And generator switch on, check."

I confirmed the proper levels of the fuel gauge and fuel-booster pump, and the steady and blinking navigation lights. I made sure I had my own flashlight on board in case of an emergency in the air or if I had to ditch the aircraft onto land or water.

I called out to my flight instructor and hailed Keith simultaneously. "Joe, my preflight checks are complete, and Keith, I am ready for engine start."

Joe climbed into the rear cockpit and secured himself into the seat behind me. We donned our headsets and boom microphones and checked our interphone communications. I acknowledged Keith's "all clear" signal and pushed the button to start the engine. It rumbled to life with a deafening roar. Keith pulled the wheel chocks away, clearing the path for me to taxi.

Using my call sign, I alerted the control tower. "Graham Tower, this is Devil-40 request taxi to holding point, runway three-six."

The tower replied, "Devil-40, you're cleared to taxi, and hold short of runway three-six."

"Affirmative. Devil-40 taxiing to runway three-six."

With goosebumps rising across my flesh and my pulse quickening, I guided the powerful T-34 across the tarmac. The slightly bumpy ride felt natural. I was only one flight away from taking the T-34 up into the skies all on my own.

CHAPTER 35
1956

WHILE IN THE cockpit and idling at the holding point, I watched a half-dozen trainees flying their aircraft through the partly cloudy, northwest-Florida sky. Then, via the T-34's interphone communication system, Joe instructed me to execute a takeoff, fly a left-hand traffic pattern, and finish with a full-stop landing.

Using the radio, I confirmed to the control tower that Devil-40 was ready for takeoff and requesting a left traffic pattern for a full-stop landing.

The tower responded, "Devil-40 is cleared for takeoff and left-hand traffic pattern for full-stop landing."

I taxied onto runway thirty-six and advanced the throttle to full power for takeoff. We were off the ground. I retracted the landing gear while ascending to one thousand feet and turned into a left-hand traffic pattern. Now it was time to land. When I passed the approach end of runway thirty-six, I extended the landing gear and completed my before-landing checklist.

The tower called, "Devil-40, you are cleared to turn base leg to the final approach and a full-stop landing on runway three-six."

I hoped and prayed for a safe, smooth landing. Several seconds later I touched down on runway thirty-six, slowed the T-34 to taxiing speed, and exited the runway.

Joe advised me to taxi over to a middle tarmac pad and stop the airplane. When I halted the T-34, the cockpit's glass canopy slid open and my flight instructor exited the back seat.

Joe stood on the left wing, smiled at me, and reached in and shook my hand. "Go do it, Vest! Three takeoffs and three landings, with the first two landings touch-and-go, and then pick me up here when you finish."

He stepped off the wing and I closed the canopy. "Graham Tower, this is Devil-44. Request taxi to runway three-six for takeoff."

The tower replied, "Devil-44, understand that Devil-40 has now deplaned. You are cleared to taxi to runway three-six for takeoff."

I double checked to make sure that I had muted my microphone. Then I pumped my fist and released a burst of delight. "*Yes!*"

For the first time in my life, I solo-taxied an airplane and approached runway thirty-six before the tower cleared me for takeoff. I advanced the throttle to maximum power and the T-34 zoomed down the runway. I lifted off, completed the takeoff, and retracted the landing gear before quickly climbing to the proper altitude and airspeed. I gazed at the beautiful sky and felt an inspiring rush of pride. Joy filled my heart and soul.

I turned left into the traffic pattern while preparing for my inaugural solo, touch-and-go landing. Ahead of me and down on the left, I spotted my flight instructor standing on the tarmac pad. I eclipsed the approach end of runway thirty-six and extended the landing gear before settling the tires of the T-34 onto the runway and cruising past Joe at fifty miles per hour. After successfully completing phase one, I pushed the throttle to full power and executed the second solo takeoff. I retracted the landing gear and wanted to cheer. But I refrained as I recalled the words of my flight instructor: "Don't celebrate in the air."

I banked the airplane left and came back around to begin my second approach at runway thirty-six. I released the landing gear and with Joe eyeballing my every move, I delivered a beautiful touch-and-go landing. I pushed the throttle to full power for the final leg of my maiden solo flight. Once again in the sky, I felt the adrenalized emotion of invincibility.

Soon, I zeroed in on the long strip of runway thirty-six. This time, I avoided glancing at Joe. Instead, I focused on executing a flawless, full-stop landing. After passing over the end of the runway, I calmly landed the T-34 and throttled it back down to taxiing speed. Elated, but staying cool, I steered the T-34 over to the tarmac pad where Joe was waiting. He hopped onto the left wing and I pulled the glass canopy open.

Joe shook my hand and said, "Well done, Vest. Excellent! Let's taxi back to the facility and park this baby. The boys are out there waiting for you. They're really excited about taking you out on the town to celebrate your first solo."

CHAPTER 36
1956

I WAS IN an especially good mood that day. Earlier, my buddies and I had been listening to the Armed Forces Network when New York Yankees slugger Mickey Mantle blasted a home run off a Washington Senators pitcher. The ball sailed six hundred twenty feet, barely missing flying over the right-field rooftop at Yankee Stadium.

During my training assignment in Marianna, Florida, I had grown somewhat accustomed to the humidity, but the bugs and chiggers were relentless. After completing nearly forty hours of flight training in the T-34, including ninety-seven landings and more than sixteen hours of flying solo, I had matured as a pilot. I was elevated into the next phase of flying. I would be piloting the more dynamic and acrobatic T-28. The thirty-three-foot-long, twelve-foot-high, three-ton airplane became my favorite between the two types of aircraft I had flown in Florida. And the sleek, silver body, forty-foot wingspan, and crisp Air Force coloring and lettering made it more attractive.

While I got into my flight suit in the training facility's locker room, a familiar voice spoke up. "Hey, Vest, what's your plan?" It was Cadet Miller.

Before grabbing my aviator's helmet, I said, "I'm getting ready for my next round of instrument flight training. What about you?"

"I'll tell you what. These last few months have been a revelation for me. I've watched several of our classmates get washed out of training or reclassified to navigator school."

"You're right on the money, Miller. Either you can fly blind or not. There is no in-between." We wished each other good luck before I left the building and walked onto the tarmac to meet my flight instructor at the assigned T-28.

In the two-and-a-half years since I walked across the University of Missouri campus to consult with my academic advisor, the breadth of my existence had catapulted from one end of life's spectrum to the other. Now that I had tasted several other parts of the world and found my true calling of becoming a pilot, I had changed into a different person.

Joe Turner was always a few minutes early for our training sessions. We had spent a great deal of time together during the last several months, and it amazed me how courageous Joe was. Virtually every day he was putting his life on the line to  do his work of training youthful, imperfect, future pilots.

Joe began his oration. "Vest, without a doubt you've taken a liking to the T-28, and honestly, it's fond of you. Your aptitude at handling her top-end speeds and powerful turns is first-rate, and you're progressing faster than most, especially during your nighttime flights."

"Thanks, Joe," I replied.

He held up his hand. "But we're only about halfway through your twenty-five hours of flight instrument hood training and this time, when we're up there and you're in the dark flying by instruments only, trust your training and rely on your experience."

I soaked in the meaning of his message.

Joe finished, "It's no different than being thirty thousand feet above the earth and descending through ten miles of storm clouds with zero visibility and everything around you is snow white, *and* you're at three hundred miles per hour."

A few minutes later we were positioned in the dual cockpit of the T-28, with Joe taking the lead in the front seat. I settled into the rear and clipped up the fabric curtains that blocked my line of sight to anything outside of my aft cockpit. Joe and I tested our interphone system to ensure it was working and all systems were a go.

Joe took off and flew the T-28 to an altitude of six thousand feet. Then he said, "Okay, Vest. The engine is running irregularly, what should you do?"

The blackout curtains prevented me from seeing anything other than my instrument panel and some gauges. I told Joe, "I'm going to enhance the mixture, and if that doesn't work, I'll switch fuel tanks."

"Good," Joe replied. "Trust your instruments and pilot the T-28. Remember, both you and the airplane want to complete the mission."

I rescanned the instrument panel. "Joe, it appears we are 1.5 degrees off our initial flight path. Can you confirm that?"

Joe responded, "If you had missed that error, two hours from now we would have ended up in Cuba or the Bermuda Triangle."

I felt a tad bit prideful, but the grueling tutelage went on without a reprieve. Joe peppered me with questions about icing on the wings, faulty altimeters and airspeed readings, odd manifold-pressure gauge readings, and a wild tachometer discrepancy that would falsify the engine's working speed.

Joe's machine-gun approach to asking questions forced me to attain a heightened sense of alertness and quickness of response that I had never experienced before. Perspiration dripped down my forehead and temples, and my armpits and upper torso were drenched in sweat.

"Good, Vest. Fine. Now let's bring her home these last few minutes. Tell me your glide-slope reading and don't be vague." We were beginning our approach back to the runway at Graham Air Base.

The horizontal guidance system on the T-28 had not failed me during this flight. It had proven temperamental only during a few minutes of my first two hooded-instrument-training flights. I examined the glide slope of the Instrument Landing System and said to Joe, "I am a half-dot low and reducing descent rate to get back to a three-degree slope to the runway."

"Confirmed," he replied. "Now you're exactly on centerline and glide slope."

Joe took over the controls at three hundred feet above the runway and landed the T-28. Once we were taxiing toward the parking spot for the T-28, I withdrew the instrument hood and folded it neatly. It took a moment for my eyesight to adjust to the lovely, orange-and-pink dusk that backlit the air base.

Joe shut down the engine and said, "By far, that was your best hooded session yet. Top-notch."

Relishing his praise but still perspiring, I allowed his words to sink in. I sat back in my pilot's seat and let out a long exhale of wonderfully soothing relief.

CHAPTER 37
1956

AT NINE O'CLOCK on a sticky Friday morning, I was the second person standing in line at a Chevrolet dealership in Marianna, Florida. I was there waiting when the chunky sales manager opened the tall glass doors to let the customers inside.

I had never shopped for a new car due to my not having enough money and the fact that my life had been geographically unpredictable.

The friendly woman at the front of the line entered the brightly lit showroom. I followed, taking in the array of colorful new sedans, Nomads, station wagons, and pickups. The sales manager took a long drag on his cigarette before swigging at his coffee.

I spotted a beautiful, silver-bodied, ivory-topped 1956 Bel Air with chrome trim. I hurried over to poke my head inside the open driver-side window and smell the wonderful new-car aroma of the gorgeous Bel Air. I pulled my head out of the car and backed up a few steps, bumping into the sales manager.

"Careful, young fella, or you'll get hurt before you get the chance to test drive this beauty," he said. "Not only is she a looker, but that monster V-8 under the hood will torch most of her competition. That is if you're courageous enough to step on the gas and really open her up."

Reeling from his twangy opening barrage, I withdrew to gather my wits. I decided to open with "I'm on a strict monthly budget."

The sales manager toked on his cigarette while examining my finely dressed civilian presence. After he discharged twin plumes of smoke from his nostrils, he shook hands with me and said, "From the good looks of you and given the fact that Bob, the owner, told me you were coming in this morning, I'm figuring you must be Air Force Cadet Warren Vest."

Impressed by his complete disregard for my opening salvo, I replied, "That's correct. And you are?"

"Cooper's the name. And thanks for being on time."

Soon we were cruising along the roads of Marianna, Florida, while Cooper highlighted the features of the coupe. I test-drove the Bel Air with a manual transmission on the highway. I was in the right-hand lane when I put the car into overdrive and punched my foot onto the gas pedal. Accelerating the whole time, I veered the Bel Air into the fast lane and whisked past slower cars and trucks, eventually achieving the posted speed limit.

Very happy with the car's performance, I began slowing down, glanced over at Cooper, and quipped, "It handles *really* well. How much is it?"

Cooper asked, "What kind of airplanes do you fly?"

I answered, "I'm going to be a transport pilot."

Cooper remained silent. Finally, I asked, "Can you give me a great deal on this car?"

He said, "I got the green light from Bob to let you have it for twenty-six hundred out the door, today. Sound good?"

"Ouch," I said. "I don't have that much saved up."

"Relax," Cooper continued. "I'm the guy that can get this deal done for you. Besides, you came in with your paperwork ready and Air Force letters of recommendation and training scores all packaged up. Bob told me to give you the best deal. You need to carry your insurance through USAA. They're the best company that services military families."

I exited from the highway and turned left to cross the overpass. A few seconds later we were slowly driving toward the dealership and Cooper was explaining the purchasing terms. "Our total price, best offer, is twenty-six hundred dollars. You'll need to put down a one-hundred-dollar deposit. After that, it will cost you fifty dollars a month until you become an officer in the Air Force. Then your monthly payment will increase to one hundred bucks a month until the note is paid off."

We drove in silence for about thirty seconds and I asked, "Can I drive it off the lot today?"

"Of course. I want you to take this beauty all the way back to Missouri to show to your family and friends. We're talking about making a deal now, today."

I steered the Bel Air into the lot and parked near the showroom's side entrance.

Overcome with happiness, I looked at Cooper and said, "You've got a deal!"

Cooper extracted a cigarette from the pack, lit up, and said, "Now we're talking. Let's go inside and write it up. Congratulations, Warren!"

CHAPTER 38
1956

I WAS ASSIGNED to return to Reese Air Force Base in Lubbock, Texas. That allowed me to rekindle some friendships I had built during my first stint at Reese.

I finished breakfast and walked across the base by the hangars where I had worked as a mechanic's assistant on the ruggedly powerful B-25 bomber. The overall mood of the coed personnel living and working at Reese had been elevated under the leadership of Colonel Travis Hoover, a famous B-25 wartime pilot who had taken off from the flight deck of the USS Hornet and expertly bombed Tokyo, Japan, in World War II. I ducked into a briefing room and joined Lieutenant Dalton and fellow cadet Ken Bratton at a large table.

"It's cold outside!" I mumbled and dropped my coat onto a chair.

Lt. Dalton, Bratton and I were there to review the final flight-plan map for our long-range training flight to California. Dalton's casual air put us at ease. Bratton's pinpoint focus made him easy to communicate with on a variety of complex issues. I would enjoy flying the B-25s with him during the last few months of training.

As we examined the flight map spread out on the table, we checked the detailed notes Ken and I had made. Lieutenant Dalton stated, "Vest and Bratton, you two developed a good route to satisfy the limitations of an unpressurized B-25 without the need to utilize supplemental oxygen during the flight." We had plotted a flight path from Reese Air Force Base in Lubbock to Seminole and El Paso, Texas, before going to Lordsburg, New Mexico, and Tucson, Arizona. We had planned a refueling stop at Williams Air Force Base near Phoenix. After refueling, we would pass over Los Angeles and land at Oxnard Air Force Base in southern California.

I grinned at Lieutenant Dalton and said, "You'll be able to personally deliver this year's Christmas gifts to your family in Camarillo."

He replied, "It has been a long time since I've seen them. Too long actually. I can't wait to get there. Bratton, it's your turn to handle the lion's share of this flight westward, so you will take us to Phoenix. Then Vest will fly us into Oxnard. When we return on Sunday, your roles will switch. I will see you both at the B-25 this afternoon. Dismissed."

At eleven-thirty that night, the three of us were in the frigid cockpit of the B-25, cruising due west at an altitude of seven thousand feet. Ken was piloting the B-25, with its growling engines, through the night sky. Lieutenant Dalton was coaching me from the right-side chair. I sat in the jump seat behind them.

With the autopilot engaged, we focused on the dark horizon and constantly checked the multitude of gauges, buttons, switches, and lights on the instrument panels in front of us, above us, and to our left and right.

Via our headset communication system, Lieutenant Dalton's crackling voice asked me, "How are your feet and hands doing? Are they still chilly?"

I responded, "Negative. They are much better than twenty minutes ago when we were at ten thousand feet flying over Blythe, California. They have thawed out."

I leaned forward to stretch out my lower back while examining the fuel gauges and oil-temperature gauge. I asked, "Lieutenant Dalton, are you getting antsy yet? We're almost there."

"Affirmative," he replied. Then he asked, "Once we touch down in Oxnard, how many landings will that be for you in the B-25, sixty-eight or sixty-nine?"

"Seventy, sir," I replied as we flew over the glittering, late-night Los Angeles skyline.

By the wee hours of Saturday morning, I had landed the B-25 at Oxnard Air Force Base northwest of Los Angeles. As the three of us strode across the tarmac toward the Base Operations Center, Lieutenant Dalton's wife and young children sprinted out of the facility to greet him.

"Mission accomplished!" he exclaimed.

Ken and I acknowledged our lieutenant's kudos as we continued our path into the main building to register with the on-duty base operations officer. By one o'clock in the morning, we had been transported via Jeep to the bachelor officer quarters (BOQ). I was asleep by 2:30.

Later that morning, Ken and I ate a quick breakfast in the mess hall and explored the grounds of Oxnard Air Force Base. We also visited with the coed personnel on duty. By 3 p.m., Ken and I had borrowed a small pickup truck from the base operations officer and arrived at the sandy, beachside parking lot of McGrath State Beach.

We rolled up our pant legs before heading across the warm sands of the surprisingly busy beach. Ken spotted a party of at least one hundred people celebrating with music, dancing, food, and drink. He said, "Let's go join that bash! There's got to be at least fifty lovely ladies there."

"I'm going to take a short stroll along the waterline," I said, "then I'll meet you there."

Ken took off and I walked in the opposite direction down the seashore. I had briefly visited Southern California—at the port of San Pedro—three years earlier. But I had not allowed myself to ponder it too much while I was piloting the B-25 from Phoenix to Oxnard.

Now I was just seventy-five miles north of San Pedro and so close to the beautiful location where I began my work of transferring Brahman cattle to Australia. San Pedro is where I had locked horns with that lazy cowboy before he quit and left me to do the job alone.

In a span of three short years my life had come full circle, unlike anything I could have imagined back when I had been constructing cattle stalls for the animals in my care.

Three years earlier I was eighteen years old. Lloyd's of London assigned me to safely deliver a herd of cattle to very appreciative ranchers in Australia. Back then I had no idea I would be standing here now as a pilot-in-training for the U.S. Air Force.

CHAPTER 39
1957

THE NASTY, FRIGID winds could not hamper my spirits after I finished my Monday-morning pushups and leg exercises. Graduation from the Air Force Cadets was just six weeks away. In just over two months I would turn twenty-two with a bright future ahead of me as an Air Force pilot.

After shaving, showering, and downing two cups of coffee, a bowl of cereal, and a banana, I knocked on the door of Ken's room. His skin was blotchy, his eyes were bloodshot, and he had a bad cough. Ken said, "Warren, I'm sick as hell, but I really want to fly today." Lieutenant Dalton had given us the go-ahead to fly the B-25. This would make the tenth time we'd be flying the plane without him.

I asked Ken, "Do you have a fever? And have you talked to Dalton yet?" He said, "I'm burning up like a raging forest fire."

"Forget it then," I said. "I'll meet with Dalton and find a replacement. Go to the dispensary, get checked, and I'll see you after my flight."

I met Lieutenant Dalton on the wintry tarmac near the parking spot of the assigned B-25. "Ken is sick." he said, "you're going to fly with Ruben Gonzales. Ruben is one of our cadets from the Cuban group."

I looked at the twin-engine craft, rated at seventeen hundred horsepower per engine and weighing twenty thousand pounds. It could fly at speeds exceeding three hundred miles per hour.

Cadet Gonzales arrived in his flight suit with a parachute pack on his back and a large camera strapped across his chest. He walked down the flight line between parked airplanes with a huge smile stretched across his face.

Lieutenant Dalton froze me with his blue-eyed stare and whispered, "Respectfully to young Cadet Gonzales, he is nowhere near your capability as a pilot. So, you will handle all the flying duties today. Ruben is there to learn, and he also wants to take a few pictures from above. You will be in the left seat for the entire two-hour flight. Got it?"

"Yes sir," I replied. I had engaged in a few small-talk conversations with Ruben, but we barely knew each other.

Twenty-five minutes later, after completing our exterior checks, I was positioned in the left seat of the cockpit and taxiing toward the runways. Ruben was completing his pre-flight checks on my right. We arrived at the engine run-up area and I initiated the run-up procedure. During the engine power check, I found the engine manifold pressure was low. After reviewing the checklist Ruben was to have performed, I discovered he had not returned the carburetor heat levers to the fully off position.

"Ruben, please check those carburetor heat levers again. And run through the entire checklist one more time."

"I'm beginning the checks again now."

After establishing our spot at the far end of the runway, the tower cleared us for takeoff. I accelerated the B-25 full-throttle down the windy runway before lifting off north into the slightly  turbulent sky. We climbed to eight thousand five hundred feet while Ruben snapped away on his camera.

Ruben asked if we could fly over Palo Duro Canyon. "I want to take pictures of the Grand Canyon of Texas," he said. "It's America's second-largest canyon."

I replied, "Ruben, I know, but Palo Duro Canyon is sixty miles out of our way. Although it's gorgeous, it will eat up too much of our training time. We will make it happen before I graduate in six weeks."

"Sounds good," he replied. Then he asked, "Can you make a hard right turn at about a sixty-degree bank, so I can take pictures of the wing and propeller pointed directly at the ground?"

"That I can do. Making steep turning maneuvers is part of my training today."

Ruben began clicking away with his camera. Smoothly, I rolled the B-25 to the right and maneuvered the airplane through the bleak sky at two hundred miles per hour.

After finishing the banking right turn, I rolled the wings back to level. Without saying a word, Ruben pulled the right engine throttle to idle, shut off the fuel, and reached overhead to push the feathering button, causing the right propeller's governor to halt the prop's rotation. He seemed satisfied by his negligent actions and snapped pictures of the non-rotating propeller.

With a rush of adrenaline, I screamed at him: "What in the hell are you doing? Put that camera away, now!"

Ruben showed a terrified look. "I'm sorry!"

I ordered him to review the restart and unfeathering-propeller procedures. The right engine started but I had zero control of the right propeller. The lame prop was wind-milling like a carnival toy and creating a crippling aerodynamic drag on the airplane.

I was determined to focus solely on flying the aircraft. My hands gained a tighter grip on the yoke and my left foot jammed down on the left rudder pressure to maintain directional control. My overloaded senses blocked out every unnecessary sight, sound, smell, and touch. The emergency-procedure aspects of my training kicked in and in a blinding flash I recalled the comforting words of Joe Turner: "The plane is your ally."

I radioed the tower to inform them of our dire situation. "Adding power to the right engine increases the drag, and I can't maintain both speed and altitude in this situation. Please, your advice."

My thoughts careened through the limited options that remained. The tower personnel brainstormed their own ideas as we descended on a fearsome trajectory. With the wind-milling propeller on the right wing and the left engine operating at maximum power, I tried to find an airspeed to give me the minimum rate of descent while keeping the tower aware of our weakening state.

A voice from the tower said, "Shut down the right engine to reduce the propeller drag."

I ordered Ruben to shut off the right engine, but his doing so only reduced our descent rate slightly. My mind calculated the time to the field, our rate of descent per minute, and how much altitude I was above field level. The tower's dedicated team was doing its own calculations and wondering how much longer my left engine would hold up revving at maximum power. I noticed that Ruben was trembling uncontrollably.

Then came a command from the tower. "Radar shows you are in a clear area *so bail out. NOW!*"

Ruben clutched both sides of his radio headset and rocked back and forth. I continued to fly the descending B-25 toward Reese Air Force Base. I advised him, "*Bail out now, Ruben. Right now!*"

Ruben climbed out of the right seat and eased himself into the small cabin aft of the flight deck. Shaking uncontrollably, he unlatched the belly stairway and it unfurled into the slipstream.

I yelled down at him, "Ruben, double-check your parachute straps!" Before I looked back at my front panels and the decreasingly low sight line through the windshield, I saw Ruben's wide-eyed but silent appeal for mercy as he tugged and pulled at the dual harness of his parachute.

I refocused all my attention on the ascending gray horizon ahead of me. I hoped Ruben's four-thousand-foot tumble would end perfectly for him. Then I barely heard his loud screaming through the barrier of my headset. "Warren, I don't want to jump!"

Ruben was shaking and crying on the bottom step of the yawning hatch. I barked at him, "Jump, Ruben! Jump now!"

"I can't do it!"

I pivoted back to my duties while failing to suppress a thought of self-preservation. *I can parachute out of this B-25 now and leave Ruben onboard.*

A voice from the tower broke my trance. "Confirm that your co-pilot has bailed out and you are bailing out next."

"Negative," I responded. "He will not jump and I can't leave him, I'm going to try to make it back."

"Affirmative," the tower replied. "Emergency ground crew personnel are ready. Good luck."

The winds at Reese Air Force Base were out of the north at fifteen to twenty miles per hour. I was coming from the northeast. There was no way I could get around to the south end of the airport to land on runway thirty-five into the wind. The only chance I had was to continue straight to runway seventeen and land with a strong tailwind. I could not chance adding extra drag to the B-25 by extending the wing flaps, nor could I afford to lower the landing gear until the very last minute. I continued to calculate the descent rate against the estimated minutes to the runway.

"Ruben, get back in your seat and buckle up. NOW!" I ordered.

Ruben scrambled into his seat.

Tethering the yoke with my hands and holding full-left rudder for directional control, I struggled to keep the B-25 flying as we lost altitude. Moments later, I lowered the landing gear just prior to crossing over the runway threshold no more than twenty-five feet in the air, with the left engine still at maximum power, no wing flaps extended to slow us down, and a strong tailwind pushing us even faster. I landed the plane in a sickeningly hard and fast thumping skip down the pavement. The aircraft screamed down the runway at a high ground speed.

I needed the entire length of the runway to bring the B-25 to a full stop near the end of the runway as a swarm of military vehicles and emergency trucks and vans surrounded us in a semi-circle of flashing lights. Taking some deep breaths, I shut down the engine as Ruben scurried out of the cockpit and fell onto the tarmac.

I seemed frozen in my cockpit seat but finally exited the aircraft through the open hatch and was greeted by Lieutenant Dalton and a maintenance officer, who asked me to sign the maintenance log for the B-25. I attempted to scribble my name on the ledger, but my right hand was quaking terribly. So, I scratched my initials onto the log book and walked away in a daze.

Dalton guided me to one of the ambulances and sat me down on the edge of its rear cabin floorboard. Then Ruben walked over, shook my hand, and said, "Thank you for saving my life, Warren."

I nodded, but I was numb, speechless, and changed forever.

Chapter 40
1957

INSIDE THE COLORFULLY decorated auditorium at Reese, after the military band concluded the national anthem, I sat back down along with fifty-seven cadet classmates. We were waiting for our graduation ceremony to begin. I winked at Cadet Ken Bratton and my buddy, Cadet Art Dickinson. Dressed in my Air-Force-blue uniform and black shoes, I looked to the right and located my family. I saw the proud faces of my mother, father, and nine-year-old brother. Even though I had visited with them prior to commencement, my heart swelled with pride because of the love we shared for one another. They had traveled by railroad through a record-breaking blizzard all the way from Missouri to attend my graduation. My brother, Lendol, was beaming with admiration. He waved at me a couple of times before I discreetly acknowledged his greeting. I returned the smiling gestures of my father and mother, then turned my attention to the elevated main stage.

As our base commander, Colonel Travis Hoover, strode toward the podium to address the crowd, I remembered some of the key points of my years in the Air Force Cadet program. In my first twenty-eight months in the Air Force, I accomplished what would have taken much longer if I had gone back to Mizzou.

Colonel Hoover adjusted the microphone and addressed the graduating class 57J and the friends and family members in attendance. He recounted his part as the command pilot of the second aircraft in the sixteen-plane formation that bombed manufacturing targets in Tokyo and other Japanese cities during World War II. The Doolittle Raiders took off from the flight deck of the USS Hornet knowing they lacked sufficient fuel to return after carrying out their mission. Some of the airmen paid the ultimate price. Others were captured after crashing their planes and then were tortured by Japanese soldiers. My confidence soared as Colonel Hoover finished telling his story. He received a resounding standing ovation. After we sat back down, the colonel began his official recognition of the graduating cadet class 57J.

"Ladies and gentlemen, it is my great honor and pleasure to award second lieutenant gold bars, and the official Air Force pilot silver wings, to our highest-rated and top cadet in class 57J. Please welcome up to the stage our newest Air Force officer, Warren K. Vest!"

The crowd erupted in a joyous ovation. I rose from my seat and walked to the stage, but I felt as if my feet were floating inches above the floor. I shook Colonel Hoover's hand and proudly accepted my shoulder bars and pilot's wings. My graduation set me onto the fresh path of my adult future.

CHAPTER 41

Present Day

MY GRANDSON GARRETT stood up from his chair in the study where we had been relaxing together. He jogged in place and shimmied around to loosen up, then extended his hand to me and asked, "Granddad, can I give you a lift up from your chair?"

"Sure, thanks," I replied. My aching, eighty-three-year-old body had stiffened up a bit as I told Garrett my life story.

After I stood up and stretched my lower back, I said, "I'm guessing you want me to tell you the rest of my story, right?"

He smiled. "Yes, Granddad. Please hurry back after using the bathroom. I want to know where you went after graduating from the cadets. Also, you said that after you nearly crashed the B-25 that it changed you forever. I want to know how you were changed."

I responded, "Sounds good. I will."

Just then my two youngest granddaughters burst through the door giggling. Talia and Peyton held up index fingers aligned over their mouths, signaling to me and Garrett to hush and remain mute. They were playing hide and seek.

I winked at them and mouthed the words, *Okay, but Granddad has to go to the bathroom.*

Talia mumbled quietly, "Please, Granddad, can't you hold it for a little bit? We want to win this last round of hide and seek."

That's when Garrett stepped next to me and kindly but firmly said, "Girls, no. When Granddad must go, then he *must go*. Please crack the door open and let him go down the hallway."

The girls playfully moved out of my way. They cautiously pulled the door open to allow me safe passage and I squeezed through the narrow opening.

Bravely, I promised them, "Never fear. If I get caught by the enemy, I won't tell them where you're hiding."

CHAPTER 42
1957

I CELEBRATED MY twenty-second birthday under the stars at a beach party in West Palm Beach, Florida. My pal Lieutenant Art Dickinson was there, along with two other Air Force officers and a quartet of attractive, civilian ladies. I was halfway through intense flight training on the C-118 Liftmaster.

During the previous three weeks spent learning the C-118's aircraft systems, along with ground-school training, flight training, and instrument flight training, I had either piloted or co-piloted the massive, four-engine, C-118 transport plane a half-dozen times. My

USAF MATS C-118

friend and fellow cadet at Reese, Art Dickinson, had graduated with me seven weeks earlier. He had finished second in class 57J. His bold charm, husky good looks, deep, resonant voice, and swashbuckling personality constantly reeled in an assortment of new friends and curious ladies for us to meet.

At noon on Sunday, the Florida sunshine and intermittent clouds cast roving shadows across the tarmac while Art and I examined the C-118. By that time, we felt at home with the sounds of the airport lifestyle that surrounded us. We were training on the Military Air Transport Service four engine C-118 at Palm Beach Air Force Base in southeast Florida. Planes were revving engines prior to liftoff, a sound that was accentuated by the squealing echoes of an airplane's tires touching down on the runway.

The other trainees from our elite C-118 training unit, Captains Robert Drevitson and Charles Harpool, guided their C-118 down the runway for takeoff. After their aircraft was safely on its way for a one-hour training flight, Art said, "Now that I've flown with you six times on the C-118 here in Palm Beach, it's clear why we finished first and second in our class. The other pilots were very good, or at least competent. But your total command of the cockpit is remarkable, and mine is right there with you." Art was looking ahead to the time we would be flying passengers who would put their lives in our hands.

"Art," I said, "you are an outstanding pilot in your own right. We're equal in every regard, without a doubt."

He and I worked our way to the fore-section of the C-118 so we could inspect the landing gear, wheel wells, and heavy-duty tires.

"You know, Art, it wasn't too long ago I was learning to fly those small T-34s and T-28s at Graham Air Base, and you were doing the same at Malden Air Base in Missouri. The T-28 was so acrobatic and fun to fly. However, we're now flying this powerful, four-engine, long-range C-118. That is pretty special, and duty at West Palm Beach is not bad at all."

We walked beneath the undercarriage of the fifty-foot-long right wing and circled back around the wingtip into the Florida sunshine. I stared at the two giant Double Wasp radial engines, each with a Hamilton Propeller mounted on its front. I inspected the hull of the outer engine and Art performed his examination of the inner engine mounted closer to the fuselage.

Finally, Art responded. "Now that we've made it this far and there are only four of us training on the C-118s, it won't be long until we're fully prepped and ready to fly these big birds overseas and cross-country. Think about *that,* Warren."

The other two pilots training on C-118s were Captains Robert Drevitson and Charles Harpool. I recalled my first encounter with Drevitson, whom we called Drevy. I had run into him in the locker room. We shook hands, and he immediately told me a joke without even asking if I wanted to hear one.

"Warren, why did the toilet paper roll down the hill?"

I replied, "Why?"

"To get to the bottom!"

Drevy walked off to locate another involuntary subject to pepper with his humor.

Art and I eventually found our way to the front of the C-118 and inspected the front tire, the landing gear, and the unobstructed wheel well. "Looks good," Art said. "It's a good day to fly, Warren."

I bumped hands with Art, signaling it was time to do some piloting. Art slapped me on the shoulder, and we strode to the portable staircase that had been temporarily affixed to the C-118's main cabin doorway. We marched up the steps and I spotted the smiling face of our flight instructor, Major John Cichoski. His effervescent demeanor always lifted my spirits.

Major Cichoski bellowed, "Time to start the day, young gents. The skies await!"

CHAPTER 43
1957

DURING THE BALMY dusk at McGuire Air Force Base in Burlington County, New Jersey, I was sitting on the porch of the bachelor officer quarters (BOQ). I was listening to Elvis Presley's hit song *All Shook Up*—the music coming through the open, living-room window of the quarters that Art Dickinson and I shared.

McGuire reminded me of an enormous beehive, or maybe an ant colony. It was a finely tuned model of frenetic efficiency that never paused or rested regardless of the obstacles that briefly interrupted the vital missions of its working crew.

"Are you nervous?" Art asked. "Tomorrow's a big day."

"And tonight is big for you, Art, flying to Iceland," I said. "But I was thinking about my family and the five-day road trip to get here that you and I took from West Palm Beach."

Art changed the subject. "Warren, it's not an accident that you're here preparing for your first international flight. In fact, your test flights for the last two days were excellent. And even though you're the youngest pilot in the 38th Air Transport Squadron, you deserve this opportunity."

I glanced at him but remained silent. Once Art figured out that I wasn't in a talkative mood, he shifted his attention to the C-118 speeding down the runway and watched it lift off.

Finally, I replied, "Counting the passengers and crew, there's going to be about sixty-five people on board my flight tomorrow."

"Correct." Art uttered.

Feeling a bit unnerved but brimming with excitement to be making my first transatlantic flight, I tapped my feet on the porch and rubbed my hands together. I found the motions to be therapeutic and somewhat settling.

"As you know," Art said, "McGuire has more than one hundred C-118s stationed here. You can take one of those birds up and polish your skills any time you want to when you're not on the clock. You know that."

"Yep," I said. "And remember what Colonel Hoover told us at graduation: 'Get on board or get left behind'."

CHAPTER 44
1957

"**MORNING, WARREN. LISTEN,** have a safe trip today!" I was on the final leg of a twenty-minute jog at McGuire Air Force Base. I sprinted toward my residence in the McGuire BOQ. Huffing and puffing and dripping with sweat, I felt remarkably ready to join my assigned C-118 crew to Europe later in the day. I entered the BOQ, which was empty because Art had departed for Iceland the previous night on his first C-118 assignment.

After shaving and showering, I spent an hour reviewing a stack of pre-flight notes. I changed into my Class A uniform, and by two o'clock that afternoon I was meeting with the C-118 crew I would join on my first military passenger flight.

The activity at McGuire was robust. Hundreds of military personnel and their families were regularly boarding airplanes or disembarking after arriving on a military passenger flight.

On my first flight to Europe on the C-118, I would join Aircraft Commander, First Lieutenant Frank Plummer; First Pilot, First Lieutenant Merle Nelson; Navigators, First Lieutenant Larry Donoho and Second Lieutenant William Mahone; Flight Engineer, Tech Sergeant Percy Montgomery; and Flight Attendants, Staff Sergeant Charles Bailey and Airmen Third Class Patricia Forester.

Flight Attendant Bailey reported, "According to the latest copy of the passenger manifest, we expect sixty-eight souls on the flight today to Germany, counting the crew."

"Does anybody else want to review other information before we meet onboard at three o'clock?" Lieutenant Plummer asked the crew.

"We need to be spot-on when logging our flight time," said First Pilot, Lt. Nelson. "We can't exceed twenty-seven duty hours." As we rose from our chairs, the final words spoken were "Wheels-up at four o'clock. Let's enjoy this trip."

I was very impressed with Lt. Plummer's briefing and thanked him afterward.

I exited the conference room and used the restroom. I then walked past the terminal gate that held the congregation of restless passengers waiting to board the C-118. I glanced at the faces of the passengers who soon would be our crew's responsibility.

Just before I reached the door leading to the tarmac, a red-headed boy about five years old dashed over and tapped me on the leg. I bent down to greet him. "Hey there, little guy, what's your name?"

He touched the gold bar on my uniform's right shoulder. Then he said his name was Gabriel. He asked, "Are you a *real* pilot?"

I nodded. "Yes, I am. I'm Lieutenant Vest, and it's nice to meet you. I have a long flight today. We're going over the ocean. How about you? Where are you off to today?"

Gabriel pursed his lips before finally answering, "Germany."

"Me too! I'm flying to Germany and I am one of your pilots." I winked at Gabriel's parents, stood up, and extracted the miniature pilot wings pendant from my pocket.

Gabriel's folks walked up. I acknowledged them and said, "You've got a good boy here. These wings are a little gift for him if that's all right with you."

Happily, Gabriel accepted the token. A few moments later I walked onto the tarmac toward the C-118. I boarded the aircraft and was surprised when the crew announced, "Welcome onboard your first MATS (Military Air Transport Service) flight!"

I was speechless. I smiled at them and proceeded forward to open the discreet door to the cockpit. Beyond that, I entered the narrow aisle between the crew bunks and the navigator's station. I poked my head through the gray curtain concealing the middle bunk, which is reserved for the rotating pilots to use during long flights. I stowed my flight bag beside the jump seat in the cockpit. I then completed the extensive, pre-flight checklist with the crew.

The flight attendants welcomed and organized the onboarding passengers. In front of me sat Aircraft Commander Plummer, and to his right was First Pilot Nelson, followed by Navigator Larry

Donoho, who was kitty-corner to me. Flight Engineer Percy Montgomery was stationed between the two pilots. Second Navigator Mahone would occupy a crew rest seat during takeoff.

After completing the pre-flight checks and securing the passengers, Aircraft Commander Plummer pulled the C-118 away from the gate while being guided by hand signals and gestures from ground-crew personnel. He taxied across the tarmac to the south end of the runway apron. I donned my sunglasses and, after waiting for two aircraft to depart ahead of us, the tower cleared us for takeoff. Lt. Plummer pushed forward on the throttles to accelerate the C-118 full-speed ahead. The aircraft rocketed down the runway at one hundred fifty miles per hour before the pilots pulled back on the yokes and lifted the aircraft into the sky. Our first stop would be Newfoundland, four hours from now.

We cruised at an altitude of fifteen-thousand feet toward Harmon Air Force Base, Newfoundland, Canada. Through my headset, I listened to the voices from air traffic control.

Once the first pilot, navigator, and flight engineer had relayed to the aircraft commander that the plane's systems were functioning properly, and radar showed our flight path to be clear of potential hazards, Lieutenant Plummer turned on the intercom and greeted the passengers.

"Good afternoon, ladies and gentlemen. This is your pilot, Lieutenant Plummer. It's my pleasure to serve you today on our flight to Rhein-Main Air Base in Frankfurt, Germany. We're cruising at an altitude of fifteen thousand feet, at a speed of two hundred seventy miles per hour. In just about four hours, we'll make a quick refueling stop along the Gulf of St. Lawrence in Newfoundland, Canada. That will be followed by an eight-hour flight over the North Atlantic Ocean and the southern tip of Greenland before making one last fuel stop in Prestwick, Scotland. After leaving Scotland, we will be in the air for three hours, going over the North Sea and Holland before landing in Frankfurt, Germany. Once again, I hope you enjoy the flight. On behalf of our flight crew and dedicated cabin personnel, we'd like to thank you for using our services today."

The crew performed well together as if they had ventured down this flight path many times. First Pilot Nelson constantly monitored communications from air traffic control and interpreted readings from the instrument panel. Navigator Larry Donoho kept rechecking our location using maps, charts, and radar to ensure we did not veer off course. Our flight engineer, Percy Montgomery, checked and adjusted the variable aircraft systems as warranted.

Aircraft Commander Plummer, upon his checking of the weather, flight status, and overall alertness of the crew, said, "All right, gentlemen, I'm going to take my rest break. Lieutenant Vest, you can replace me in the left seat."

While the C-118 was on auto-pilot with First Pilot Nelson monitoring everything, I slid into the left seat.

I looked out the window at the two Double Wasp engines on the left. For the next two hours, we continued our course toward Harmon Air Force Base while passing over Nova Scotia.

Thirty minutes prior to landing, Aircraft Commander Plummer returned to the cockpit and replaced me in the left seat. The dark, blue waters and a rocky coastline made for a spectacular view as he smoothly landed the C-118 and slowed the airplane before taxiing to our assigned gate to refuel.

About one hour later, at nine-thirty in the evening, Lt. Plummer taxied the C-118 to the runway. The runway lights guided our takeoff, and we flew into the starry, night sky. As we traveled through the black skies over the North Atlantic, my training had me on the lookout for potentially hazardous weather, for aircraft that might create a midair collision or any other type of in-flight malfunction.

Flying while using only the readings of my instruments had become second nature to me. I trusted my abilities to operate an airplane equally well only with the help of my instrument information coming at me.

While passing over Gander, Newfoundland, with the edges of the windshield a bit frosty, Aircraft Commander Plummer asked First Pilot Nelson to get some bunk time. I assumed my next position in the right seat. We flew the C-118 underneath a blanket of stars shining brightly.

Suddenly, without receiving a warning from any of the air traffic in our area, we encountered rough air and battled a formidable amount of turbulence. Aircraft Commander Plummer turned on the "Fasten Seat Belt" sign for the passengers and crew. The cockpit vibrated, rumbled, and shook. The aircraft's long fuselage and broad wingspan bucked unnaturally.

Plummer and I jostled with the yokes and kept our feet near the rudder pedals while monitoring the controls. The turbulence thrashed the aircraft for eighty seconds before we returned to calm air.

In the wee hours of Tuesday morning, June 11, Aircraft Commander Plummer issued the order I had been dreading. "Lieutenant Vest, it's time for you to take a rest."

I replied, "Yes sir."

First Pilot Nelson vacated the crew bunk and we completed our switch. I heard Navigator Donoho snoring away on the top bunk while the other navigator, Second Lieutenant Mahone, handled navigation duties.

Lying there on my back with a pillow under my head, I could have been anywhere in the universe. I had supreme confidence in my fellow crewmembers operating our C-118. After a few minutes of restlessness, I dozed off at fifteen thousand feet above the earth.

CHAPTER 45
1958

FOR MORE THAN a year at McGuire Air Force Base, I had been assigned to work with different flight crews. We had flown C-118s to Germany, Iceland, Scotland, Canada, Greenland, and Nova Scotia, in addition to various cities in America.

I was twenty-three years old and wanted to gain as much piloting experience as possible in the shortest amount of time. Over the past year, on my own time, I had checked out unassigned C-118s at McGuire so I could practice takeoffs, landings, and instrument approaches. I was always accompanied by a second pilot and a flight engineer.

By this time, Art and I had rented a two-bedroom home in Browns Mills, New Jersey, about seven miles from McGuire. Late one Sunday morning, I scooped up my flight bag, jangled my keys, and opened the front door. I was ready to begin my afternoon of flying.

I glanced at Art and his fiancée, Laura. "Okay, you lovebirds," I said. "It's time to say goodbye. You'll only be apart for a couple of days."

Laura smiled and waved at me and kissed Art again, longer this time. Art mumbled while kissing her face. "I'll meet you out front in two minutes, Warren. I promise."

I walked out into the manageable humidity and strolled up to my shiny Bel Air. I tossed my flight bag onto the back seat before sliding into the car and starting the engine. Art arrived and slid into my car. He had a smear of Laura's red lipstick across his left cheek.

"She gotcha good, Art," I chuckled, pointing at his face. Art shook his head. "I love that woman," he said. He then took a handkerchief from the glovebox and wiped his face. "When Laura and I get married in five weeks, I hope you're going to be okay," Art said to me. "By the way, have you found a place to live? It's getting kind of close."

I drove northwest up Texas Avenue, nodded my head, and said, "Yes. In fact, last night I was with Felix, Bob, Ron, and Terry, and the five of us found a big house with a large back yard in Bordentown. It's perfect, and we're moving in right after your wedding in late July."

"Excellent," Art said, obviously relieved. "You and I have been flying so much, and you're grabbing a lot of extra hours on your own. But it seems like we haven't had a lot of time to catch up with each other. Tell me, how was your VIP Flight as first pilot with the European delegates from the Federation Aeronautique Internationale?"

"It went well," I said. "We flew from New York to Washington, D.C., and from there to Fort Worth, Texas, and then to Los Angeles. Those delegates have a cushy life. They were being welcomed by important people, from John Dulles to Bob Hope; from Charles

Lindbergh to Henry Cabot Lodge and Cardinal Spellman. And they had lunch at the Aero Club in D.C. with President Eisenhower."

As I drove toward the entrance to McGuire Air Force Base, Art asked, "Anything else to report?"

I responded, "Yes. On the way to Los Angeles, we had renowned female pilot Jacqueline Cochran in the cockpit as we flew over the Grand Canyon. An amazing view, truth be told. Oh, and Colonel Jimmy Stewart welcomed us in California."

"Sounds like fun," Art said. "Good for you."

I pulled my Bel Air into the shady confines of the three-story officers' garage. Before we left the car, Art tugged at my arm and asked, "Has it ever crossed your mind when you fly that it might be the last time you will ever see your loved ones?"

For the first time since I had known him, Art had a pensive expression on his face. I could tell he was worried about his fiancée and the uncertainty of his fate while flying for the Air Force. I paused before answering. "Did I tell you about the World War II pilot I met in Perth, Australia, just over four years ago?" Art shook his head. "Jake from Boston, who runs a beachfront café in Perth, flew fighters in the war. After the war, he cashed in his assets and moved to Australia to open a lovely beachfront cantina."

"I met Jake while I was strolling alone on the beach in Perth, wondering about the path of my life. Jake was surf fishing without a care in the world. He reeled in a beauty right in front of me. He dragged the fish onto shore and knocked it senseless. Then we walked to his diner to join my friends for an amazing, grilled lunch."

Art asked, "What does that have to do with the question I asked you? Understand that I'm a bit more worried now. I sometimes think I might not ever see my beautiful Laura, or you, again."

I gripped his right hand firmly as if we were going to shake hands. "During that great afternoon at Jake's beachside pub, he pulled me aside and we had a very serious conversation, one-on-one, for about ten minutes."

"What did he tell you?" Art asked.

"You're an excellent pilot, Art, and this is the first time I've ever seen you worried," I said. "I understand why you're so anxious but trust your skills."

"I appreciate that Warren, but what did Jake tell you?" He really did want to know.

Firmly, I uttered, "He said, 'Don't ever get into the cockpit if you're thinking about dying'."

CHAPTER 46
1958

AFTER THE SERIOUS conversation I had with Art, we headed off to our separate activities. I was single-minded and tenacious about accruing supplemental hours flying the C-118. I wanted to increase my skill level and hopefully ascend the piloting ranks more rapidly within the Air Force.

I met my flight engineer for the afternoon's flight, Percy Montgomery, in the terminal cafeteria at McGuire. We nibbled at a light lunch in the busier-than-usual diner while reviewing my short list of items that I wanted to improve upon during the upcoming flight. The list included smoother landings and a variety of instrument approaches.

The clear white surrounding Percy's brown eyes was accentuated by his black skin, and his pearly teeth were his pride and joy. He loved it when people commented on his dazzling smile. After lunch, we grabbed our flight bags and strode through the terminal's entrance.

On the tarmac, we couldn't escape the late-June humidity rising from the pavement. Maintenance personnel were revving airplane engines.

"It's steamier than a crawfish boil out here," Percy lamented. "The mugginess in this type of air always takes it out of me and slows me down."

"It is bad," I replied, "but it's definitely better than the God-awful humidity at Graham in Marianna, Florida. Down there, it was by far the worst I have experienced."

We arrived at the mobile stairway hooked up to the foot of the cabin doorway. I gestured to my flight engineer to hustle up the stairs ahead of me. In the cockpit, we were greeted by the youthful, freckled face of the second pilot, Lieutenant Roger Osgood. "I got here early and completed several of my pre-flight checks," Roger said, "even though I realize we'll have to reconfirm all of them."

I nodded. "Let's take care of business and get this bird into the air. Percy is an outstanding flight engineer, so let's focus on our checks and take off as soon as possible. It's only the three of us onboard today, so we have very little room for any type of mistake."

I slid into the left seat, as the flight's first pilot, and we commenced our checks. After we finished, Roger Osgood said, "Based on your notes for our flight plan, it appears we're going to shoot some landings here at McGuire and instrument approaches. Does that cover it?"

"Affirmative," I replied. Minutes later I taxied the C-118 to the runway holding area and waited for the control tower to clear us for takeoff.

Percy chuckled. "When Warren is determined to do something, by golly, he is going to get it done come whatever may be!"

Osgood grinned and replied, "Understood."

The tower cleared us for takeoff. I pushed forward on our throttles, with Percy backing me up, and accelerated the hefty C-118 down the runway and lifted off into a clear sky.

To the west, seven minutes into our flight, I flew the C-118 to four thousand feet and slowly rolled the airplane to the left, banking it southwest over Springfield and eastward above Pemberton, New Jersey, before passing far above the little home Art and I were renting in Browns Mills.

As I prepared to turn the C-118 left, a surprising command came from the control tower. "MATS 818, please be aware one of our tactical fighter jets just landed with a failed landing gear on runway two-four. McGuire has been closed indefinitely. Please contact MATS Transport Control Center (TCC) to coordinate your intentions."

I nodded at the two men with me. "Affirmative, tower. This is MATS 818. We have received your message and are coordinating with TCC on a plan."

Percy was computing how many hours of fuel we had, and I got on the radio with the MATS Transport Control Center. Percy calculated we had six hours of fuel remaining, and I passed this information on to TCC. They checked the weather on the East Coast and recommended we go to Dow Air Force Base in Bangor, Maine. TCC filed a flight plan from McGuire to Dow and said to coordinate our training in the Dow Air Force Base area. Upon completing our training, we were to land at Dow, refuel, and return to McGuire.

The TCC controller said, "This should give McGuire sufficient time to clear the runways and be operational."

I pulled back on the yoke while pushing forward on the throttles to climb to thirteen thousand feet. I turned northeast, in the direction of Maine. We flew over the eastern seaboard of the United States, cruising above Long Island, New York, and then over Newport, Rhode Island. Then it was on to the fishhook-shaped peninsula and harbor of Plymouth and Provincetown, Massachusetts. To my far right, the vastness of the dark-blue Atlantic Ocean awaited, just as it had when I sailed home from London, England. As we flew over the craggy coastline of southern Maine, we began our descent over Rocklin and Searsport on route to Bangor.

I communicated with Dow Air Force Base's approach control and advised them that we desired to do some training in the area.

Dow replied, "MATS 818, please confirm your intentions."

"Affirmative. This is MATS 818. We want to make some instrument approaches and touch-and-go landings, then land at Dow to refuel prior to returning to McGuire."

"MATS 818, please proceed on your current heading for vectors to an ILS approach."

"Affirmative. 818 will stay on our current heading for vectors for the ILS."

A few minutes later I flew the C-118 over the winding Penobscot River on approach to Dow Air Force Base. Second Pilot Osgood lowered the landing gear. On the ground below, I noticed an armada of fighter jets, transport planes, and bombers impeccably aligned and parked in their assigned spaces. I could see airmen scurrying throughout the base.

Percy said, "I've adjusted the systems and we're on a vector for another approach." Then he added, with a smile, "Hey, boys, wouldn't it be great if we suddenly had a minor maintenance problem and we had to spend the night in Maine? We could chow down some big, fat lobster tails drowned in butter."

For the next ninety minutes and with the cooperation of Dow's approach control, we completed nine approaches and eight touch-and-go landings. Following our ninth approach, I smoothly executed a full-stop landing. I taxied the C-118 to our assigned parking spot before Roger Osgood and Percy Montgomery and I shut down the aircraft. Then we conducted our post-flight checks and disembarked from the C-118.

In the Base Operations Office, we were confronted by a very perturbed Air Force captain. "What are two green second lieutenants doing flying a C-118 into Dow Air Force Base?"

He picked up a telephone and called someone he addressed as a colonel. He asked the senior officer to come to the Base Ops counter. After slamming down the receiver, the captain continued to question our authorization to fly the C-118. To this point, I hadn't been given a chance to explain the situation.

A tall lieutenant colonel arrived. We saluted him, and the lieutenant colonel asked me, "Lieutenant Vest, did you have consent to fly out of McGuire this afternoon?"

It took me a moment to gather myself. I answered, "Yes sir."

The still-unsatisfied captain challenged me. "You had better be telling the truth, Lieutenant Vest, or you and your cohorts will be spending the next fifty years at the federal penitentiary at Leavenworth." Both of the Dow Air Force Base officers were trying to detect if I was lying or telling the truth.

I decided to speak up. "McGuire instructed me to divert up here to Dow," I said.

The captain glared at Second Pilot Osgood and Flight Engineer Montgomery. They remained silent, and he eventually turned his attention back to me.

He moved in closer and asked, "Do you pull this type of unannounced maneuver often, Lieutenant Vest? Gallivanting around America, hopping from base to base? Is that your M.O.?"

Crisply I replied, "No sir! This type of situation has never happened to me before, sir. In fact, every chance I get, I try to gain extra flying time in the C-118. The truth is, sir, my goal is to become an aircraft commander. I'm scheduled to begin training for that in the very near future, sir."

The lieutenant colonel frowned at my reply, but he seemed to relax. After a lengthy pause, he asked, "Lieutenant Vest, do you happen to know a Colonel Donald Kohl?"

"Yes sir! Lieutenant Colonel Kohl commands my unit, the 38th Air Transport Squadron. I can provide you with his phone number if you need it."

The lieutenant colonel said, "He and I go back a long way. We played on some of the same sports teams together growing up. A good man."

He continued, "At ease, gentlemen. I'm going to give Lieutenant Colonel Kohl a quick phone call to verify your story. Dismissed."

I gave him Lieutenant Colonel Kohl's phone number, and we saluted him. The three of us took a step back, and the officers from Dow went into the captain's chambers to call my superior.

Under his breath, Percy said, "Boy oh boy. I can almost taste those juicy lobster tails I was dreaming about."

CHAPTER 47
1958

LESS THAN A week after I moved into a five-bedroom house with three pilot buddies and a navigator pal, I collapsed on my bed, elated, but needing a break before my housemates and I hosted a massive party later that night.

By noontime, my new roommates wanted me to join them in a pre-party celebration. However, I was drifting off to sleep. I pictured my Uncle Glenn sitting on his front porch pretending to read the *Kansas City Star* exactly four years earlier.

Back then, in the summer of 1954, I had been treading water. My soul passionately yearned for only one career—to be a pilot—but I was doing nothing to move toward my goal. Fortunately, Uncle Glenn pointed me toward a job assembling airplane wings. He understood that moving into the aviation field, even if it was putting rivets in B-47 bombers, would improve my chances of someday becoming a pilot.

My subconscious mind took me home to Buffalo, Missouri. I saw my aging mother and father and my younger brother, who was eleven years old. Our family quartet was working on the farm during a sweltering summer day. We were tending to the horses and working the fields with our temperamental mules, Jack and Jill. My father and I repaired some broken fence, and my mother, my brother, and I chased a pair of crazed, white chickens that had escaped the coop.

It was a stirring daydream that seared a permanent mark in my soul. It represented a way of life that might have been my calling. But my dream of flying airplanes professionally drove me. I was convinced that training as a pilot would enable me to exercise the true depths of my life's freedom.

A series of loud shrieks and the sound of hearty laughter startled me awake. When I opened my eyes, I realized tiny rivulets of tears were running down my cheeks. I wiped the dampness from my face before stretching and collecting myself.

My roommates had cranked up the stereo. The Connie Francis song "Who's Sorry Now" was playing loudly, booming into our yard. I popped up from the bed and walked to the front bathroom to shave and shower.

By four o'clock I was dressed in khaki shorts, tan topsiders, and a polo shirt. I sauntered into the kitchen and was welcomed by my four roomies. They had decorated the back yard. I realized that I'd be in charge of clean up after tonight's bash had culminated.

Terry Gautsch, my housemate and an Air Force navigator, handed me a cold beer. I noticed three kegs strategically positioned in our yard.

"Cheers, Warren," Terry said. We toasted and took a drink. Terry was known for his good looks and warm personality. He routinely attracted the ladies, no matter what party we attended or what part of the world we had flown to.

Normally, Terry found the best parties for us to hang out at. But this Fourth of July, everybody would be coming to our place.

Felix Gomez, another housemate, grabbed a cup of beer. Bob Malone and Ron Hall, fellow pilots and housemates, joined in the banter. We laughed and joked, each of us holding a cold beverage.

I hoisted my cup of beer and proudly said, "Here's to us, gentlemen, and to our new House of Pilots!" We touched beer cups, and Terry said, "And one navigator!"

"Here, here!" we shouted as one.

We were expecting seventy-five to eighty party guests to start arriving at five o'clock. We had less than an hour to double-check the backyard lighting, the barbeque, and the kegs and snack trays.

Bob cranked up the stereo to a thumping beat. A couple of neighbors set off fireworks, and at five o'clock cars and trucks began turning onto our street. Partygoers of all types were toting bottles of liquor and appetizer platters. They walked into the house and the back yard as if they owned the joint. I knew an outstanding party had commenced.

Within a few hours, more than one hundred people were having a blast. I walked into our torch-lit yard and headed toward the food table. But my plan was interrupted by the sight of a young, dark-skinned woman. I swear she was smiling at me from across the yard.

I headed in her direction. She never took her eyes off me, and I bumped a few people as I made my way to her side. She was wearing a light blue sundress and I saw that she was taller and lovelier up close. I opened with "Hello, I'm so glad you made it to our little party tonight. And happy Fourth of July. My name's Warren."

She flashed me a dazzling smile. "It's nice to meet you, Warren, and thanks for hosting such a great party. I'm Darlene."

The festivities surrounding us, and the neighbors' fireworks all seemed to go mute. I focused my attention on Darlene's dark hair, dark eyes, and wonderful face.

She asked, "Did it take you a long time to become a pilot? I don't want to be crass, but I'd like to be a pilot someday."

I couldn't believe it. She was pretty and personable, and she wanted to fly! By now my level of interest was revved up. But before I could answer Darlene's question, a handsome airman whom I'd seen at McGuire snaked between us and planted a long kiss on Darlene's lips.

Crestfallen doesn't begin to cover it. I swigged at my beer, tried to gather my wits, and introduced myself to Darlene's fiancé. We exchanged pleasantries, then I answered Darlene's questions about becoming a pilot.

CHAPTER 48
1958

ON THE SAME day that famous singer-songwriter Buddy Holly married his receptionist, I nervously entered the conference room at McGuire Air Force Base Headquarters. I was dressed in my officer's blue uniform and polished black shoes. I saluted the six, high-ranking officers standing behind the review board's table. From my left to right, the officers were Colonel C.O. Williams, Group Commander; Lieutenant Colonel Donald Kohl, 38th Air Transport Squadron Commander; and the most powerful man in the room, Brigadier General George Dany, Commander of the 1611th Air Transport Wing of MATS. To his left stood a major and a captain I had not met. A flight surgeon was on the far end to my right.

After the officers acknowledged my salute, Lieutenant Colonel Kohl said, "Lieutenant Vest, please find your seat at the small table up front."

I removed my cap and took a seat in the chair in the middle of the room. I noticed the serious faces of the men sitting behind the table reviewing their notes. Brigadier General Dany's strong facial features, salt-and-pepper hair, and stoic expression highlighted the seriousness of the moment. After eyeballing each of the men and trying to gauge their demeanor, I gave up.

General Dany opened the meeting after conferring with his colleagues. "Lieutenant Vest, and all officers present, let the record show we have convened here at McGuire to review the possibility of

Lieutenant Vest becoming an aircraft commander in the United States Air Force. Furthermore, and according to the records that I have been given, when Lieutenant Vest joined the 38th Air Transport Squadron on June 7h, 1957, he was the youngest pilot in the unit. Is that correct, Lieutenant Vest?"

I replied, "Yes sir. That's the same information I was told."

The general continued. "In June of this year, the flight examiner presiding over your training recommended that you be considered as a candidate to become an aircraft commander. Is that correct, Lieutenant Vest?"

"Yes sir. It was my honor to obtain his reference."

The officers on the review board checked their notes. My commander, Lieutenant Colonel Kohl, whispered to General Dany.

The general nodded, then focused his attention on me. "Lieutenant Vest, our records indicate you have successfully finished the upgrade training and line checks and the required two full days of observation spent at the New York Air Traffic Control Center, and one day in the Altitude Chamber Training Facility at Hempstead, New York. Is that correct?"

"Yes sir," I responded.

The officers made notes and spoke among themselves. The major I had not met leaned toward the general and spoke in a hushed tone.

General Dany frowned. Then he asked me a surprising question. "Son, what color are the bars on your shoulders?"

"Gold, sir," I said.

Clearly embarrassed about something, my commander dropped his gaze and resignedly rubbed his face with his hands. After an uncomfortably long pause, a displeased General Dany stated, "Gentlemen, we have a young Air Force officer who meets all of the stringent requirements to be a C-118 aircraft commander for the Military Air Transport Command. All, that is, except one."

The faces of the five men at the table flanking the general flushed with shades of red. The general continued after allowing the full weight of the error to sink in. "The oversight here, gentlemen, and it's no fault of the young officer, is the requirement for aircraft commanders to be first lieutenants. Therefore, my question for the review board is this: "How quickly can Lieutenant Vest be promoted to first lieutenant?"

My commander, Lieutenant Colonel Kohl, murmured into General Dany's ear. The general advised me to remain seated while several of the senior officers hustled out of the room to make telephone calls. The flight surgeon huddled in an alcove in a far corner of the room with General Dany and the two unknown officers.

After a fifteen-minute break, during which I wondered about the fate of my desired promotion to aircraft commander, the group of men reconvened behind the table in front of me.

General Dany glanced at my commander, Lieutenant Colonel Kohl, who stated: "We have confirmed that by the order of the President, Lieutenant Vest can be promoted to first lieutenant on September 28, 1958."

General Dany nodded. "Very good. All those in favor of Lieutenant Vest receiving his promotion to first lieutenant and to C-118 aircraft commander on September 28, 1958, please raise your hand."

Each of the six officers raised his hand, and General Dany said, "It's unanimous!" The general smiled at me and continued, "Congratulations, Lieutenant Vest!"

Raw emotion zipped through my body, heart, and soul. It took me a moment to reply, "Thank you, sir! I am deeply humbled and honored by the unanimous consent of the review board. Thank you all very much!"

General Dany and the other officers rose to their feet. I stood and saluted them, and the general informed me, "Lieutenant Vest, I will confer with Lieutenant Colonel Kohl on the time and location on September 28 where you will receive your promotion. I will personally see you there. That is all, Lieutenant Vest. Dismissed."

CHAPTER 49
1959

TIMES WERE GOOD for my Bordentown, New Jersey, roommates and me. Three of my fellow pilots and housemates, Felix Gomez, Ron Hall, and Bob Malone, had all earned promotions to become aircraft commanders. Our other roomie, Navigator Terry Gautsch, had been promoted to first lieutenant. And several months earlier, I had been promoted to first lieutenant and aircraft commander.

We had worked many months of long-haul shifts flying for MATS from McGuire to Germany, England, Greenland, Iceland, Spain, and France. Over the past several months, each of us had saved enough money for a month-long vacation in Europe. All of us, that is, except Ron Hall. He elected to visit his family in Chicago before spending a couple of weeks soaking up the sun along the southern coast of California.

Felix, Terry, Bob, and I began our holiday in Frankfurt, Germany. We rented a car to travel the roads of Austria, Italy, France, and Switzerland before driving back to Frankfurt.

All of us had packed our tennis gear. We received some clay-court pointers from a German tennis pro at the Eibsee Hotel in Garmisch-Partenkirchen, Germany. Every day we played doubles or singles matches against one another, either on the grounds of our various hotels or at a nearby park if the hotel courts were booked.

One day, following our final doubles match in Rapallo, Italy, Terry and Felix came around the net to congratulate Bob and me on our hard-earned victory.

We walked off the court toward the hotel lobby in the Mediterranean sunshine. Terry spoke up. "This trip has been better than I could have imagined. We've partied almost every night and met some nice ladies in Innsbruck, Venice, and Rome. And even though there is no way in hell we could tour Europe for five dollars a day, as that little handbook said, it has been wonderful. The book should have read, 'Five dollars per day and fifty dollars per night.' But it's all good anyway!"

As we neared the lobby entrance, I wiped sweat from my face. "It has been fantastic, Terry. And we have three days left in Rapallo."

The four of us entered the rustic foyer of our hotel, which had been in business for more than two hundred years. We meandered into the main breezeway, where we beheld the striking image of a remarkably attractive family of four. The parents of the two lovely ladies turned left in the direction of the poolside outdoor café. Their daughters followed behind them.

Felix uttered, "Oh my God! Those two gals are the best-looking ladies I have ever seen!"

I asked my buddies, "How old do you think the taller one is?"

Bob said, "I'm guessing she must be twenty-five or twenty-six."

Terry guffawed. "Not a chance! She's probably twenty-two at best. But it doesn't matter, my dear friends, because after I shower and put on some fresh duds, the game shall be over. That beauty will be all mine for the next couple of days."

I was determined to meet the lady I found to be the more attractive of the two, even though they both were very appealing. The one who piqued my interest was about two inches shorter than me, with wavy, copper-colored hair, bronzed skin, and vibrant green eyes. The race between my buddies and I was officially on. We zoomed to our hotel rooms, agreeing to meet up in the lobby in thirty minutes.

Felix and I played rock, paper, scissors to determine who got the first shower. I won, so I was first to shave and shower. Twenty-five minutes later I found myself in the hotel lobby, awaiting my three friends. With time on my hands, I asked the desk clerk if she knew anything about the family of four relaxing in the outdoor restaurant by the pool.

"They're a sweet family from New Zealand," she said.

As my trio of buddies exited the elevator, I joined them, and we walked out to the poolside lounge. We took the circular table next to the family of four that, by then, was enjoying their lunch.

A few minutes later, after our waiter had delivered drinks and appetizers, I'd overheard enough to know that they were certainly from New Zealand.

We hadn't yet worked out a strategy when Felix excused himself to go use the restroom. The attractive woman I was most interested in followed Felix with her eyes; then she caught me gazing at her.

It was time to do something. I came up with "Hi, I'm Warren. Pardon me for saying this, but I really like your accent. Do you happen to be from New Zealand?"

She responded with a grand smile. "Yes," she said. "How did you know that? I'm Catherine."

CHAPTER 50
1959

IT WAS NOON on Wednesday in Rapallo, Italy. Over the last two days, I had spent considerable time with Catherine and her younger sister, Jenny, and their parents, William and Mary Scott. On this day, I waited for Catherine to join me at the far end of the hotel's front desk while I read the *New York Times*.

A *Times* article reported that Stan "The Man" Musial, of the St. Louis Cardinals, had been tagged out between second and third base at Wrigley Field. Musial wasn't aware that at home plate the umpire had offered up a fresh ball to the Cubs catcher who then gave it to the pitcher. The ump had overlooked the ball that still lay at the backstop after Musial had chosen not to swing at it during his recent at-bat. When Musial saw the ball lying at the backstop, he decided to steal second base. The pitcher tried to throw Musial out at second using the new ball, but the throw went over the second baseman's head. So, Musial decided to head to third. Before he made it to third base, the Cubs third baseman had retrieved the original ball and thrown it to Ernie Banks at shortstop, who then tagged Musial out. It was a rare event in major league baseball when two balls were in play.

"Hi, Warren!" I looked up from the newspaper and saw Catherine walking toward me. She looked radiant dressed in a crème-colored sundress and white sandals. Her hair was in a ponytail.

A handsome front-desk clerk followed Catherine's smiling gaze with his eyes. Then he settled his sardonic stare on me. He shrugged in a subtle but disapproving manner, indicating his opinion that I should not be the one to pair up with the pretty New Zealander.

I came around the corner of the front desk. "Catherine, you look wonderful, really beautiful."

We kissed and embraced, then held hands and walked out into the afternoon sunshine. A cab was waiting, so I opened the passenger-side door to let her in before I followed.

The brusque Italian taxi driver asked, "Portofino, Signore?"

I nodded, and he punched on the gas pedal. We were on our way to the charming seaside fishing village.

Catherine and I snuggled in the back seat. "I'm so excited we're going to spend today in Portofino!" she exclaimed. "I've heard it's wonderful."

The cabbie wove the car down the road along the rocky coastline, then zipped us through a series of alleys and quiet streets. We passed any number of majestic, centuries-old Italian villas overlooking the Mediterranean Sea. Catherine and I marveled at the tiny fishing vessels, mid-sized yachts, and sailboats anchored in the small harbor.

Before one o'clock in the afternoon, the driver stopped the cab a block from the piazza. I paid him, and he reminded us in his thick, Genoa-accented English: "Pesto! Eat the pesto frutti di mare!"

I nodded appreciatively. "We'll have seafood pasta for dinner."

Catherine and I walked along the boardwalk overlooking the waterfront. Then we left the beaten path to head down the narrow, curving roads in the ancient village of Portofino. The smells of the portside town were intoxicating, as was the clamor of fishermen as they negotiated with local buyers who were interested in the fresh catch of the day.

We discovered a little delicatessen two blocks from the main beachfront. We bought a loaf of focaccia bread, cheese, a stick of salami, and some chocolates, along with a chilled bottle of Prosecco. By three o'clock we had wound our way through the seaside vendors and shopkeepers asking for our business. Finally, we ended up at a smaller, less-crowded beach.

Catherine removed her sandals as we strolled through the ankle-deep surf. "I'm going to miss you, Warren," she said. "It's hard to believe it's been three days."

"I agree. But with your parents renting a flat in London through October, and with my MATS flights bringing me to Europe three times a month, we can see each other quite a bit and in different cities."

She looked at me with tears forming in her eyes. "Even though I'm twenty-one years old, my parents still worry about me. And not to fret, they like you. However, my father is concerned that we're trying to create something more substantial from what he calls a "vacation relation."

"Not me, Catherine, and no offense to your dad. I want to see what happens between us. We may fizzle out or we might be together forever. We owe it to ourselves to find out the real answer."

She wiped tears from her face. Finally, she said, "I want the same thing. Let's give it a go!"

I hugged and kissed her and lifted her off the ground. She looked down at me with a bright smile. I set her back down and we held each other closely in the ebbing tide.

I noticed a tiny, vacant cove farther down the beach. I suggested, "Let's celebrate our decision in a more secluded spot."

"Good idea," she replied and passionately kissed me.

CHAPTER 51
1959

ON A CRISP, breezy, misty fall afternoon in Paris, Catherine and I sat together in an arthouse movie theater off the Rue de Rivoli. We were there to see the French film *Les Amants* (The Lovers), starring Jeanne Moreau. We were sharing a large container of buttered popcorn and a Coca-Cola®.

The picture had been playing for a year in France, but recently it had been released with English subtitles. The other two dozen moviegoers in the smallish theater were focused on the big screen. Due to a man in front of us who was smoking, we moved to other seats.

We enjoyed the movie. Afterward, I helped Catherine slip into her jacket and we joined hands and kissed. I glanced up to the right and saw the Eiffel Tower piercing the gray sky in the distance. The vast structure lorded over the gold and burgundy leaves still clinging to the trees that lined the park.

"What a tragic but great movie that was," Catherine said. I agreed. "The ending really surprised me." We were walking down the Rue de Rivoli at 3:30 in the afternoon. We made a few turns and arrived at our place of lodging, the Hotel Normandy.

"A quick drink before we visit the Louvre for the second day in a row?" Catherine asked. "I could spend a week in there just poking around. How about it, Warren?"

"*Oui, oui*, sounds good!" I replied.

In the hotel lobby, I waited for Catherine while she freshened up in the ladies' room. Hotel guests generated palpable energy with their conversational buzz and constant movement through the hotel.

Catherine returned, and we walked into the lively Normandy Bar. A big band was playing, and around one hundred carefree patrons were singing, partying, and dancing.

A waiter plucked two flutes of champagne from the tray he was carrying. He bowed slightly and offered them to Catherine and me. "Mademoiselle and Monsieur, compliments of the hotel. Salute!"

We toasted our flutes and sipped at the bubbly.

I spotted a couple leaving their small table, so I caught Catherine's free hand and said, "Let's see if we can grab those two seats; then we can dance!"

We reached the table at the same moment as a group of loud men. The tallest one, a good-looking, older guy glared at me. But when he noticed Catherine gazing at him, his demeanor changed. He took a step back and smoothly pulled out one of the chairs.

Catherine glanced at me and then said to the man, "Thank you, sir."

When he had reached for the chair, I had noticed a military symbol tattooed on his left forearm. I asked him, "U.S. Army? Did you serve?"

He looked at me with displeasure. "Yep, did my twenty years. But, that's over with."

I responded, "Air Force for me, active. And thanks for serving our country. It's always nice to meet a fellow patriot and former military member."

The man rose to his full height. The tension between us was increasing. The hair on the back of my neck pricked up, and a zinging sensation careened through my body. I braced myself on the balls of my feet, ready to join the battle if that's what was coming. I stared into the dark eyes of the retired Army man.

At that moment I expected the Army man to try to get me out of the picture, Catherine spoke up. "Excuse me, lads, but my boyfriend and I would like to be alone. And thank you for giving us your table."

The Army man blinked and let out a whooshing breath of liquor-tainted air. Through clenched teeth, he muttered, "Enjoy the evening with your pretty lady, flyboy." He nodded over at Catherine before leading his cadre out through the bar's exit.

The adrenaline speeding through my body could find nowhere to expend itself. I downed my glass of champagne, then helped Catherine out of her jacket before removing my coat.

"I'm sorry about what just happened," I told her. She shook her head while holding up her index finger and sipping her champagne.

"That was not your fault," she said. "He was a jerk, and I'm glad he's gone."

I reached for Catherine's hands and said, "Let's boogie."

The band's catchy beat pulled me back into the wonderful day I had been enjoying with Catherine. We found an opening on the packed dance floor and began to shake and jive like there was no tomorrow.

I lost track of time, but Catherine and I had been dancing so long that we were perspiring and happy. We held hands and walked back to our table to grab our garments before leaving the bar. We took the elevator to the second floor, and I opened the door to our room.

Catherine peeled off her sweater, pumps, and slacks. When she was stripped down to her lace bra and panties, she slid onto the king-sized bed.

I tore off my shoes and socks and pants on the way to the bed, yanked my damp shirt over my head, and landed next to Catherine wearing only my briefs.

I kissed Catherine's slender neck. She said to me, "Warren, you know I'm falling in love with you. But I don't know if this is going to last for as long as I want it to. We live on opposite sides of the world, and I'm afraid it won't work out."

"I love you too, Catherine. And I don't know what's going to happen either."

We wrapped our arms and legs around each other in a tender embrace. For the next couple of hours, we made love and forgot about everything else.

CHAPTER 52

Present Day

"GRANDDAD. HEY, ARE you okay?" Garrett and I had been talking in the study for six hours.

A tear made its way down my cheek, and I wiped it away. My vivid recollections had pulled me back into the pivotal moments of my young-adult life. I looked through the window and realized a rosy dusk had appeared. As my emotionally spent senses returned to the current time, I removed my glasses and rubbed at my balding head. I was still choked up, so I didn't try to speak as I gathered my wits.

Garrett was looking at me. "You had me a little worried, Granddad. It felt like you were someplace else while you were telling me about that vacation in Europe with your buddies and spending those times with Catherine."

I nodded, still unable to speak without a quiver in my voice. Garrett asked, "Whatever happened to Catherine? You didn't finish that part of your story."

I slipped my glasses back on and said, "People come into your life for a reason, a season, or a lifetime, Garrett. It's impossible to know the reasons why in advance, especially when you encounter someone new.

"Catherine and I grew very fond of each other, and we seriously discussed creating a future together. When my time in the Air Force was due to probably come to an end, I considered moving to New Zealand to join her. I could have finished my university education while she completed her studies."

"Wow!" was all Garrett said.

"Let me tell you plain and simple: it's better to dive headfirst into a potentially loving relationship and to have it last a few short months, rather than to walk away from it and never know what might have been."

Garrett asked, "When was the last time you saw Catherine?"

Suddenly I was pulled back into 1959. "Catherine and her family and I met again in London to plan their trip to the U.S.A. Everything was arranged. I would meet them in Toronto and proceed to New York for our two weeks together. However, two weeks before this was to happen, I received orders from Air Force headquarters to report to Stead Air Force Base in Nevada for top-secret code school. I was not able to get my orders changed or delayed. My leave was canceled, but my squadron commander gave me a few days off before I transferred to Nevada. I flew to Toronto and met the Scotts. I had two special days with Catherine in New York.

"After leaving New York, I flew to Nevada and completed the code school. But as it turned out, I never needed to make use of that training. I had to wonder why that ended up being the glitch that interrupted my planned two weeks with Catherine in New York.

"She and I continued to correspond by telephone and letters from halfway around the world as I continued my Air Force career."

Three knocks echoed from the study door. The door opened, and my youngest son, Brian, walked in followed by his lovely wife, Drue.

"You guys have been in here for a long time," Brian said. "I was about to send in the SWAT team." He continued, "We've still got a million things to do before we move to Texas, so we're going to get going. I just wanted to say goodbye for now, and we'll see you for dinner on Wednesday."

My son offered me a hand up as I groaned from the stiffness of sitting for several hours. I hugged him and Drue and said, "Love you both. I'll see you on Wednesday."

Although I had exercised regularly throughout my adult life, my elderly body had slowed down considerably. By typical geriatric health standards, I was in relatively good shape. However, even though I did my best to keep Father Time's grasping hands away from me, with each new day I understood he was closing in.

My other pretty daughter-in-law, Caroline, entered the study while assisting my darling wife of fifty-six years, Ingrid. She moved slowly while favoring the leg with a damaged femur, which she had broken ten months earlier. Ingrid's limp was heartbreaking for me to watch.

Caroline and Ingrid were followed by Garrett's sisters, Gentry and Kinnon. Now my three oldest grandchildren were in the study. I turned on the table lamp and smiled from the surprise of the group's unexpected arrival. I said to my grandson, "Garrett, we have been invaded by the Vest females."

I was concerned about Ingrid. It had been a long, busy day visiting with our children and grandchildren. Caroline must have seen the concern in my eyes. "Your wife is a trooper, Warren. She's a tough bird."

Ingrid grinned at me, then asked, "How much longer are you going to be, Honey?"

"Just a couple of more hours," I said. "I promise."

I kissed Ingrid, then stepped over to Caroline, Gentry, and Kinnon and pecked each of them on the cheek. Gentry asked me, "Granddad, what have you and Garrett been doing in here all this time?"

Before I could respond, Garrett replied, "He's telling me about his life, and he was almost to the point where he met Grammi."

Kinnon spoke up, "Cool. Can we join you, Granddad?"

"I would love that," I said warmly. I motioned for Garrett to pull over two more chairs. He arranged the chairs in a semi-circle next to his seat and bracketing mine.

"It's getting kind of late, Honey," Ingrid said. "You don't have much time left."

I nodded at the double entendre, then watched Caroline and Ingrid turn slowly. Before they left the study, Ingrid grinned at me. "Honey, make sure you tell them how you pursued me all over the world."

I smiled. "I will, Dear, don't you worry."

CHAPTER 53
1960

EARLY ON A frigid Friday morning, I shuffled past one of my roommates, Ron Hall, who snored loudly while sleeping on the TV-room couch. I moved into the kitchen, trying my best to stay warm while dressed in flannel pajamas and thick, sheepskin slippers.

I brewed a pot of coffee and eased back into the TV room and back past the still-snoring Ron. Outside, I snatched up our copy of the *New York Times*. Within a few minutes, I was at the kitchen table, sipping coffee while reading the front section of the *Times*. I was about to begin reading the sports section when the telephone rang, startling me at this early hour.

I picked up the receiver.

"Good morning, this is Steedman Hinckley, assistant chief pilot for Overseas National Airways (ONA). I'm calling from Idlewild Airport in New York. I'm trying to reach Bob Malone. Is this Bob?"

"No, I'm afraid not. Bob is away in Europe, flying until Wednesday, I believe."

"Well, that's unfortunate," said Steedman Hinckley. "With whom am I speaking?"

"This is Warren Vest."

Hinckley replied, "Nice to meet you over the phone. Bob mentioned that he lived with a few other pilots. By chance do you happen to be a C-118 pilot?"

"Yes sir. I'm an aircraft commander and flight examiner on the C-118."

Hinckley turned from the phone to speak to another person. Then he asked, "How would you like a job as an airline captain flying DC-6s, and flying internationally between New York and Frankfurt, Germany?"

"That would be great," I said, "but I'm still in the Air Force. And what about Bob?"

"It's first come first served, and Bob knows that," Hinckley replied. "Vest, could you come to New York tomorrow to meet with me at noon?"

"Yes," I said. "I'll be there at noon tomorrow."

By noon the next day, I had driven the ninety miles into New York City, arriving at Idlewild Airport. An hour later, I was advised that Captain Hinckley had not returned from a training flight. Instead, I was introduced to Captain Starkloff, the chief pilot at ONA. We went into his office, where we had a long conversation. Starkloff learned a lot about me, and I discovered more about ONA. He said that he would be taking two co-pilots out for their annual flight checks and asked if I would like to tag along.

I told him I would love to.

Not long after, Assistant Chief Pilot Hinckley returned from his flight, so Starkloff and I walked across the tarmac toward a DC-6. "Even though you do not currently have an FAA pilot's license," Starkloff said, "when I saw your Air Transport Rating exam results, I was impressed."

"Yes, sir. When Bob and I took the ATR test together, both of us scored very well. And to be candid, I always keep it in my wallet."

Three hours later, having observed Starkloff's expertly administered flight checks of the two young DC-6 pilots, we were at the holding point at MacArthur Field prior to takeoff.

Captain Starkloff set the parking brakes, exited the captain's seat, and asked me to take that seat. The co-pilot got out of his seat and was replaced by Captain Starkloff. He said, "I want you to show me just how good your Air Force training has been."

The DC-6 was virtually identical to the Air Force's C-118. After familiarizing myself with the minor differences on a couple of gauges, I guided the DC-6 down the runway for take-off.

Starkloff waited until I went through my initial checks, then he ordered, "Head northeast just outside the perimeter of MacArthur Field and turn southeast over the Atlantic. We're going to test your skills over the big blue yonder."

"Affirmative," I responded. I banked the aircraft to my right at six thousand feet above sea level and then headed out over the Atlantic Ocean to do air maneuvers.

For the next two hours, Starkloff cross-examined me and tested my flying abilities and reactions. It was the most intensive check ride of my career. His rigorous checks involved all the typical things I had experienced up to that time in the Air Force. However, his simulated failure of a second engine during an engine-out ILS missed approach was entirely new.

After completing his rigorous check ride and the impromptu *what-ifs* during the two-hour flight, we returned to Idlewild. I landed the DC-6 on a dark, wet runway. I taxied back to the parking spot, and we shut down the aircraft. I followed Starkloff into the dispatch center.

Captain Hinckley was waiting for us. He asked Starkloff how things had gone.

Rather than answer Hinckley, Starkloff asked me, "How soon can you fly your first flight for ONA? You're a good pilot and we need you."

"If I had my FAA license," I said, "I could start as soon as possible. But only if I'm no longer on active duty for the Air Force."

"Well, I'd like you to know I'm an FAA flight examiner," Starkloff said. "You now have an FAA type rating to fly the DC-6 and DC-7. I'd love it if you could start tomorrow."

I shook his hand again and did the same with Hinckley. Then I clarified that I needed to meet with my squadron commander to figure out the timing. Also, I had to decide if I really did want to leave the Air Force.

"Understood," Starkloff replied. "Please call me tomorrow with your answer."

In an adrenaline-charged daze, I drove back to my home in New Jersey and wondered about the course of my piloting career. The house was empty, but I was too jacked up to lie down in my room. I put on a winter coat and walked around in the neighborhood, attempting to figure out my next move. While walking, I realized that my having taken the phone call meant for Bob could possibly have been fate calling me toward a new direction in my aviation career. After a long stroll under black skies, I returned to the house and went to my room. I fell asleep after a few hours of reviewing the virtues and drawbacks of a military career in contrast to a civilian piloting career, and vice versa.

After a hasty shave and shower the next morning, I was in the office of my squadron commander by nine o'clock. During our discussion, Lieutenant Colonel Kohl did his best to keep me from leaving the Air Force.

"Lieutenant Vest," he said, "the Air Force has been very good to you, and you've been good for it. Without a doubt, your career in the Air Force is limitless. Of that, I am absolutely sure."

"Thank you, sir," I replied. "Your opinion means a great deal to me. That's why I'm here."

"In the Air Force," he continued, "you are guaranteed a full-time job with a full slate of planned routes, journeys, and destinations. That is impossible to find in the civilian world, no offense to our civilian counterparts."

"Commander Kohl, may I use the conference room to think things through?" I asked. He opened the door to the vacant conference room. I walked around the long table while watching a variety of aircraft taking off and landing on the busy runways at McGuire.

I pondered and prayed. I searched the depths of my soul for the right answer. An hour later, I reentered Commander Kohl's office.

I saluted before stating, "Sir, I've made my decision. I want to sincerely thank you and the Air Force for making the last few years of my life so great. But now I'm ready to be an airline captain for ONA and to become a civilian once again."

Shortly after departing Commander Kohl's office, I reflected on the phone call from ONA. That call was meant for Bob but, as *fate* would have it, that call changed my destiny from military to commercial flying.

CHAPTER 54
1960

ON A CLEAR Wednesday morning at nine o'clock, I was in the left seat of the cockpit and flying a white-and-brown DC-6 at an altitude of fifteen thousand feet. We were on route from Shannon Airport in southwest Ireland to Frankfurt, Germany. The plane was carrying ninety-five trusting passengers.

During the past three months, I had flown this route nine times. We would depart from Idlewild Airport in New York City to fly to Gander, Newfoundland. Then we would cross the Atlantic to land at Shannon Airport in Ireland. We would lay over there for a mandatory twenty-four hours. After the layover, I would fly the DC-6 over the

Overseas National Airways DC-6

United Kingdom and cross the English Channel before flying over Antwerp, Belgium, and into northwest Germany. Eventually, we would land in Frankfurt, Germany.

On this day, we had just crossed the English Channel and the aircraft was operating smoothly, when my co-pilot, Frank, asked, "Captain Vest, did you plan on being a lifer in the Air Force, or did you always want to be a civilian pilot?"

"I'm not sure," I said. "If I hadn't picked up the phone the morning that Steedman Hinckley had called looking for one of my housemates, who knows what might have happened. I could have spent the next two or three decades flying for the Air Force."

"It truly is strange how *fate* can drop opportunities in front of us," Frank said. "Then we have to decide whether to take the chance."

"It's unwise to try and predict the future," I said. "In my opinion, it's better to build a plan and adjust along the way than trying to foresee outcomes and continue down the wrong course. That's my overall philosophy most of the time, anyway."

We passed over the northwest coast of Belgium, then Frank said, "I know we don't get to interact with our flight attendants very much outside of our normal in-flight duties but let me ask you a question if that's all right with you."

I nodded, and Frank waded in. "I know that all three of our flight attendants are lovely. But if you had to pick just one, who would it be: Carol, Inga, or Susan?"

I remained silent while contemplating my answer to Frank's innocent but pointed question. He was obviously interested in at least one of the ladies.

"Let me tell you," I began. "I could have left the Air Force to pursue a budding love affair with a young lady in New Zealand. But when this career opportunity came about, she and I discussed it at great length. We agreed that I should pursue a career in commercial aviation, and she should complete her final years at Victoria University."

Frank nodded, and we enjoyed some good-natured banter before trouble arrived. Our flight engineer, Paul, returned from using the lavatory. He sat down between Frank and me, then said, "Captain, we've got a problem with engine number one. The engine analyzer shows no ignition in the number two cylinder."

I acknowledged the information as we initiated our descent for landing at Frankfurt. I reduced power to idle on the malfunctioning number-one engine. At 10:30 in the morning, I landed the DC-6 at Frankfurt Airport. After slowing to the plane's taxiing speed, I steered the aircraft to the ONA ramp location.

After concluding our post-flight checks, I exited the DC-6 and briefed maintenance personnel about the number-one engine. Then I went to the ONA office with Frank and Paul. Shortly, ONA

maintenance personnel advised us of the need to replace the defective cylinder, and our estimated departure delay was eighteen hours.

The ONA ground hostess on duty, Ingrid Bakker, walked into the office to confirm the eighteen-hour delay. I looked at the pretty brunette, dressed in her blue

Ingrid

uniform, and said, "Yes, that is correct."

Ingrid frowned. "Then I'll need to arrange for bus transportation and hotel accommodations for the ninety-five passengers waiting to depart. The passenger list includes dependent women and children who need supplies such as extra baby bottles and diapers to cover them during the delay."

I saw the concerned look on Ingrid's face. I appreciated the challenge she was facing, and I volunteered to help her.

Her light-gray-green eyes lit up, and she smiled at me. She replied in slightly accented German-English, "Ah, yes, Captain Vest. I'm the only one on duty today. Thank you! Do you mind helping me with gathering enough diapers and formula after we get the passengers settled into the hotel? Because the requests will be coming in for these items very quickly after that."

"It would be my pleasure," I said. Ingrid and I walked out of the office and approached the delayed passengers, who were waiting for more information from us.

Ingrid whispered to me, "Captain Vest, I believe we can buy most of the supplies we'll need at the Rhein-Main base exchange."

"Sounds like a good idea to me," I replied. "And by the way, when we're not on duty, please just call me Warren."

CHAPTER 55
1960

SEVERAL HOURS LATER, after getting the delayed passengers securely checked into a hotel, Ingrid and I hurried to the base exchange to buy bundles of diapers, along with baby formula and an assortment of other supplies. Once we were done, we were free to enjoy an early evening together at the hotel coffee shop. Due to the influx of our passengers and flight crew, the hotel suddenly had nearly one hundred unexpected guests. The modest diner was rather busy. However, Ingrid and I secured a small table near a window. From the lounge across the lobby, I could hear a jazz band playing catchy music.

I sipped at my cup of coffee and scouted Ingrid's pretty face and dark hair. She was sharing some of her unique background and upbringing. She had a radiant smile, which fit well with her captivating eyes. Her charming personality exuded a natural warmth. I found her openness and bluntness alluring, and even though we had met previously a few times during my two-hour turnarounds at Frankfurt, due to our busy schedules we hadn't been able to talk much and get to know each other.

While we were having coffee, Ingrid said, "You know, Warren, my being born at the beginning of World War II in Karlsruhe, Germany, wasn't ideal. But as I grew up, my mother somehow managed to make things work for us, including my two younger sisters, Heide and Lilo. My father was a German Marine POW who was captured in England. Our house was built by my grandparents, and the brick-walled basement had a reinforced ceiling with thick poles jutting into it, in case we got bombed. Often, the city's air raid sirens blared across town. My mother would shuttle us down to the cellar and close the thick doors behind us. It was terrifying. I remember one time when my mother stashed my sisters and me down there and locked us in. Then she went upstairs to listen to our hidden radio to get news about the war. Hitler forbade all families from having radios, but my mother kept one anyway."

I nodded. "Hitler controlled the messaging, and he was an awful master manipulator."

"Yes, he was a monster, as we now know," Ingrid said. "Most of us Germans did not realize what Hitler was really doing inside our own country. It was terrible."

The waitress stopped to top off our coffees. "When my sisters and I were locked in the cellar, I fell asleep. Later, I woke up in that pitch-black cellar, and I was terrified. I thought my mother had forgotten about us, or that something terrible had happened to her. I screamed for a long time before she realized what had happened, and she came running downstairs to retrieve us all."

"It must have been harsh," I said.

Ingrid's face grew sadder, and her eyes welled with tears. "Oh, yes. My mother had us three little girls to care for. She couldn't just pack up and leave like many of our neighbors did. One time, when the Russian army came through town, a few of the soldiers barged into our home with their rifles. They pillaged our place looking for food and valuables. I thought we were all going to die."

"What happened," I asked. "How did your family survive the Russians?"

She sipped at her coffee. "My mother told us that Russians were occupying many of the homes in our neighborhood. One night, she took a couple of Russian soldiers into the bedroom and pointed at the three of us little girls sound asleep. The soldiers decided not to kill us. After the Russians left our home, my mother collapsed onto the floor and cried with relief."

I sat back in my chair, transfixed by Ingrid's account of her life.

She continued, "I know it's hard to imagine. But between watching and hearing those whistling bombs drop from the sky to destroy nearly everything around us, and the Russians taking over, and then the French coming into town for a bit.... Well, it's a miracle that I'm sitting here with you tonight. If it weren't for the Americans leading the way to win the war and then occupying our area, I would not be here now. That's for certain. As a matter of fact, things got so bad during the war that the first time I ever developed new friends was with American military children after the war. The first time I ever tasted a piece of candy was when a sweet, American soldier gave me a wintergreen mint. I ran home to show the candy to my mother before eating it."

The waitress returned to our table with two slices of warm apple pie. Each one had a slice of cheddar cheese on top. The waitress indicated a smiling couple waving at us from the opposite corner of the room. She said, "Compliments for a job well done today."

Ingrid and I acknowledged their generosity, and I forked a piece of pie into my mouth. It was fabulous. I asked Ingrid, "Did you learn to speak English so well from the children of American military personnel?"

She nodded, and I asked about her dad. She dabbed at her mouth with a napkin and answered, "My father was a troubled soul. After the war ended, he was released to come back home. He regularly lost his temper during his drinking binges, and he would sometimes go missing for a day or two. One night, my mother sat my sisters and me down in the kitchen. She told us that our father had died after falling backward onto a cobblestone street and hitting his head. Obviously, he'd been drinking and lost his balance. He was only forty-two years old."

"I'm very sorry to hear that," I said.

Ingrid stared at me with a poised but pleasant look on her face. "I appreciate that, but I didn't really know my father well. For the most part, it was just my mother and us three girls growing up. We used to walk everywhere, and we didn't have a car. We would stroll with our mother to the train station on workday mornings, and we'd be there waiting for her each night when she returned. She was always waving hello to us as the train pulled into the station."

I could not wait any longer. "Ingrid, can I see you again?"

CHAPTER 56
1960

EARLY ON FRIDAY morning at sixteen thousand feet, I flew a DC-6 on the assigned air route over the North Atlantic from Shannon, Ireland, to Gander, Newfoundland. I had ninety-five passengers onboard and was reminiscing about my long conversation with Ingrid two nights earlier.

Even though I found her to be very beautiful, what drew me, even more, was Ingrid's personality and her tough upbringing. My heart rate increased whenever I thought of her. My ponderings about Ingrid also forced me to confront an undeniable truth pertaining to much of my dating life. For some reason, I seemed to be attracted to women from other countries.

At times, my mind would highlight the lovely and amiable foreign women I had spent time with. I would recall pleasing moments with them that would hopefully stay with me forever. But why had I been drawn over the years to international women?

I donned my sunglasses and sipped some water while my co-pilot and navigator conducted routine in-flight checks. The navigator confirmed our position at twenty degrees west longitude, and the co-pilot was preparing to report our position to air traffic control via Shanwick Radio. The sky was clear, and from our cruising altitude of sixteen thousand feet, I spotted a ship on a westward course toward North America.

Again, I looked back on my life. It felt as if the past half-dozen years had gone by in a flash. At times, memorable flashbacks would come to me unbidden.

I conferred with my co-pilot. He had finished his position report, everything was looking good, and we were one minute ahead of our flight plan. I informed my crew that they would be running the show for the next couple of hours. I needed time to think.

Maybe I was just like any normal soul living on Earth. It's likely that I wanted to merely discover sincere forms of love and companionship to ease the sometimes-heavy burden of life. That might explain why I spent three nights cuddling with Marlene on lounge chairs upon the aft deck of the Queen Elizabeth when I was cruising from England to New York.

During much of my time in the Air Force, I had gone on dates with nice women in Florida, Texas, and New Jersey. But even then, I had been drawn inexorably to yet another foreign woman, Catherine. She was a New Zealander, but I met her in Italy.

Relaxed in the cockpit, my contemplations moved to my outstanding meeting with Ingrid a couple of nights earlier. Ingrid's honest portrayal of her formative years in Germany outlined an upbringing vastly different from my own. But I noticed two distinct similarities we happened to possess. Both of us were basically tough and we grew up without much in the way of financial resources. However, without a doubt, Ingrid had it far worse than I ever did.

While enjoying coffee and apple pie that night in Frankfurt, I had asked her how she had become an ONA ground hostess and reserve flight attendant. "Several years after the war ended and when I was fourteen years old," she said. "I became sick with a terrible fever. In one of the magazines my mother gave me to look at while I was recovering, I read a love story about a flight attendant and a pilot. Then during my high school years, I loved jazz music, and we turned a friend's basement bomb cellar into an underground jazz club. We spent lots of time there. However, I always remained interested in going to an aviation school in Frankfurt that taught general aviating. So that's what I did."

As my co-pilot guided our DC-6 on toward Newfoundland, images of Ingrid's pretty face and attractive smile kept scrolling through my mind. I felt myself tumbling into the familiar lair of much-needed sleep. Right before my conscious mind gave way to the rush of my subconscious mind, another handful of Ingrid's charms popped into my head. Like me, Ingrid had an innate desire to see the world and to experience the different cultures that each country and its people had to offer. She was fearless about wanting to travel and unafraid of the big commitment needed to accomplish her globetrotting goals. She possessed a set of core values that had been forged by years of surviving hard lessons in a tough environment, but her mother's deep love established the bedrock she relied on.

It's little wonder that nearing the end our coffee and conversation in Frankfurt, I had asked Ingrid if I could see her again.

She had responded to my overture with "Yes, I would like that very much." Once again, I was captivated by a foreign woman.

CHAPTER 57
1960

SINCE MEETING INGRID as the result of an Overseas National Airways maintenance stopover in June, I had looked forward to each of my flights into Frankfurt. Even if I could see her only during a two-hour turnaround, it would be more than worth it.

Far more fulfilling were the occasions when Ingrid was called on to replace a flight attendant who had fallen ill. In those instances, she would work the flight back to New York. Her New York layovers normally lasted only twenty-four hours, but we took full advantage of every opportunity to deepen our bond and strengthen our relationship. I took Ingrid to visit with my buddies at our House of Pilots in New Jersey. Later, I rented a Kew Gardens apartment in the borough of Queens, New York, to be closer to Idlewild Airport. That made it easier for me to operate short-notice flights.

After I moved to Queens, Ingrid had two more New York layovers. However, ONA's contract with the military was set to expire in October, so we wondered if this might be her final layover in New York for the foreseeable future.

On a pleasant, fall afternoon in Queens, I listened to the noise of occasional sirens and the steady stream of vehicles passing outside. While shuffling around the kitchen, I realized that unless there was a major emergency nearby, the screaming echoes of police and fire vehicles no longer bothered me. A newscaster's voice on the kitchen radio reported that Democratic presidential candidate John F.

Kennedy had proposed creating a new Peace Corps if he were elected in a few weeks.

Ingrid was relaxing on the couch watching a soap opera, one of her recent discoveries. I grabbed two cold bottles of beer and popped off the caps. I poured one in a glass for Ingrid and carried our drinks into the living room. As I walked toward Ingrid, she remained focused on her daytime show.

I placed her glass of beer on the coffee table and sat next to her on the sofa. She patted my leg affectionately, thanked me for the beer, and said, "My soap opera is almost over. Only two more minutes to go. This is intense!"

I nodded. "I know. As the World Turns."

I munched on potato chips until Ingrid's favorite television drama ended. She reached for her glass of beer, sipped at it, and said, "I can't believe that Lisa is pregnant with Bob's baby. And now they're going to elope!"

Pretending to be intrigued, I replied, "Is that a good thing or a bad thing?"

Ingrid rolled her pretty eyes and waved me off with a flirtatious laugh. We sat for the next several minutes enjoying our time together in silence. She took another sip of her beverage and set down the glass. She turned toward me, and we kissed before she gently pulled back. "Warren," she began, "these last four months with you in

Frankfurt and New York have been great. But what are we going to do now that the ONA contract with the military is about to end?"

"I'm all in for you, Ingrid. I want to keep building our relationship. You are kind, beautiful, and smart; and you've been proactive about immigrating to the United States."

She smiled, but there was a hint of doubt in her expression. She rested her hands on my shoulders before replying. "If we are going to develop a foundation with each other, it should be for more than six or seven days per month. Don't you think?"

"Yes, of course," I said, "but our way of life is not normal. The lifestyle we've chosen is unique, and it's not easy. It's also liberating and somewhat romantic."

Ingrid raised her eyebrows. "That's true. I've had a lot of fun with you in New York and Germany. And I must say, I'm very excited about immigrating to the United States."

I pulled her closer and we kissed and explored each other's bodies through the barriers of our clothing. After getting overheated, we took a break and stretched out together on the couch. We laughed and told stories about our ONA co-workers as the late-afternoon sunshine gradually shifted to mid-September dusk.

Ingrid rolled on top of me. Her hair tumbled and framed her lovely face. She playfully said, "I'm hungry!"

I replied, "Me too. Do you still want to go out for dinner, or do you want to cook something here? I've got some nice steaks in the fridge."

"Hmm," she mused. "Since you don't have a grill, I will cook them German style in that iron skillet of yours. Does that sound good?"

"Done," I said.

We arose from the couch and straightened up our disheveled selves before making our way into the kitchen. I grabbed the steaks and some mixed vegetables from the fridge. Ingrid located my iron skillet and a small saucepan and placed them on the burners. She poured olive oil into the skillet and streamed water into the saucepan, dumping raw vegetables into it. She turned on the burners, then spun the dial on the kitchen radio to find music to her liking. Immediately, she cranked it louder. Chubby Checker's new hit tune exploded from the radio. "Come on baby, let's do the twist!"

I prepared a rub of garlic, pepper, and salt for the steaks, and watched Ingrid groove around in my kitchen. She was sexy and vibrant, and she did not appear to have a care in the world.

I wiggled my hips back and forth and quietly sang my passionate and devilish thoughts about Ingrid. "Come on baby, let's do the twist!"

The music was booming, and Ingrid couldn't hear what I was saying. The olive oil bubbled to life, and I "assisted" as Ingrid placed the seasoned ribeyes into the frying pan. A wonderful aroma rose into the air as I moved to the counter to carve up a head of lettuce for a salad.

Ingrid flipped the steaks over and cut off a piece of ribeye for me. It tasted great.

We turned off the burners and carried the food to the table. Chubby Checker's hit song had faded, and a disc jockey said something. Then I heard Elvis Presley singing "Stuck on You."

Halfway through our meal, she stood up and circled behind me, wrapping her arms around me. The intoxicating scent of her perfume was incredibly appealing. She kissed the back of my neck and seductively began working her way around to my face.

She whispered into my ear, "Warren, do you want me to make some coffee, or would you like to go straight to dessert?"

I stood up and we embraced. I kissed her neck, and she said, "It's time for dessert!"

"Agreed," I said, as I led Ingrid out of the kitchen.

CHAPTER 58
1961

THE ONA MILITARY contract had expired at the end of September 1960. I had flown my final ONA flight into Frankfurt during the last week of the month and had seen Ingrid during my two-hour turnaround. She assured me that her paperwork to immigrate to the United States was in order and approved by the American Embassy. She planned to travel to New York on the last ONA flight from Frankfurt on October 1.

It was unfortunate that I was simultaneously being transferred from the ONA operations in New York City to Oakland, California. I rented an apartment in Hayward, California, and had flown my first ONA DC-7 flight out of Oakland on November 8, the day John F. Kennedy was elected president of the United States.

Upon her arrival in New York, Ingrid had been invited to share an apartment in Manhattan with an ONA flight attendant. Ingrid found work at Fieldcrest Mills, Inc., in lower Manhattan. She enjoyed her job very much, but she dreamed of becoming a stewardess with an international airline. That way she would be able to visit her family in Germany.

We were living almost three thousand miles apart on opposite coasts, so we wrote letters to each other and spoke on the telephone regularly. However, the unplanned shift in our living arrangements put a strain on our relationship.

In mid-February 1961, for the first time in my piloting career, I was unemployed. ONA had furloughed my position after its business on the West Coast had been reduced. While talking with Ingrid on the phone to wish her a happy Valentine's Day, I mentioned that I was no longer an airline captain for ONA and was looking for a job. At the same time, there was good news. Ingrid was preparing to move to Kansas City to begin flight-hostess training for Trans World Airlines. TWA would be lucky to have her, and TWA would be great for Ingrid.

Later that day, I drove to a grocery store and bought every Bay-area newspaper I could find. With my anxiety increasing over being jobless, I raced home to scour the help-wanted ads. I couldn't shake the advice given to me by my former squadron commander, Lieutenant Colonel Kohl. When I had met with him to discuss my future—either in the Air Force or in the civilian world—he had tried to talk me into staying in the Air Force, pointing out the guaranteed job security.

I had scoured the Bay-area newspapers and two Bay-area magazines, finding nothing. I was about to give up hope for the day but then noticed a tiny advertisement in the Hayward newspaper.

Pilot Wanted was all the ad stated. Below the heading was a phone number. I dialed the number and talked with a quiet-spoken man, who set up an interview appointment in Walnut Creek the following day. I spent the next twelve hours trying to sleep. By ten o'clock the following morning, I was sitting in an office in a nondescript building. A large man who said his name was Stan had been thorough in probing the details of my piloting background.

He had my file spread out in front of him. "Warren," he said, "just to be clear. Your meeting with me has gone extremely well, so I'd like to share some information with you. We at International Aviation Development Corporation, IADCO for short, recently purchased two DC-6s from American Airlines. We need a chief pilot for the planes. That's why you're here today."

"I appreciate your sharing that information with me, Stan. But may I ask a question?"

Stan nodded, and I asked, "Can you tell me why I need to take a lie-detector test to fly DC-6s? (Stan had mentioned almost in passing that the following day I would need to go to San Francisco for a polygraph test. But he also had said he'd already confirmed my employment and flight records with the Air Force and with my former employers at ONA).

He leaned back and looked at me from behind his desk. "IADCO only hires the best people and the most trustworthy individuals to assist our government with some of the more discreet and important duties that it tasks us with."

The cryptic answer caught me off guard. Stan wasn't finished. "Assuming that you pass the lie-detector test, Warren, you would become IADCO's chief pilot for the DC-6."

I straighten up and asked, "Where would I be based?"

"Air Jordan of the Holy Land in Amman, Jordan, and maybe another location in the Middle East."

I was surprised, but I tried not to show it. All I said was "When would I start flying?"

Stan didn't hesitate. "Two weeks from now, and that's when you need to be in Jordan."

CHAPTER 59
1961

THREE-AND-A-HALF months after being hired by IADCO at the age of twenty-six, I entered my apartment on a hot day in the hilly city of Amman, Jordan. There were no supermarkets in Amman, so I had carried in a bag of food items purchased at a specialty shop. I shopped sparingly out of necessity.

I scooped up letters and postcards from Ingrid and read them again. Her tender writing warmed my heart. I recalled my drive back to Missouri in late February to drop off my belongings and my 1956 Chevrolet at my parents' home. I had visited with Ingrid in Kansas City, where she was training to become a TWA flight attendant. She met my parents and my brother during their short weekend visit to Aunt Mary and Uncle Glenn's home in Kansas City.

Back in Amman, the incredibly loud, echoing call to prayer sounded from the community prayer sirens atop minarets above the city's mosques. The piercing wails boomed across Jordan's capital city and summoned Muslims to commence one of the five mandatory sessions of prayer.

I left the apartment for my daily jaunt to the Air Jordan office. Like other days, I would be flying to one of our busiest airports at Beirut, Lebanon.

By the time I entered the building, my assistant had completed his midday prayers. He greeted me with a broad smile. "Warren, I've got good news. Our street-runners have already sold fifty-five tickets today. I totaled up the dinars and they match perfectly with the exact number of fares."

He handed me a fat envelope filled with money. I shook his hand. "Thank you, Mohammed. Well done. I'm relieved that I will have enough cash to pay for our gas in Beirut when we refuel, instead of my having to write another personal check and then wait for Air Jordan to reimburse me."

Mohammed smiled knowingly. "Allah has bestowed his blessings upon us today."

I asked, "Will any members of the royal family be joining us on the flight to Beirut?"

Mohammed shook his head. "No, the royal family is dealing with a personal matter today. But his Royal Highness, King Hussein, sends you his best wishes for a safe journey. He also said for me to thank you again for taking him along during your amazing feat yesterday."

The day before, we had flown a DC-6 at one thousand feet *below* sea level. We were only three hundred feet above the Dead Sea. Apparently, King Hussein had enjoyed the experience. Shortly afterward, he had "Below-Sea-Level Flying Club" business cards created.

BELOW-SEA-LEVEL FLYING CLUB

AIR JORDAN CERTIFIES THAT السيد جون ل. تراڤلر
YOUR NAME IN ARABIC

IS ENTITLED TO FLY 1000 FEET BELOW SEA
LEVEL OVER THE DEAD SEA AND JERICHO

John O. Traveller

IS THEREFORE AN HONORARY MEMBER OF B.S.L.F.C.
AND HAS THE EXCLUSIVE RIGHT TO ASK

HOW LOW CAN YOU GET... AND STILL FLY?

SIGNED THIS   DAY OF   195
IN THE HASHEMITE KINGDOM OF JORDAN
AIR JORDAN CAPTAIN

I went into my office to retrieve my flight bag, and I double-checked my scheduled list of flights for the next two weeks. Destinations included Beirut, Jerusalem, Cairo, Kuwait, and Bagdad. I stuffed the envelope packed with dinars into my flight bag, said goodbye to Mohammed, and caught a taxi to the Amman airport.

By four o'clock that afternoon, I was positioned in the left seat of the cockpit of the familiar Air Jordan DC-6. We were scheduled to land in Beirut, Lebanon, on the eastern shore of the Mediterranean Sea. My co-pilot, Amin, and flight engineer, David, executed their duties, and once our in-flight checks had been confirmed, I flew the DC-6 at an altitude of eleven thousand feet. We had sixty-two passengers and crewmembers on board.

After flying over Damascus, Syria, and starting our descent to Beirut, I viewed the gorgeous, turquoise waters of the

Mediterranean. The white sand beaches were dotted with beachgoers enjoying the late-afternoon sunshine. Rising up behind them was a skyline of hotels and condominiums.

We landed and taxied to the gate, where the flight engineer said, "Captain Vest, I assume the maintenance facility will have their people tow the aircraft to the hangar for its scheduled maintenance check."

"Yes," I said, "our maintenance personnel in Amman coordinated with Trans Mediterranean Airways." After a pause, I continued, "Our agent has arranged for a van to take our crew to the hotel. Then I'll buy all of us dinner. It's my treat before we fly back to Amman tomorrow."

By seven o'clock on that warm evening, I was seated at a table with Amin and David and our two lovely flight attendants, Farah and Hala. We relaxed on the bustling veranda of my favorite Beirut restaurant, which overlooked the dazzling shoreline. Our waiter kept bringing us platters of excellent food, and I sipped at my glass of iced tea and watched hordes of passersby walking down the boardwalk.

"This place is breathtaking!" David exclaimed, and we toasted our non-alcoholic drinks.

"It's like the Paris of the Middle East," I said.

The usually quiet Farah chimed in, "Thank you, captain. This is a nice surprise, and these grilled prawns and yogurt dip are excellent."

"My pleasure," I said. "Since David had never been outside the United States before joining Air Jordan this week, I figured this would be a nice little detour."

We ate deliciously grilled vegetables and assorted seafood. I had to pause to let the meal settle in. The palatial structures of the Phoenician and St. George hotels took on a reflected glow in the sunset. The street lamps and dangling lights adorning beachfront eateries glimmered to life.

David said, "Now that you've been flying movie stars all over Jordan and back and forth to Wadi Rum, give us some insight into what Peter O'Toole and Omar Sharif are like."

"Mister Sharif is a class act, a total gentleman and a heavy intellectual, a deep thinker. Peter O'Toole, on the other hand.... Let's just say O'Toole is not a fan of the desert, not in the least bit. He loathes the dry climate and he can't wait until they wrap up filming in a couple of months. Still, he understands that *Lawrence of Arabia* is going to be a big hit in the States."

We started talking about our favorite films. Then Hala asked me about my social life; what it was like having a solid relationship while traveling all over the world.

"It can be tough," I said, "but if you're dating someone who works in the airline industry, then you might have a better chance of success because they understand the unique lifestyle and the gaps of time in between seeing each other."

Hala nodded, and David said, "The gal I was hot and heavy with dumped me two weeks ago when I told her I was taking this job. What a drag that was." My thoughts turned to Ingrid, who was now living in New York City and working as a flight hostess for TWA.

Farah asked, "What about you, captain? Do you have a special lady in your life?"

"Yes, I do. Her name is Ingrid. We've only had the chance to see each other a couple of days in New York during the past few months, but I truly believe she wants the same things I do. I have a good feeling about us."

"And what's that?" David asked.

"Love, of course."

CHAPTER 60
1961

IN ADDITION TO flying passengers to destinations around the Middle East for Air Jordan of the Holy Land, I had been instructed to transport huge shipments of emergency medical supplies from the United Nations distribution facility in Cairo, Egypt. I flew the supplies into the heart of Africa, landing at Stanleyville in the Congo. Ever since the assassination of the Congo's prime minister, Patrice Lumumba, in January, the bloody war in the Congo region had caused massive devastation and famine.

It was stressful flying over the vast, green canopy and then having to descend into the armed chaos of Stanleyville. On my previous trip, after landing the DC-6 in the dangerous airport, I had been met by a large group of communist-backed rebels in need of our free medical supplies, and by a U.S. consular officer from Leopoldville, who was waiting for the local U.N. Peacekeeping Force to unload the goods from the airplane.

On the current approach to Stanleyville, as I prepared to land, I was guided only by a smattering of dim lights that faintly outlined the darkened runway. I cautiously set down the DC-6 on the battered runway.

Hitting berms and bumps along the way, I taxied the jostling airplane toward the terminal area. My co-pilot, Jimmy, finally let out his breath in relief. But his sense of calm was premature. As I steered the aircraft in the direction of the terminal, twin flanks of floodlights suddenly came to life. Between blinding walls of light, I braked the airplane to a stop.

"What the hell?" I muttered.

"This does not look good," Jimmy agreed.

I squinted at what appeared to be a heavily armed rebel army. The Congolese irregulars surrounded the plane, and every man had his gun pointed at us.

Jimmy estimated there were several hundred soldiers. The rebel army's leader instructed some of his men to offload our supplies. We stayed inside the cockpit with explicit orders not to move. About two hours later, the rebels allowed us to refuel and leave. Even though I had to take a leak awfully bad, I piloted the DC-6 through takeoff and up to a safe altitude before allowing Jimmy to fly the plane while I took a much-needed break on route back to Cairo.

Eight days later back in Amman, in part due to a "misunderstanding" involving the U.S. consular officer from Leopoldville, we received notice that all flights pertaining to the use of aircraft owned by Air Jordan of the Holy Land would no longer be allowed to operate. Just like that, we were grounded.

American Airlines had major financial liens on the two DC-6 aircraft, but the director of civil aviation would not release the planes from Jordan. About a dozen American employees and spouses, plus several Egyptian mechanics and their families, were stranded in

Amman. There was no air service to Cairo or Beirut, and Egypt and Syria were at war. All of us were in limbo.

In the midst of all this chaos, I received a call from a former airline executive, Allen Barry, who was familiar with the politics of the Middle East. He asked what it would take to get the two DC-6s out of the country.

I told him I would get back to him within a day. Then I discussed a few ideas with a fellow pilot, Bill Piles. We came up with a plan that would take about four weeks to execute. We convinced the Jordanian authorities that the DC-6 aircraft engines had to be operated at least once a week to preserve their mechanical integrity. Every time we would run the engines while the airplanes were parked, we would ask the Amman airport authorities for enough fuel to run up the engine. The result was that every week, Bill and I were adding fuel for our planned escape flights to Beirut. During the month-long-plus clandestine operation, Bill and I would secretly position spare aircraft parts and some of our employees' personal effects on board the planes each time we did an engine run-up.

In five weeks, Bill and I felt we were ready to pull off our unauthorized flight out of Amman. We orchestrated the plan to conduct our engine run-ups on both DC-6s at the same time on Sunday evening, October 1.

That afternoon, Bill and I gradually positioned the terrified American employees and nervous Egyptian families onto both aircraft without being noticed. We used a pair of maintenance vans, transporting four, five, or six people at a time. Somehow, and probably with divine providence intervening, we were able to get all the passengers and crew onboard the DC-6s undetected.

Under the cover of early darkness and complete radio silence, Bill and I used a series of hand signals to communicate. We started our engines simultaneously. I was dripping with sweat and fighting back a nauseating feeling. I taxied the DC-6 onto the runway and advanced the throttles to maximum power as we took off for Beirut, with Bill's DC-6 hauling ass into the skies right behind me.

A few minutes after takeoff, as we crossed the Syrian border, I noticed that my aircraft was losing oil in all four engines. I radioed Bill and alerted him to the situation. He confirmed that he also was experiencing oil loss. Someone in Jordan had probably added some type of detergent to our oil tanks in their attempt to sabotage the aircraft.

We couldn't turn back to Jordan, and if we landed in Damascus, Syria, our Egyptian passengers would likely end up dead or imprisoned. Bill and I agreed not to shut down any of our engines until the oil temperature pegged out on the gauge. If we could keep at least half the engines on each plane running until we topped the mountains between Damascus and Beirut, we could make the Beirut airport.

Roughly fifty-five minutes later, Bill and I landed our DC-6s at the Beirut airport with only one engine shut down on each airplane.

Tearful passengers hugged me before exiting the plane, and within minutes both DC-6s were turned over to the Trans Mediterranean Airways maintenance facility.

Our Beirut Agent arranged hotel accommodations for us. The following morning, I contacted several airlines that Air Jordan had interline accounts with. I discovered that SAS owed Air Jordan several thousand dollars of credit, and they were willing to give our U.S. citizens free tickets on SAS flights to the States. And even though our account balance with Egypt Air was minimal, they showed great humanity and provided free travel from Beirut to Cairo to our Egyptian families. Furthermore, SAS coordinated with their contacts in Beirut, enabling our dozen American crew members and family to obtain temporary lodging in Beirut while everything got sorted out.

I was exhausted from the intrigue and uncertainty of the past five weeks in Amman. Even though Bill and I had managed to transport fifty people to safety, my body was still tense from the emotional stress of the ordeal.

Upon arriving at our temporary lodging, I stripped off my clothes and took advantage of the walk-in shower. I let the frigid water rain down on me from above. I flinched from the shock, but the cool water felt good, and I was thrilled to be alive. I continued to bathe under the soothing cascade, and my normally positive thoughts returned to the woman I loved and missed, Ingrid.

CHAPTER 61
1962

FOLLOWING OUR SUCCESSFUL, five-week-long, cloak-and-dagger repatriation of two DC-6s and our grateful American and Egyptian

DC-3 in Libya

families, I spent October 1961 in Beirut debriefing IADCO senior leadership. Once the IADCO brass was up to speed on what had transpired in Amman and Beirut, I was reassigned to Tripoli, Libya. I would be flying DC-3s in support of oil explorations for major international oil companies.

Tripoli, a coastal city on the northwestern edge of the country, was hot and dry. The occasional sand storm made for difficult flying conditions over the parched Libyan terrain. Tripoli could not measure up to the refinement and world-class cultural ambience of Beirut. The sobering reality of my new assignment was compounded by the fact that I was only a few hundred miles south of Mount Etna, Italy, and several hundred miles west of the Suez Canal in Egypt. Eight years earlier, I had enjoyed these uniquely beautiful places on my world cruise home from Australia.

In Libya, I shared a rented house with Captain Paul Soha and Bob Williams, director of maintenance. They had been transferred from Amman a few months earlier. The house came furnished and included the assistance of a servant, a young man named Khalid. He cooked and cleaned and slept in a guest house out back.

Our flying schedule called for us to fly Monday through Saturday, with Sundays free. Saturday night was our time to relax and have a few cold beers. Our houseboy, Khalid, approached us one Saturday evening while the three of us were relaxing on our rooftop patio. He looked pensive, and I asked if something was wrong.

"I am very sorry for asking you all for this," he said, "but may I please have an advance on my salary? My brother wants to get married to his woman, but the girl's parents will not consent until her older sister is married off first."

I shot a glance at Bob and Paul. Then I asked, "Has your brother convinced you to marry the older sister? Is that why you need the advance?"

He nodded. "Yes, Mister Vest. It is my duty."

Bob buried his face in his hands. Paul drank some beer and shook his head. I took out my wallet and grabbed some cash, then collected equal sums from my roommates.

I handed the wad of bills to Khalid, and we wished him all the best. He thanked us profusely before quickly leaving the house.

Two weeks later, during our Saturday-night beers-on-the-rooftop-patio ritual, Khalid knocked on the back door. Once inside, he bounded up the back staircase and joined us on the roof.

He was livid, waving his arms in a disgusted rage. It took all three of us to calm him down.

Finally, Khalid explained that the older sister he had agreed to marry kept her face covered by a burka. He wanted to help his brother, so he followed through with marrying the woman. "Then," he said, "after I married my new wife and lifted the veil, I saw that she is cross-eyed. And they cannot be fixed!"

I swallowed a laugh. Paul and Bob were shaking their heads in disbelief. We all felt sorry for Khalid. To me, this was the outcome of an extremely hasty move combined with buyer's remorse. With that, we commiserated with Khalid over a round of beers.

Ingrid was in New York, continuing her career with TWA. I missed her terribly. If she and I were meant to be together, then something would have to change. Things never stay the same: they either get better or they get worse. I had Ingrid send me a job application for TWA. I wrote a detailed resume and mailed it to TWA.

In the meantime, I found contentment learning to fly the DC-3 in Tripoli. I was in the air six days per week. At times I flew at night when supplies and materials were needed immediately due to major equipment breakdowns. I often flew to Benghazi on the northeast coast and made frequent trips to remote desert locations such as Sabha, Awbari, and Murzuk.

I enjoyed flying into the village of Sabha, four hundred miles south of Tripoli and famous for the Fort Elena Castle, built during the Italian colonial period. Our mid-day arrivals left time to visit an amiable cafe operated by a Frenchman and his wife, both of whom were great company.

The hostile climate of the Libyan desert meant low population density and paltry, third-rate, flight facilities. One time, I flew the DC-3 at night across the vast desert and finally landed on a sand airstrip lined with gasoline-soaked rags that had been stuffed into empty beer cans. The rags had been set ablaze to illuminate and outline the pitch-black sand runway.

I reflected on my forebears, one of whom had served the United States on a mission in Libya in 1805. My distant cousin, U.S. Marine Lieutenant Presley O'Bannon, had led seven fellow Marines and a few hundred mercenaries across the desert from Alexandria, Egypt, to Derne, Libya. His mission was to break the hold of the Barbary Pirates, who had interfered with American shipping in the area. The Americans engaged the enemy and, after hours of close-quarters combat, Lieutenant O'Bannon and his comrades won the gruesome battle. He was the first American to plant the American flag on foreign soil during wartime. He was hailed as the Hero of Derne. Prince Hamet presented O'Bannon with a sword, which, in 1825, became the model for the regulation sword that is part of the modern Marine Corps uniform. The Marines' Hymn includes the words "to the shores of Tripoli" as a tribute to Lieutenant O'Bannon's heroics. The major bank in my hometown of Buffalo, Missouri, is the O'Bannon Bank, founded in 1901 by my O'Bannon relatives.

In February, after I had returned home in the early evening, Khalid greeted me. "Mister Vest, a businessman from America called the house looking for you."

"Really? Who was it?"

Khalid shook his head. "I could not understand his name, so I wrote down his telephone number and the company information. The businessman said it was about a job."

"Where did you put the note?" I asked. Khalid indicated it was on the dinner table. I reached the dining-room table and picked up the note. I read the trio of letters in disbelief. TWA! Was fate calling again?

CHAPTER 62
1962

LATE THAT EVENING in Tripoli, when I knew the TWA offices in America would be open, I called the number on Khalid's note. I reached a woman in TWA's personnel department. She said TWA had completed its due diligence, expedited by my having provided a resume and references. The woman said my employment was finalized, assuming I could get myself from Libya to Rome, where TWA would provide transportation to their offices in Kansas City.

"Consider it done," I said. "And thank you!" TWA planned to assign me to the company's operations in Jeddah, Saudi Arabia.

I felt as if I were living in a dream. I was longing to see Ingrid and my family. It had been nearly a year since I had seen them. With Ingrid, our months of courtship through letter-writing and postcard correspondence was at best satisfactory. Our long-distance phone calls helped to ease the pain of my loneliness. And I was thrilled to commence my fresh TWA opportunity in Jeddah, but again we would have to carry on our courtship from a great distance. Still, I was determined to build a successful relationship with her, regardless of our temporary geographical challenges.

I called Ingrid in Boston to give her the great news and to have her meet me in Kansas City. Before ending the call, she told me, "Don't worry, Honey. I'm already packing for K.C. and I can't wait to see you!"

I hurried to wrap up my business affairs in Tripoli. Luckily for me, the executives at IADCO granted my release and arranged for my flight into Rome. I spent one chilly evening in Rome, which I welcomed after having spent months in the heat of North Africa. I strolled through a quiet section of the city and located a tiny bistro. I walked in and treated myself to a hearty dinner of spaghetti carbonara, garlic bread, and a glass of Chianti.

While savoring my dinner, I pondered the next phase of my life. TWA was hiring me to fly as a captain for the Saudi Arabian Airline, which TWA managed out of Jeddah. It was another big step in my aviation career.

The portly Italian café owner sensed my happiness. When he delivered the check, he asked in his heavily accented English, "Americano, yes?"

I smiled and nodded. "Yes, American, and I'm an airline pilot. Not only that, I'm headed to Kansas City to meet up with the woman I want to marry."

He grinned and replied in his bellowing voice, "Amore!" Then he snatched up the check before I could pay. The café owner winked and crumpled up my tab while backing away and joyfully singing, "*In bocca al lupo!*"

I was humbled by his generosity and good wishes. I truly believed it was a sign of great things to come. The next morning, I caught my flight to Kansas City via New York. From the airport in New York, I called Ingrid to ensure everything was on track. All was good, and since TWA needed two days to complete my paperwork and the renewal of my FAA first class medical certificate, there was time for my folks to meet us in Kansas City. All of us would stay at my Aunt Mary and Uncle Glenn's home.

But before all that, I eagerly reunited with Ingrid in our Kansas City hotel room. I was looking forward to our time together and the impending get-together with my family. She had met them only briefly during her TWA training twelve months earlier. This would be a wonderful opportunity for her to really get to know them.

I kissed her and said, "I'm so happy that you're finally going to get to know my family better."

"I hope they like me," she said. "I really do." For the first time that day, I saw a flicker of doubt flash across Ingrid's pretty face.

"They will love you," I assured her. Then I pulled her closer and enjoyed the warmth of her sweater against my body. Early the next morning, my parents and younger brother, Lendol, met us in the hotel lobby.

"Hello, big brother!" Lendol exclaimed while striding over to us. I was amazed at how much he had grown since I had last seen him. My fourteen-year-old sibling was now my height.

Soon, I saw the beaming faces of my mother and father. I rushed over to greet them and saw that my mother had tears of joy in her eyes. My folks had aged a bit since my last seeing them, and my father appeared to be moving a bit more slowly than before.

Father Time is undefeated, I thought.

"Warren! I'm so glad you are home!" my mother cried out. I hugged my parents tightly, then reacquainted them to the love of my life.

My mother happily took Ingrid by the hands and asserted, "We had so little time to learn about each other last year! This is going to be a great weekend together!"

"I'd love that," Ingrid replied.

I stood face-to-face with my father while neither of us said a word. There was a deep impression of kindness and pride emanating from my father's gaze. It seemed as if he wanted to tell me something fantastic but couldn't muster the words. I waited patiently for him to speak.

Finally, he said, "I'm so glad you are home, son. Let's have a great time at Glenn and Mary's. Then I'd like you and Ingrid to spend a couple of days at home with us."

I told him we'd love that. Then we loaded ourselves into my parents' car and headed to my aunt and uncle's home.

Two days later, after a great weekend of visiting, Ingrid and I joined my parents at their home in Buffalo, Missouri. Ingrid had begun to build a bond with my parents, and things were going very well. Our visit was topped off with a nice surprise: Granddad Vest arrived and spent time with us at my parents' home. His unexpected presence was an excellent way to accent the entire experience.

After breakfast the following morning, my father was waiting for me in the entryway. He quietly said, "Come on, Warren, let's take a walk around the farm while the ladies do their thing in the kitchen."

Lendol and our granddad followed us outside, and we headed towards the hayfields and barnyard. My father spoke, as Lendol and granddad walked behind us, "Ingrid's a lovely woman, son. She seems to have a really good head on her shoulders to go with her pretty face."

I nodded. "Yes, she's blessed with outstanding common sense and intelligence. She and her family survived some terrible things during World War II. Now that she's working for TWA, Ingrid truly appreciates everything she's accomplished. She's loving life right now, and so am I."

My father nodded appreciatively. Then, with a wry smile, he patted me on the back. "One day you were off to Australia, then you went around the world before joining the Air Force, then came Jordan and Libya, and now Saudi Arabia! Can you believe it, son? You've come such a long way in a relatively short period of time. It's hard to believe."

"I'm excited, Dad. It's a huge opportunity for me professionally. TWA has advised me that the captain of the Royal

DC-6 will become the captain of the Royal Comet, and I will be serving the Saudi royal family as captain of the Royal DC-6."

We stopped walking at the barnyard fence and rested against the wooden planks. Lendol and granddad drifted off together to examine something of interest. My father looked at me with a loving but serious expression. He asked, "Is she the *one*, son?"

I replied, "Yes, Dad. Ingrid is the one. I'm going to ask her to marry me, no doubt about it."

He smiled and shook my hand. "Congratulations, son! I'm so happy for you!"

CHAPTER 63
1962

ON APRIL 4, Ingrid and I announced our engagement to be married. With our wedding plans set for December, we were less than nine months away from transitioning from Ingrid being my fiancé to her becoming my wife.

I had a job with TWA as supervisory pilot and captain of the DC-3 and Convair 340 for Saudi Arabian Airlines. I was also captain of the Saudi royal family's DC-6.

I relocated to the Middle East, living in Saudi Arabia in the seaport city of Jeddah. This was the gateway for millions of Muslims who make their pilgrimage to Mecca. In my work, I trained Saudi pilots and others, along with carrying out piloting duties for the royal family. I also flew out of Riyadh on a variety of domestic and international trips to Egypt, Oman, Ethiopia, Yemen, Iraq, and Iran. And I'll never forget the flights to a multitude of sand-strip villages throughout Saudi Arabia.

Ingrid was living in a house in Cambridge, Massachusetts, with a good friend of hers, Tove, a Norwegian flight attendant also employed by TWA. The letter-writing campaign and postcard exchange between us became more intense and colorful now that our impending nuptials were on the calendar.

The searing heat in Riyadh, Saudi Arabia's capital city, often made me feel as if I were walking through a massive solar oven.

Protective cotton keffiyehs adorned the heads and covered the necks of Saudi men, while women wore the customary hijabs and black abayas, which cloaked their bodies and heads.

In the early morning of July 20, I piloted the royal family's

Saudi Arabian Airlines DC-3

DC-3 down a darkened runway and lifted off from the Riyadh airport. Captain Ralph Robinette managed his co-pilot duties beside me in the snug cockpit.

After turning the airplane due west and ascending to an altitude of ten thousand feet, I confirmed with Ralph that our course toward the Hijaz Mountains was on target. I transferred control of the airplane to Ralph as the sunrise filled the skies with a bright yellow glow. I glanced down and spied nothing but an ocean of sandy terrain. Once again, I was amazed that any type of creature, human or otherwise, could thrive in such an unforgiving habitat.

Ralph asked, "Have you ever been on an ibex hunt, Warren?"

"No, this is my first time," I told him. "But Crown Prince Faisal has mentioned that we'll probably hunt for ibex a few times this season."

I excused myself and left the cockpit, making my way down the aisle of the cabin toward members of the royal family. I approached

King Saud bin Abdulaziz and the crown prince, who greeted me with warm smiles.

"It's a beautiful morning, Captain Vest," said the crown prince. "How can I help you?"

Even though the crown prince had asked the question, when I answered I focused much of my attention on the king. "Well, so far so good," I said. "We should touch down in Al Rathaya, about twenty-five miles east of Medina, at seven-thirty this morning. We'll be right on time."

"Very good," the crown prince replied with a nod of his head. "Our hunting party and our two guides eagerly await us. In fact, they are thrilled that you and Captain Robinette are joining us on this ibex-hunting excursion."

"Me too," I said. "It's an honor." Just then the aircraft passed through a patch of turbulence. Expertly, Ralph steered the DC-3 through the bumpy air. As the aircraft bounced, the king's eyes grew wide with concern. I took his cue and excused myself before hustling back to the cockpit.

Ralph asked me, "How did it go back there?"

I grinned. "Fine, and you did a nice job of getting us through that bumpy air. But for a moment, I thought the king was going to have my head served up on a platter for making too much small talk."

A few hours later, after I landed the DC-3 in Al Rathaya, we joined up with the royal family's hunting party and the two ibex guides. By nightfall, our caravan of jeeps and a supply truck had wound its way into the gorgeous foothills of the arid Hijaz Mountains. The servants and cooks quickly set up our campsite on a bluff overlooking a stunning, watery ravine.

As we sat around one of the campfires, a mindful servant brought Ralph and me an assortment of flatbreads and hummus, barbequed-chicken skewers, a yogurt beverage, and tea. We devoured the delicious meal while the crown prince told engaging stories about his growing-up years in the royal family.

Then without warning, he raised his tea and focused a serious gaze on Ralph and me. The crown prince smiled broadly, and his white teeth shimmered in the flickering light. He said, "To my good friends, Captains Vest and Robinette. I cannot thank you enough for giving me such peace of mind each time you fly the royal airplanes. And Captain Vest, every time you fly my children to and from their schooling in Geneva, Switzerland. When they return home, I say a prayer to Allah in your honor. Thank you!"

Humbled by the unexpected expression of appreciation, I replied, "Your Highness, the pleasure is all mine, and I am grateful for your recognition."

Soon, the veteran members of the hunting party were telling about their best ibex-hunting trips. We would set out on a new hunt at dawn tomorrow.

Much later, even though I tried my best to fall asleep, I tossed and turned in my tent. Quietly, I crawled out through my tent flap and crept toward the lip of the bluff. I peered at the broad, cavernous, canyon below. The blackened sky was alive with a swath of twinkling stars; it was easily one of the most amazing nighttime skies I had ever seen. As I stood there, my thoughts returned to Ingrid. I hoped she was missing me as much as I was longing for her. I finally grew calm and returned to my tent and fell asleep.

At just past six that morning, I was positioned with Ralph and the crown prince behind a small  outcropping of rocks. We were about fifty yards behind the king and his personal hunting guide. A warm breeze washed over me, and nobody dared to speak a word. Slowly and expertly, the king's guide peered through his field glasses. The guide pointed to our left, directing the king to focus his attention about halfway up the mountainside.

The king peered through the scope of his hunting rifle and took aim. I found myself tensing up. I was impressed by the king's silent patience.

Without warning, the deafening blast of the rifle shook the air. A large, male ibex tumbled down the side of the mountain face. The fallen animal settled into a heap less than one hundred yards below us.

Ralph, the crown prince, and I jumped out from behind our rocky hideout and sprinted toward the king and his hunting guide. We climbed down to the felled ram, and I was amazed by the massive set of curled horns sprouting from its head. It wasn't hard to understand how such a creature had become a trophy to hunt and, eventually, to dine on.

We congratulated the king, and after taking pictures and recounting thrills of the hunt, we climbed back into the jeeps for the rough ride back to our campsite. The guides stayed behind to dress and pack the ibex, which they hauled back on a flatbed truck.

From the front passenger seat in our jeep, the crown prince turned toward us and exclaimed, "Tonight, Captains Vest and Robinette, you will truly eat like kings! Grilled ibex is delicious, and my father is going to honor you both by giving you the best part to eat."

I was excited at the thought of tasting my first ibex. And I couldn't help but ask, "Which part is the best?"

The crown prince grinned and shouted, "The penis!"

Stunned, I turned to Ralph in disbelief. Meanwhile, the Jeep veered toward our campsite.

CHAPTER 64
1962

AFTER SEVERAL MONTHS of training pilots in Saudi Arabia, I found myself flying arms to the village of Najran on the Saudi Arabia/Yemen border. War had broken out in Yemen and, in addition to flying arms, I was transporting Egyptian prisoners to camps for internment in Bisha. It was exciting, but after flying from daylight to dark between Riyadh and Najran every day for two weeks, I was exhausted. I asked my buddy Ralph to ensure that my flight schedule was covered for a few days while I took time off from the turmoil in Yemen. I contacted the Sabena airlines crew—which had been flying arms from Brussels to Riyadh—and bummed a ride to Belgium. I made a connection with TWA in Brussels and arrived in Boston in a matter of hours. I wanted to surprise Ingrid.

Even though the Beantown climate was damp and frigid, my spirits were high. I took a taxi to Ingrid's house in Cambridge and bounded up the stairs to knock loudly on the door. I could hear a panicked commotion inside the house. Ingrid's current roommate, Nancy, started grilling me from behind the locked door. "Who is it? What do you want? Go away!"

I replied, "It's me, Warren! I'm here to see Ingrid."

Nancy and Ingrid started talking to each other in hushed tones. Then the door opened slightly. Ingrid's pretty eyes fixed on me, and I thought she was going to faint from surprise. I put my arms around her, and we embraced and kissed to make up for all the months we had been apart.

"Oh my God!" she said. "This is the biggest surprise of my life. Nancy and I thought you might be the Boston Strangler. It's been a spooky time around the city lately."

I smacked my forehead and apologized for failing to send word of my trip. After clearing the air, Ingrid and I talked late into the evening, even though she had a very early flight the next morning. Her flight had a layover in Pittsburgh, so rather than cancel her trip she asked me to join her. While we were in the Steel City, we went out to dinner with a former military buddy, Bob Malone, and his wife, Carole. Bob was now flying as a corporate pilot for U.S. Steel. During dessert, Ingrid and I told Bob and Carole we had decided to tie the knot.

Ingrid and I returned to Boston on Sunday afternoon with an overwhelming desire to get married immediately. On Monday, I tried to obtain a marriage license and the clerk informed me that Massachusetts had a mandatory five-day waiting period. When I explained that I had to leave soon for Saudi Arabia, the clerk scribbled a telephone number for an officer of the court in Exeter, New Hampshire. The Live Free or Die state had no waiting period for people who wanted to get married.

I dialed the phone number to Exeter. The man who answered the phone said, "If you can get here by six o'clock, you can get married. However, given the weather conditions, I recommend that you plan on being married tomorrow."

I rushed back to Ingrid's house and informed her of the news. She immediately called her closest friend, Tove, now based in New York, and asked her to catch an Eastern Air Lines shuttle so she could join us for our wedding the following day.

Ingrid held the phone away from her ear so I could listen. "I would be honored to join you," Tove said, "and I'll let you know which flight I will be arriving on!"

The following afternoon, we picked up Tove at the airport and headed north to Exeter in a nasty mixture of snow and rain. Ingrid looked radiant. I was bolstered by her poise and calm demeanor even though we were about to legally join our lives.

"Even in these awful conditions, we should be in New Hampshire by five o'clock," Ingrid said while fidgeting with her gloves.

Tove's natural charm and her positive comments from the back seat made the drive seem shorter. More than once, she said, "I'm so happy to be sharing this day with the two of you."

Merrily, Ingrid and I responded, "We love you, Tove!"

The drive finally ended with us parked in front of a very old courthouse in Exeter. We scurried into the building to commence our marriage-license appointment.

The older gentleman who processed the paperwork pointed us in the direction of the place where we could be married. "The justice of the peace is right down there a few blocks," he said. "You can't miss it."

We thanked the kind man and headed toward our new destination. By six o'clock, the three of us were standing at the front door of the justice of the peace's dwelling. I rapped on the door, and a pleasant-looking, middle-aged man opened the door and greeted us.

"My wife thought she was done for the day," he said, "but no worries at all. Please come in and have a seat."

Nervous and excited, we entered the quaint living room. After a few minutes of polite talk, the justice of the peace joined us.

"She's *beautiful*," Ingrid whispered in my ear.

The striking-looking woman had exceptionally white hair, but her youthful face belied her age. After greeting us and without waiting to be asked, she began speaking. "You know, Warren and Ingrid, getting married is a very serious matter. It's not something to be taken lightly or to rush into. Patience is justified when it comes to marriage."

My mind flashed back to the day on the beach in Perth, Australia, when I talked with Jake from Boston. I called to mind one of his mantras: "You don't have to marry everyone you date, but you better date the woman you marry for life!"

Overcome with emotion, I was listening to the justice of the peace, but my mind rattled back and forth between her words and a quick review of how I arrived at this point in my life. After Ingrid and I confirmed that we wanted to get married, things kicked into gear.

With Ingrid on my left and Tove as our witness, the justice recited the required verbiage. It seemed to take forever, but in just under five minutes Ingrid and I had become husband and wife!

We kissed, and Tove cheered us on. We thanked the justice and her husband, and after a few minutes the three of us were back in the car and headed to an inn on the Hampton Harbor beachfront.

After settling into our rooms, Ingrid and Tove made themselves up. The inn's bar was alive with partygoers. Droves of people were dancing and living it up. I informed a guy that we had just been married, and our little group within the club exploded in heightened celebration. A table was soon cleared for us.

Everything felt intoxicating to me. Ingrid looked incredible! I was now her husband, and the festive ambiance of the bar was invigorating.

Ingrid and I hustled onto the crowded dance floor and celebrated into the wee hours of the night. It was an awesome feeling to be a newlywed husband to the woman I loved.

Late the next morning, after taking a hot shower and shaving, I felt somewhat rejuvenated. Ingrid was sitting on the bed combing her hair. She flashed me a fantastic smile and I blew her a kiss. Just then, Tove strolled into our room through the adjoining doorway. She winked at me and coyly said, "Good morning, Warren. Did you get some sleep? Oh, by the way, I ordered us some food and coffee."

There was a knock at the hotel room door, and a man's voice stated, "Room service."

I opened the door only to be met with the young man's knowing grin. I stood there unaware of the reason for his devilish manner. Then it hit me. I had a damp towel around my waist, and I was in a room with two beautiful women who were wearing bathrobes.

I stepped to the side so the waiter could bring in his trays loaded with food. On his way out, I tipped the grinning waiter a couple of bucks and whispered, "Hey, this is not what you think it is."

The bemused waiter pocketed the tip before twitching his eyebrows at me. His last words were "Sure, buddy."

CHAPTER 65
1963

AFTER MARRYING INGRID sooner than expected and enjoying our brief few days together as newlyweds, we had to postpone our honeymoon. I returned to Saudi Arabia to arrange housing for us in Jeddah.

I hated being halfway around the world from my new bride. With desirable lodging hard to obtain and the war in Yemen still ongoing along the southern border, I did a lot of soul-searching about bringing Ingrid to this part of the world.

I finally decided to resign my position with TWA/Saudi Arabian Airlines. However, due to my involvement in training Saudi co-pilots, my position was considered critical. As a result, my exit visa was denied. It took U.S. embassy officials six weeks to obtain a visa allowing me to leave Saudi Arabia.

On January 15, 1963, I sent a telegram to Ingrid: "WILL START OUR MARRIAGE NEXT WEEK. ETA SUNDAY 20, ALL MY LOVE, WARREN." Finally, I happily returned to the United States and joined Ingrid in Boston.

I was without a job, but confident that given my unique flying experience and Ingrid's loving support, it would only be a matter of time before I would be employed again. My greater concern was the healthy development of our marriage.

Luckily, I received a timely call from IADCO, the company that had hired me for the Jordanian piloting job in early 1961. As it turned out, the American Airlines DC-6s that Bill Piles and I had commandeered out of Jordan were now operated by International Airlines, Inc., which was moving its base of operations from Rome to Berlin, Germany.

After talking it over with Ingrid, I accepted an offer to become the chief pilot for International Airlines, Inc. My only condition was that they transport our car and personal belongings to Germany ahead of our arrival. IADCO handled the arrangements, and Ingrid took a three-week vacation from TWA to make time for our honeymoon in Miami.

During our fabulous, three-week honeymoon, I took time to conduct test flights in the Miami area. I was testing a third DC-6 that International Airlines had obtained.

In the South Florida tropics, Ingrid's skin took on a light-brown hue, which made her brunette hair and grayish-green eyes even more vivid. We frolicked and swam together in the gentle surf. I was in love, and I wanted nothing else in the world to change from that moment in time.

I could tell that Ingrid wanted to say something. "I'm going to quit my job at TWA so we can move to Berlin without anything holding us back," she said. "I don't want to have an intercontinental marriage. It's better for both of us if we are living our lives together, and I'm tired of being separated from you."

I cupped her face in my hands and said, "That's exactly what I want. Let's go for it!"

Holding hands, we trudged our way out of the water toward the beachfront. Ingrid's two-piece bathing suit made her look even more stunning, and I felt a surge of pride as we walked on the beach. Even though Miami Beach was loaded with beautiful people, Ingrid's natural beauty drew attention. We eased onto our lounge chairs, and I put on my sunglasses. I turned my head to face Ingrid, who was clearly happy.

I said, "West Berlin, here we come!"

"Yes," she said, "but it's concerning that we'll have to enter East Berlin to get our visas just to visit my family in Karlsruhe, even though they are in West Germany. The much scarier part is that we cannot go into East Berlin together. You, as an American, must use the Checkpoint Charlie gate. And for me, as a German, I'll have to enter through the Frederickhof gate. This means we'll be separated while in East Berlin, and that is frightening."

"It will be worth it for us," I said, "even though I've heard terrifying stories about Americans' completing their visas quickly, while their West German spouses often are delayed for several hours."

CHAPTER 66
Present Day

THREE OF MY grandchildren—Garrett, Gentry, and Kinnon—excused themselves and hustled off to use the bathroom and grab some refreshments.

I peered out through the window of the dimly lit room and watched the last few partygoers walk back to their cars. It was way past my normal bedtime hour, and I felt tired but not totally spent. I was ready to enjoy a few more rounds of recounting parts of my life with some of my grandkids. Every time I had asked Garrett or Gentry or Kinnon if they wanted me to continue, they had eagerly replied in the affirmative. I've always believed that every life on earth is worth discussing, whether an individual lived only for a day or for more than one hundred years.

The door of the study was pushed open. A piercing beam of bright light struck me in the eyes.

"Jeez! Who goes there?" I asked. "Close the door, please, and come into the room. That bright light is brutal!"

"Oops, sorry about that, big brother," Lendol said. "I didn't know you had the lights dimmed in here."

"That's all right, Lendol. Where have you been all night?"

He shut the door behind him, and I examined my seventy-one-year-old little brother. He was dressed in a pair of blue jeans and a sweatshirt. His roundish face and wavy, gray hair gave his appealing look a disarming appearance. Without a doubt, he was one of the sincerest individuals I had ever known, sibling or not.

"It's nearly midnight, Warren," my brother said. "Do you think it might be time to wrap things up and go home? Ingrid's asleep on one of the couches and Lord knows you must be incredibly tired as well."

I thought it might help if I explained myself. "I just finished telling them about marrying Ingrid and our honeymoon in Miami before we moved to West Berlin."

"That means you've not yet reached the point in your life when Tim was born in February '65? Am I right about that?" Lendol asked.

"Correct," I said. "In fact, we had moved International Airlines, Inc. from Berlin to Shannon, Ireland, in November of 1964 and Tim was born in Limerick, Ireland, on February 19. I remember double-checking the visa stamps in my passport and discovering that Ingrid became pregnant during one of our getaways to Malaga, Spain. With Ingrid occasionally working back then as a third flight attendant on some of my flights, we had some nice, quick weekends throughout Europe, the Canary Islands, and Egypt. But yes, when we were visiting Gibraltar and staying in a little inn overlooking the Alboran Sea, that's when Tim was conceived."

Lendol grinned and said, "I remember you telling me that."

We shared a chuckle. "It's hard to believe, now that Tim is a pilot and has flown to all seven continents, that his first trip across the Atlantic Ocean was in a Porsche 356B when he was five months old."

I recalled that day when I was flying an empty DC-6 from Ireland to Baltimore. Once I delivered the airplane, another crew would fly it to Leopoldville in the Congo. I had loaded my Porsche onto the main deck of the DC-6 with the idea that I would drive it from Baltimore to Florida. I planned to take Ingrid, her sister Lilo, and baby Tim down to visit my family. With Tim asleep in his bassinette, Ingrid strapped him into the passenger seat of the Porsche, where it was much quieter. He woke up over Gander, Newfoundland, after having completed his first Atlantic crossing.

I had carried on too long, and Lendol's gaze was adrift. I asked him, "What's going on in that head of yours?"

My brother looked at me and leaned against a bookcase. "I'm just remembering the time after I graduated from high school in '65, and you had me flown over to Europe to stay with you for a few weeks. That was unforgettable. So many memories, like our dinner at Five Flies restaurant in Amsterdam and the ascent out of Innsbruck, Austria, with the Alps on both sides of the airplane."

I smiled at the recollection. "When International Airlines, Inc. (IAI) did some contract work for a Dutch airline, I rented that cute little house outside Amsterdam that you liked so much. You and I flew to Spain, Italy, Austria, Denmark, and Norway. That was such a great experience, and I loved it."

"As did I," Lendol agreed. "And don't forget Greenland. Going there was like traveling back to the ice age. Quite remarkable, especially given the fact that I would later end up spending a year in Thule, Greenland, with the Air Force."

International Airlines DC-6 in Sondrestrom, Greenland

Old memories tumbled through my brother's mind. We remained silent for a moment. Then he said, "What a trip that was when I got to pass through Checkpoint Charlie and tour East Berlin on my own. Crazy times back then, and I can't believe I was so bold."

As if on cue, both of us then uttered, "And then Grandfather Vest passed away." We looked at each other, and he said, "Summer of '65 was incredible. Thanks again, Warren, for making it happen for me. It's bizarre, but right now it feels like that was just a couple of months ago instead of fifty-four years ago."

I rubbed my eyes. Even though fatigue was wearing me down, I replied, "You know what, Lendol? When International Airlines began talking about relocating yet again and moving operations to San Antonio, Texas, in the fall of '65, I wasn't sure what was going to happen. It caught me by surprise."

Just then, the trio of young-adult grandchildren reentered the cozy confines of the study. he gave each of them a hug goodbye. Then he winked at me and said, "Love you, big brother. Don't stay up too much longer. Remember, you're no spring chicken."

"Love you, too," I replied. My grandchildren looked at me expectantly, and Garrett asked, "What's next?"

I pondered for a moment. "Let me tell you about my time at World Airways, and how all of that came about."

CHAPTER 67
1965

ON A PLEASANT, Thanksgiving Day afternoon, after a sixteen-hour trip from Shannon, Ireland, to San Francisco via New York, I was almost an hour into an important job interview. I was meeting with two of World Airways Incorporated's most powerful executives, Doug Larsen, vice president of flight operations, and Assistant Vice-President Kenneth Healy, a highly respected pilot of the emerging jet-airplane era.

It was just the three of us in one of the World Airways conference rooms at Oakland Airport. I was beyond excited about the potential opportunity before me, but I forced myself to remain businesslike as our conversation jockeyed back and forth.

Sitting across from me, the salt-and-pepper-haired Doug Larsen said, "Warren, do you really want to move to San Antonio for International Airlines, Inc. and fly DC-7Cs back and forth from Texas to Southeast Asia? We think our offer is much better, and we would really like you to be a captain on our DC-6 operation from here in the Bay area for the Domestic Military Logistics Air Transport."

I paused to calibrate my thoughts. "Jet airplanes," I began. "I'm ready to join World Airways, but only if I can immediately train to fly the B-707. I want to pilot the new Boeings, and jet-powered travel is the future of commercial aviation. I have a young family to support now, and I want to be a part of our industry's future. That's why I'm here with you gentlemen right now. My desire is to fly jets."

Larsen remained silent and shot a glance to Captain Healy. I realized that Kenneth Healy was smirking at my bold statement.

Eventually, Healy said, "As we touched on earlier, the three of us know many of the same people. We have found that their recommendations of you are top-notch. Captain Ralph Robinette, and of course our senior VP of marketing and sales, Bill Hardenstine, your former director of operations at Overseas National Airways in New York, both said they would trust you with their lives."

Healy continued, "After being your chief pilot with ONA here in Oakland during the winter of 1960-61, I concur with their opinions of you."

"Thank you," I responded. "The same goes for me about them. They're good men."

Doug Larsen rejoined the discussion. "Warren, you have a lot of the same traits as one of our DC-6 captains, James Reese. A sharp man."

"I don't know him," I said. "But I look forward to meeting him—very soon."

"You've certainly got the brass to fly jets," Healy said. "Even though I was your boss for a short time, I never had the opportunity to fly with you at ONA. But everyone I have talked to about your flying in the Middle East has told me that you've got nerves of steel. Now I'd have to agree with their assessment."

"Thanks," I replied. My guts were churning. I desperately wanted to become a jet airline pilot.

Larsen and Healy looked at each other across the table from me and exchanged a quick nod. They stood up, and I rose quickly on my side of the table.

Larsen extended his right hand and bellowed, "Warren, the final decision must be approved by the owner, Ed Daly. If Mr. Daly, who is presently in Europe, gives it the green light, then we would love to have you join World Airways as our newest first officer of the Boeing 707!"

I was covered with goosebumps. My mouth had gone dry, but I managed to reply, "Yes! Thank you!"

I shook each man's hand. "Warren," Larsen said, "you've had a very long stretch during the past twenty-four hours. Go back to your hotel, grab an early dinner, and then get some rest. We'll call you tomorrow morning with Mr. Daly's answer."

I ate a good meal and then took a short walk around the hotel grounds. Back in my room, I lay on my back and stared at the popcorn ceiling. I couldn't help but dream about flying B-707s all over the world. This would be an excellent start to building the next phase of my life with Ingrid and our nine-month-old son, Timothy.

CHAPTER 68
1966

I HAD JUST completed a flight assignment into Seattle and positioned to Oakland via United Airlines for my scheduled days off. Prior to departure from Seattle, I received a message from World Airways dispatch. Captain Healy was going to conduct a training flight to administer a captain proficiency check for Captain George Merrill. Healy indicated he would like me to join them. I confirmed my acceptance and said I would report to dispatch at 8 p.m.

During my flight from Seattle to Oakland, I wondered why I'd been asked to participate in the training flight. Five months earlier, I had graduated from B-707 training and was not due for another proficiency check until March the following year.

Arriving in Oakland at 6:15 p.m., I went to the terminal's restaurant for dinner still wearing my airline uniform. Afterward, I would report for the training flight. I had just ordered my meal when a young man approached me. He had long hair and an unkempt goatee. He was dressed in a tie-dyed shirt, bell-bottom jeans, and platform shoes.

The hippie stopped a few feet from my table. He smiled at me and asked, "Do you mind if we visit for a while? I'd like to ask you about becoming a pilot. I promise not to ask you about the Vietnam War."

Surprised by his disarming tactic, I replied, "Sure. I have a few minutes before I've got to be at my flight dispatch center. Take a seat."

The hippie dropped his backpack and shook my hand before taking a seat. He was cleaner-smelling than most of the hippies I had encountered across the country. I surmised he had regular access to a decent home with a place to shower and sleep.

"So, what would you like to know about becoming a pilot?"

He grinned. "I'd like to hear about your journey. I've thought a lot about flying, and I think I'd like to be a pilot after the war. In fact, everywhere my friends and I go to protest the war, they're always getting down on me for talking to pilots when we're hanging out at airports. My friends tend to think all pilots are just another extension of The Man."

I nodded, and the hippie continued. "How long have you been flying those big turbo-jet airplanes?"

His innate charm and inoffensive demeanor intrigued me. "Just six months," I said. "In fact, I have a check ride tonight." I found myself enjoying our unexpected conversation, and it seemed the hippie did as well.

"When did you become a pilot?" he asked.

"Well, I joined the Air Force in November 1954 and began my primary flight training in April of '56."

The airport's public-address system boomed from the speakers and momentarily halted our discussion. After a series of announcements ended, the hippie said, "That last call was about my flight to Chicago. I've got about ten minutes before I've got to split. But keep going."

"Sure thing," I said. "In the Air Force, I worked my way up to flying C-118s. Then, after leaving the military and returning to civilian life, I flew DC-6s out of New York and in Middle Eastern countries. After that, I attained the rank of chief pilot for International Airlines before finally joining World Airways here in Oakland."

In the distance, one of my companion's hippie friends shouted his name and waved his arms. But the hippie kept up our conversation. "How did you end up in Oakland?" he asked.

"Back in December," I said, "I got a call from Ed Heering, the DC-6 chief pilot of World Airways. He wanted me to begin my flight training for what I thought was going to be the 707. At the time, I was training crews in San Antonio, so I hit the road and drove up here in two days. But when I got to Oakland, there had been a mix-up. The training was for DC-6s, not 707s. I was already fully qualified to fly a DC-6."

The hippie reached for his backpack but remained seated. "That must have been a real drag," he said. "What did you do?"

I shrugged my shoulders. "The company sorted out the error, and I filled in as an instructor for the DC-6 ground school. But I made sure that I got fitted for the brown 707 uniform and not the charcoal DC-6 outfit. After the New Year, I began training on the 707."

Politely, the hippie reached across the table and shook my hand. Then he donned his backpack and said, "Thanks for sharing part of your story with me. I think it will take me one step closer to becoming a pilot. You're probably the twentieth pilot that I've talked to in the past year. Thanks, man."

I nodded. "You're welcome. And do you mind if I ask you a question?"

He said, "Anything you want."

"What's waiting for you in Chicago?"

"My family," he said. "That's where I'm from. I've been accepted into Northwestern University for the fall semester."

"Good for you, and best of luck," I said. "But don't wait forever if you want to be a pilot. I suggest you enroll in the ROTC program at Northwestern, then be as persistent as I have been if you really want to be a pilot. You'll need to dedicate yourself to it as a profession."

The hippie held up his right hand and flashed me the peace sign. Then he hustled away to board his flight.

I paid the check for my dinner and walked to the shuttle pick-up area for transport to the World Airways dispatch center. I checked in at 8 p.m. to join Captain Healy, Captain Merrill, and Chief Flight Engineer Hanson for Captain Merrill's captain's proficiency check ride.

CHAPTER 69
1966

NEARING 10 O'CLOCK at night, at an altitude of twelve thousand feet, we were maneuvering above the Farallon Islands thirty miles west of the Golden Gate Bridge. I sat in the cockpit jump seat behind Captain Merrill, while Captain Healy administered a captain's six-month proficiency check for Captain Merrill. We were flying a four-engine, B-707 jet airliner.

I still had no idea why I had been asked to participate in this check flight. We flew through dark skies at various speeds and performed a variety of flight-test maneuvers. I observed Captain Merrill closely, with a keen desire to learn from his performance. I scanned the bank of gauges, levers, and buttons on the instrument panels, and all systems were functioning properly.

While Captain Merrill prepared for his next maneuver, Captain Healy said, "Warren, I've heard that you and your wife bought a nice home in Dublin. That's a good location and not far from the Oakland Airport. A smart move, if you don't mind me saying so."

I nodded and said, "We love it. We moved into our new home on July fourth. It was a very special day for us."

Captain Healy shifted his attention to the check flight. "George," he said, "your proficiency check is complete, so please let Warren take your place in the left seat."

I moved into the left seat and assumed primary control of the aircraft. I looked at Captain Healy, awaiting instructions. "Please perform a captain proficiency as you just observed," he said. I complied with his command, then asked if he had any further request. "Please just remain on course," he said.

"Affirmative," I replied. I guided the B-707 through the sky while double-checking my instrument-panel readings. I flew the jet due south, feeling as if I could perform any maneuver I needed to do.

"She's amazing, isn't she?" Captain Healy asked, sensing my total immersion in handling the jet. "When Doug Larsen and I interviewed you on Thanksgiving Day, it was obvious that you were hungry to begin flying jets. We had other highly qualified candidates who wanted the position, and now it's clear that we made the perfect hire in bringing you onboard."

I allowed Captain Healy's kind remarks to sink into my soul. I expressed my gratitude for his welcoming statement. During the next ninety minutes, he put me through a demanding check ride.

I banked the B-707 through a series of steep turns and maneuvers as if it were second nature to me. As my hands worked the yoke and my feet pressed down on the hydraulic rudders, I felt as if I were somehow part of the aircraft. After executing more than a dozen maneuvers, Healy had me perform a few stalls of the aircraft. To my surprise, I was calm, even though my level of concern through each delayed recovery of the heavy jet was high.

Just before one-thirty in the morning, I landed the B-707 on Runway 27 at Oakland Airport. I taxied to the World Airways maintenance facility and powered down the B-707. Captain Healy and I conducted our post-flight checklist, and by two-thirty in the morning we headed to the dispatch center.

Healy looked at me. "You're probably wondering what is going on with your having to do a check ride after having only six months serving as a first officer."

I replied, "Sort of. I didn't realize first officers were getting check rides every six months."

"You're right about that," Healy replied. "But you got a *captain's* check ride. You'll be completing formal training to become a captain in a few weeks. Congratulations, Warren!"

CHAPTER 70
1966

SINCE PASSING MY surprise captain-proficiency check ride two months earlier, I had flown the maximum allowable hours in September and October. I was eager to begin the formal captain upgrade process.

Having already finished an initial training program, I was allowed to complete an abbreviated ground school and another captain proficiency check with an FAA examiner. That enabled me to earn a B-707 type rating, which authorized me to operate as a captain.

I was scheduled for my first route-qualification line check with Captain Bill Keating, who was the chief pilot. My ten crewmembers and Captain Keating reported to World Airways dispatch at Oakland Airport on November 1. We were transported by van to Travis Air Force Base, a one-hour drive north of Oakland Airport.

My crew and I completed the necessary preflight paperwork, weather briefing, fueling, and aircraft preflight inspection for a scheduled 6 p.m. departure. We boarded one hundred sixty-five military passengers who ultimately were destined for Tan Son Nhut Air Base in Saigon, Vietnam. The trip would have an intermediate stop at Yokota Air Base, Japan, for a change of flight crew and refueling.

Our routing would take us over the northern Pacific Ocean, eventually tracking about sixty miles off the Russian Kuril Islands. It was not uncommon to encounter headwinds approaching two-hundred miles per hour in this region.

The navigator became the center of attention as he computed our ground speed and kept us clear of hostile, Russian airspace. We arrived in Japan radar coverage exactly on course, and I could feel the tension dissipate because we had confirmed that our remaining fuel was right on plan and we had safely skirted the Russian Kuril Islands. We began our descent for landing at Yokota Air Base as the sun rose behind us. My crew and I were looking forward to a good rest at the hotel before our flight to Da Nang, Vietnam, early the next day.

The following morning, our departure was on time for a five-and-one-half-hour flight to Da Nang, replete with one hundred sixty-five military passengers.

During our climb to cruising altitude, the majestic, snowcapped Mount Fuji, twelve thousand three hundred eighty-nine feet high, was just off our right wing. We continued along the southern coast of Honshu, over Okinawa, just east of Taiwan, across the South China Sea and south of Hainan Island into Da Nang.

Da Nang Air Base had been transformed into a bustling United States military compound. Bombers, transport planes, and helicopters created relentless air traffic around the airport. Since Da Nang was centrally located on the coast of Vietnam, this had become one of the busiest and most dangerous airports in the world. Upon landing, we were directed to a spot close to the base operations office. A bomb shelter was located nearby.

After shutting down the engines, I noticed a group of GIs playing basketball with a makeshift hoop. A sudden memory made me laugh out loud. My mind had darted back to my teenage days in Buffalo, Missouri, when my friends and I would shoot baskets at the old rim nailed to the side of my dad's barn. Watching soldiers play a game of hoops near a bomb shelter reminded me that, as kids playing in Daddy's barnyard, the biggest danger we faced was slipping on a pile of cow manure.

We offloaded our passengers and prepared for our return flight to Yokota. While boarding new passengers, three young Air Force officers asked if they could look at the spacious cockpit. They were F-4 pilots.

I answered a few questions about the B-707. I then said, "Since you gentlemen are F-4 pilots, tell me if you might know of a good buddy of mine. His name is Douglas Peterson—Doug to his buddies." I knew Doug from our pre-cadet days back in 1955.

After a long pause, one of the officers said, "I'm so sorry to be the one telling you this, captain, but I was one of Pete Peterson's wingmen during a night mission out of Ubon Air Base, Thailand, in September. We were flying "radar in-trail" and had just completed our mission and were climbing to altitude on our way back to Ubon. During the ascent, we entered a heavy layer of clouds that prevented everyone in the formation from seeing a surface-to-air missile until it was too late to out-maneuver it. Pete's aircraft was hit by the missile explosion."

"But are you sure Pete Peterson is *Douglas* Peterson?" I asked. I couldn't accept that my friend was MIA.

The lieutenant replied, "Yes, Pete is Douglas Peterson. Our squadron and the command are concerned that he and his co-pilot did not survive."

I got up from my seat, shook hands with the young pilots, and wished them all the best in their future service. The passengers were still boarding, so I took a slow walk around the aircraft to compose myself.

A fighter formation passed overhead, which caused me to glance up. There at the top of our B-707's vertical tail fin was the American flag. I saluted the flag and silently praised Doug for what he had sacrificed for our country. I also prayed that somehow, he had survived.

I returned to the cockpit to do my part in flying troops to their next destination. It was my opportunity to demonstrate appreciation for soldiers who had been standing in harm's way for our country.

I spoke to my crew. "Let's start engines and get these heroes on their way home to their loved ones."

CHAPTER 71
1970

IN THE NEARLY four years since I was promoted to captain for World Airways, my piloting life had been pleasantly routine. The charter flights to Europe, South America, Hawaii, and other domestic destinations were a rewarding experience. And the flights to support the Vietnam effort kept my flying schedule busy.

Ingrid and I had settled into our new home in Dublin with our young son Tim. Timmy had attended pre-school and kindergarten, and Ingrid was a stay-at-home mom.

The World Airways transport contract with the United States military had ensured the growing company and its employees an uncommon level of stability in our industry. But even in the best of times, it seems that all good things change eventually.

Since the pilots, flight engineers, flight attendants, and aircraft mechanics had unionized four years earlier, tensions had escalated between World Airways senior management and the Teamsters Union. Negotiations to renew the union agreement bogged down, leading to a strike in September 1970.

I was concerned about the lengthy impasse between the company and the union. With that in view, I had accepted an offer to fly to Tokyo to interview for the position of captain on the DC-8 for Japan Airlines. My interview and check ride in the DC-8 simulator went well, and I returned home with a job offer in hand.

However, when I told Ingrid about a job in Tokyo, she said, "Not going to happen." We had a son and a home in a community that we liked, and we'd been putting down roots. So, I turned down the Japan Airlines offer and focused my energies on trying to help end the strike. I got involved in the stalled negotiations.

During pre-strike negotiations, I had served as a backup alternate to the captain representative on the committee. My input had been limited out of respect for the ranking captain. However, the situation had reached a point of being a financial burden on the company and was jeopardizing the well-being of the employees. I made my case to the union and was assigned to be the captain representative at the negotiating table in future meetings with management.

Talks had been at a standstill for two weeks when we resumed negotiations in October. The sessions normally started late in the morning and continued well past midnight. The usual team of negotiators for the company were Jerome Byrne, from the law firm of Gibson, Dunn and Crutcher, LLP, plus various members of management. The union team consisted of Flight Engineer Glenn Iverson, an experienced negotiator who previously had served with a flight engineer union; First Officer Donald Treichler, who had been involved since the beginning of negotiations; Dan Porter, our Teamsters agent and an experienced negotiator; and me, the newcomer at the table.

We got underway and were making minimal progress when, shortly before midnight, Mr. Ed Daly, the owner of World Airways, entered the conference room. Even though he was only forty-eight years old, Daly showed the signs of a stressful life. He seemed disgusted with the lack of progress in negotiations. He puffed on a cigarette, nodded at us, and muttered, "Good evening, gentlemen. Now we can finally cut out the small talk and get down to serious business."

He pushed aside a stack of folders and set his drink on the table. After he rearranged some documents, he removed a .38 caliber revolver from his coat pocket and placed it on the table with a thud.

My eyes darted around at each person sitting at the table. The gun was pointed directly at Donald Treichler, who calmly reached over and turned the firearm to point toward an empty wall.

A moment later, Mr. Daly, while shuffling papers, caused the handgun to return to its original position, pointing at Mr. Treichler.

Again, Don turned the gun away and said to Mr. Daly, "Ed, I'm a former Marine, and when a gun is pointed at me it better be used. Otherwise, I will put it where the sun doesn't shine."

Finally, I offered my best shot at breaking the tension. "When I came by the airport this morning, I spoke with Captain Jim Reese, and he asked that I pass along his feelings. Gentlemen, it's time for us to get a deal done, period. This ugly strike has dragged on long enough."

The attorney, Jerome Byrne, curtly responded, "Mr. Daly is not made out of money, Warren."

I shot Byrne a stern glance, but before I could respond, Daly held up his hand and cut me off. "Relax, Warren. Jerry is just doing his job of trying to protect me and the airline. Tell me, what do you have in mind?"

I took advantage of his invitation, rattling off a list of reasonable demands and highlighting other issues essential to ending the strike. The union's demands included outlining exact pay scale and guaranteeing penalty pay for being scheduled for excessive duty time periods.

He interrupted me. "Aren't you just nickel and diming us with this penalty pay for over duty time?"

I responded that it was our desire to never collect a penny of such pay. I added that the provision was being proposed to influence the crew-scheduling department to *not* schedule flight crews for more than sixteen hours of duty—for safety reasons. After I concluded my presentation, He leaned back in his chair. Finally, he took a sip of his drink while extinguishing his cigarette. Nobody else dared to speak until Mr. Daly was ready to talk.

After the lengthening pause became too much to bear, Glenn Iverson cracked an innocent joke to bring some levity into the room. "If we don't get this deal hammered out soon," he said, "my wife is going to throw me out of the house. I'll be sleeping on your couch, Ed."

Don Treichler and I stifled our laughter, and then Ed began to chuckle. "No thanks, Glenn. My couch is doing just fine without you on it. But I tell you what, a lot of Warren's ideas make sense. Combined with the issues already raised by Don and you, this deserves further discussion. It seems to me we're on the right path. Notwithstanding the stares of your union rep, who has been glaring at me all night."

Luckily, our union agent kept his mouth shut, and Ed went on. "Tell you what, boys. Let's take a quick break, and I'll have some dinner brought in for us. We can burn the midnight oil and work out the nuances of each detail."

I exhaled with satisfaction at the thought of finally ending the strike.

Ed Daly - Founder and CEO of World Airways

CHAPTER 72
1971

SIX MONTHS AFTER the World Airways strike ended, my peers elected me to the position of Union council chairman. That was an honor, but after the grueling, tug-of-war negotiations to end our strike, it wasn't the way I wanted to spend hours of my time.

On a Thursday, I arrived at World Airways headquarters for a meeting in Ed Daly's office. He stood to greet me before walking around his desk to shake hands. I glanced to my right and saw the World Airways president, Retired Air Force Four Star General Howell Estes.

"I've asked Howell to join us," Daly said. "I know the two of you have worked closely together since you became chairman of the union council, so I figured you wouldn't mind."

I told him, "I don't mind at all."

Howell Estes said, "Hello, Warren. It's good seeing you again."

We moved to some chairs positioned around a coffee table. Mr. Daly stared out through an office window, then said, "Warren, how would you feel about becoming vice president of the Far East for World Airways and moving to Japan?"

I had just turned down a job offer from Japan Airlines. I collected my thoughts. "First of all, sir, let me tell you how honored I am by your offer. It's truly humbling and very exciting."

Ed remained silent, but Howell said, "It's really an amazing opportunity, Warren."

I told them, "During the strike, I was offered a captain's job by Japan Airlines. Truth be told, when I talked to Ingrid about it, she was not happy with the idea of living in Japan."

Ed leaned forward and slapped his right hand on my left knee. "I understand, and it makes sense. Even though Ingrid is very well-traveled, not everybody wants to relocate overseas, especially with a young child about to start first grade."

He continued, "When I bought World Airways in 1950, it cost me fifty thousand bucks, and plenty of folks thought I was crazy. But look at us now; we're planning to build our own maintenance center here in Oakland. When it's completed in a couple of years, the facility will house four 747s at one time. We're growing, boys, and we've got planes in the air crisscrossing the globe at any given time, seven days per week."

He was putting on the full-court press, giving me his best sales pitch. Howell stepped in and remarked, "Warren, both Ed and I agree that you are the best choice for this assignment. Even though it would require you to move overseas for a while, I firmly believe you and Ingrid, and even little Tim will find it to be a very rewarding experience."

Ed had more to say. "You will be responsible for a huge area west of Hawaii all the way to Bangkok, Thailand, and from Korea south to Australia."

I replied, "I'm quite familiar with the Far East routes and, from what I've seen, our 727 flights would serve Japan, Taiwan, Korea, the Philippines, Vietnam, and Thailand."

"Correct," Ed said. "And the hub of our operation is located at Yokota Air Base, as you know. So, given the fact that you'll be located just west of Tokyo and overseeing our large group of B-727 cockpit and cabin personnel, it will be a tremendous career opportunity for you."

Howell jumped back in. "Even as compared to my time in the Air Force, I've got to say that our Japanese maintenance supervisors and their teams are the best I've ever seen."

Ed said, "Plus, while the war's going on, you and your pilots will be responsible for delivering the *Stars and Stripes* for the military each day on the B-727s. The troops absolutely love it."

I knew already that we also had a 727 operating Air Vietnam's flights out of Saigon. So far, it seemed to be going fairly well.

Ed leaned forward and pushed a piece of folded paper across the table in my direction. He sat back, then both men waited for me to open it.

I unfolded the note and looked at the salary figure written there. Then I let out a deep breath.

Ed and Howell grinned at my non-verbal response. "Warren, I understand that Ingrid might not be eager to move to Japan," Ed said.

"But talk this over with her. Let her know that I will guarantee all the perks of a nicely furnished home with maid service, a personal car, and a private driver to make your relocation as smooth and enjoyable as possible."

"I will, sir," I told him. "This is a very generous offer indeed."

Howell rejoined the discussion. "Warren, a few months ago you mentioned that you and Captains Holt, Villano, and Wilson had put down some money on a big ranch in Idaho, with an option to buy it in two years. Seems to me this promotion might help you to exercise that option."

"Yes, it could," I agreed.

Howell Estes and Ed Daly stood up. Ed extended his hand to shake on the deal. He said, "Warren, your new assignment begins in September, which will allow time for you to be qualified as a B-727 captain and FAA-designated check captain."

I shook both men's hands and replied, "I hope Ingrid will appreciate your generous offer as much as I do. If all goes well, you will have a definite acceptance within a few hours."

CHAPTER 73
1973

NEARLY TWO YEARS had passed since the negotiation with Ed Daly and General Estes. Fortunately, when I had approached Ingrid about the possibility of our moving to Japan, we decided to take advantage of this new opportunity and relocate our little family. However, we would keep our house in Dublin, California, to ensure that we always had a home in America.

The additional compensation that came as a result of my promotion enabled us to cover all our financial obligations in

Lolo Creek Ranch partners (L-R)
Uncle Kelly, Pete Villano, Russ Wilson,
Warren, Hank Holt and Tim (front)

addition to moving forward on our commitment to purchase the Lolo Creek Ranch, along with my Uncle Kelly and three World Airways pilot friends. In July 1971, Ingrid, Tim, and I took a quick trip to the Idaho ranch so they could experience it before we moved to Japan. The joy radiating from six-year-old Tim was heartwarming. He loved exploring the mountainous ranchland, which drove home the fact that we had made a good financial decision. Beyond the wise investment, there was the future enjoyment that would be coming our way for years to come.

The Lewis and Clark expedition had spent the winter of 1806 in Kamiah, Idaho, waiting for the snowmelt in the mountains. They resumed their eastward trek the following May and passed through the area of Lolo Creek Ranch to meet up with their Nez Perce Indian guides. The group had survived the brutal Kamiah winter by hunting elk and catching steelhead trout from the Clearwater River. The Lolo Creek Ranch was named after Lolo Creek, which borders two miles of the ranch's north boundary line.

Ironically, after acquiring the ranch, I learned that William Clark is a distant cousin of mine through my mother's side of the family. This made it extra special for me, knowing that I own land that Clark traversed two centuries ago.

We returned to California from Idaho, and I completed my qualification as captain and check pilot on the B-727. Then we made our move to the Far East. The furnished home provided by World Airways was located near Tachikawa Air Base and only a ten-minute commute to my office at Yokota Air Base. The timing for the school year allowed us to enroll Tim in the Christian Academy of Japan for first grade.

As I settled into my new job, I also was traveling all over the Far East. In addition to the daily duties of being a vice-president for

World Airways, I was flying regularly and served as the company's representative to the American Chamber of Commerce in Japan. In that role, Ingrid and I attended formal functions in Tokyo. We honored the Joint Armed Forces of Japan and the USA at the USO Gold Star banquet, attended a Chamber of Commerce dinner with then-California Governor Ronald Reagan and wife, Nancy, and attended the grand opening of Wells Fargo Bank in Tokyo.

Amid our overbooked schedules and the adjustments to a new culture, in early 1972 Ingrid learned she was pregnant with our second child. Our first son, Tim, had been born in Limerick, Ireland, and Ingrid decided she did not want to give birth overseas a second time. She and Tim returned home to Dublin, California, in August.

A couple of months passed, and I couldn't escape the fact that I was lonely and emotionally adrift. With Ingrid at my side, I had immersed myself in our new lives in Japan. But now I was alone in Japan and missing Ingrid and Tim, so I threw myself into my work. I planned to fly home for Ingrid's delivery, but the baby beat his estimated time of arrival and was born on October 4, 1972. I made it to the hospital a day later. I remained home in California with Ingrid until she was comfortable, then I returned to Japan.

Two months later, in early December, Ingrid packed Tim and newborn Brian and returned to Japan. With all of us back together as a family, she organized and hosted a fabulous Christmas party for more than one hundred twenty children of our Japanese and American employees. It was a tremendous Christmas, especially for me because I had my family back.

Now, on the sunny, humid afternoon of February 12, 1973, at Clark Air Force Base in the Philippines, I was the captain of a World Airways B-727. The crew and I were preparing to depart with a load of passengers headed to Japan.

But the tower called, "World 361, please be advised we have an inbound C-141 from Hanoi carrying American POWs scheduled to arrive in five minutes. Therefore, all departures have been delayed until the POWs have been deplaned. Please stand by for further instructions."

Surprised and delighted by the news, I glanced at my co-pilot, Al Brandon. "That's the best reason I've ever heard for causing a flight delay, Al."

"Agreed, Captain Vest," he said. "Good news for sure."

We watched the skies until a long, grayish MATS C-141 Starlifter transport plane approached the landing strip. After it landed and taxied to its parking spot, about two hundred yards away, Al and I watched a stream of American POWs filter out of the aircraft and stride toward waiting officials and medical staff. I had to look down at my hands, momentarily averting my eyes from this overwhelming scene. My thoughts returned to memories of my long-lost Air Force buddy, Doug Peterson, whose fighter jet had been shot down over North Vietnam several years earlier.

"Warren, is something the matter?" Al asked me

I replied, "I was just thinking about an old friend from back in the day. Let's get ready to start engines when the tower gives us the green light." I spotted the last few POWs ambling toward the terminal area as the tower cleared us to start engines.

The following morning after our return flight to Japan, I was puttering around the house. I sat down at the breakfast table and sipped a cup of coffee. I picked up a copy of the *Stars and Stripes* and found a list of names for the POWs who had been safely delivered to Clark AFB the day before. I read the list twice and found no mention of Doug Peterson.

But my hopes were rewarded a few weeks later when I learned of Doug's release. The POWs had initially been liberated on a first-in-first-out schedule. After the first group departed Hanoi on February 12, the Vietnamese prepared a group of twenty prisoners for discharge. But because the North Vietnamese had abandoned the first-in-first-out policy, this second group of POWs had refused to comply. Their boycott of the rigged process caused a huge uproar and paralyzed the process for a couple of weeks.

Finally, Doug Peterson and others were brought home. After so many years, my short prayer on the ramp at Da Nang airport in 1966 had been answered.

CHAPTER 74
1974

THINGS DON'T STAY the same. After more than two years as vice-president of the Far East for World Airways, I was approaching my thirty-ninth birthday in April. While the work kept me hopping, Ed Daly had been right in saying that the experience of living in Japan would be a fulfilling adventure.

But not everything had gone smoothly. In the summer of 1973, while I was administering a line check on a B-727 evening flight, a wicked bolt of lightning struck our jet, and the reactive plasma of St. Elmo's Fire covered our cockpit's windshield. The wash of bluish flames finally extinguished itself, and we found that the nasty electrical hit had short-circuited two of the three generators that powered our aircraft's electrical systems. It goes without saying that such a circumstance could jeopardize the lives of passengers and crew. Captain Sims, his crew, and I called on our combined years of emergency flight training to minimize every nonessential aircraft function to hopefully reserve enough electrical power to fly the B-727 without alarming the people onboard. Fortunately, we made a successful landing at Kadena Air Base in Okinawa.

That fall, while U.S. President Richard Nixon was under investigation for the Watergate scandal and Henry Kissinger had signed accords to end combat operations, senior management and I agreed that my director of operations, Chet Miller, could manage the reduced operation in Japan. Ingrid and I moved our small family back to Dublin, California. I accepted a position in flight-operations management at the World Airways headquarters at the Oakland Airport.

Rebooting our lives in the United States took place against a backdrop of fluidity in my career at World Airways. With U.S. military involvement officially curtailed in Vietnam, the World Airways contract with the U.S. military would be greatly reduced. The World Airways pilots needed to stay busy flying to keep the company financially healthy.

Ed Daly's background as a successful entrepreneur served us well, and our airline prospered even after the plentiful flights of the Vietnam War era were scaling back. World Airways negotiated a contract with Indonesian Airlines and became a leading airline company for thousands of Indonesian Muslims making pilgrimages to Mecca, a religious obligation known as the Hajj. The long air route from Indonesia to Saudi Arabia matched up with our long-range B-707s' capability. Any number of airlines were providing flights for pilgrims to Mecca, but such flights out of Indonesia were the province of World Airways.

I enjoyed keeping busy. I had flown Hajj routes before from Kuwait to Jeddah, Saudi Arabia, during my assignment as chief pilot for Air Jordan of the Holy Land, and while living in Saudi Arabia in 1962.

It is critically important for Indonesian Muslims to make a pilgrimage to Mecca at least once during their lifetime. I was familiar with Islamic customs, values, and practices from my time living in Jordan and Saudi Arabia in the early 1960s. So, for me, it was humorous to observe the reactions of crew members during discussions about the nuances of proper discourse during Hajj operations.

At our hotel in Jakarta, Indonesia, I was relaxing at a poolside table with two coworkers. Other members of the World Airways flight crew were enjoying themselves in the pool.

Flight Engineer Harry Smock was thumbing through the World Airways Hajj Program Manual. Taking a drink of beer, Harry asked me and Flight Attendant Pat George a question. "Are you two up for a game of Hajj trivia? I'll buy the next round of drinks for today's lucky winner."

We agreed to join in, and Harry held his Hajj manual close to his chest. "Ladies first, Pat," he said. "Please name the Five Pillars of Islam."

"That's easy," she said. "It's faith, prayer, charity, fasting, and...pilgrimage."

"Bingo!" Harry said. "Warren, or should I say Captain Vest? Can you recite all the rules covering Do's and Don'ts when working the Hajj in the Kingdom of Saudi Arabia?"

"C'mon, Harry," I replied. "You only made Pat answer five!"

Pat laughed, and I pondered my answer. "I'll start with the 'Don'ts.' Don't discuss religion; don't stare at someone when they are praying; don't step on a prayer rug; don't cross your legs or rest your feet to show the bottoms of your shoes, and don't take photographs."

"Impressive," Harry said.

"The four 'Do's are: 'Do know how to refuse a refill of Arabian tea or coffee by placing your hand over the cup or shaking the cup from side-to-side while handing it to the waiter. Do remember that Saudi Arabians have no official celebration for anniversaries or birthdays. Do understand that during Ramadan, most Muslims are fasting, so try to avoid eating, drinking, or smoking in public or when in the company of Muslims."

I paused after giving three of the four rules governing what to do. My memory returned to an unpleasant time several years earlier in Saudi Arabia. Harry pointed out my delay in giving the final "Do."

"Unfortunately," I told him, "I know the last part of the answer all too well, and that is: 'Do fully understand that once you surrender your passport to Jeddah Immigration, as a crewmember entering Saudi Arabia without a visa, you are allowed only to travel between your hotel and the airport."

Pat and Harry left to join up with colleagues. Now seated alone at the table, I ordered a large glass of iced tea. Left to myself, I entertained pleasant mental images of Ingrid and our two boys, who were more than 8,600 miles away. Deep in my heart, I prayed that my family was safe, and I dearly hoped they were missing me just as much as I was longing to be with them.

I had so much to be thankful for, and I avoided trying to guess what might come next. I concentrated on enjoying the day.

Picture from the World Airways Hajj Program Manual. World Airways served the Muslim community for nearly three decades. Service ended in 2000/2001.

CHAPTER 75
1975

I WAS COMPLETING the DC-8 pre-flight checklist with Co-Pilot Larry Dulich and Flight Engineer Bill Badders. We awaited clearance from the tower to taxi for takeoff from the Minneapolis airport. The destination of our two-hundred-nineteen-seat jet that day was Acapulco, Mexico. On the trip south we were flying with a full crew but no passengers.

"Since we've got a few minutes to fill before the tower clears us," Larry said, "can you tell me about the rest of the things that happened during that crazy time in Saigon a few months ago?"

I took a deep breath and began telling what had occurred weeks earlier when an onslaught of bloody chaos overtook Vietnam. On March 28, while I vacationed with my family in Maui, I received a phone call from the World Airways corporate headquarters. Ed Daly needed me to get to Saigon, pronto.

But in a second phone call, I was told that the situation in Saigon had turned dire, and I should finish my vacation and prepare for a busy schedule upon returning home.

The U.S. government grew nervous and shut down all flight operations in Saigon. However, Daly would not give up on a vital cause all that easily. He ordered three B-727 jets from Saigon to Da Nang in a courageous attempt to save as many women and children as possible. North Vietnamese soldiers and Viet Cong irregulars were closing in on the former capital of South Vietnam and threatening to overrun Da Nang airport. Under the circumstances, only one of the B-727s was able to land. Nearly three hundred people rushed onboard the one-hundred-five-passenger aircraft. They filled the seats and the lower baggage compartments. Ed Daly, with a pistol in his hand, warded off several desperate South Vietnamese soldiers who tried to enter the aircraft on the aft stairway. This was taking place as the passenger jet sped down the taxiway under machine-gun fire before finally taking off. A few days later, on April 2, Daly had Captains Ken Healy and Bill Keating and crew fly a cargo-configured DC-8 out of Saigon carrying fifty-seven Vietnamese orphans. He ordered the aircraft's cabin to be remade so that it more closely resembled a nursery playpen. The secretive flight took off under the cover of darkness and eventually arrived at the Oakland Airport.

Moments after I finished my recollections, the tower radioed that we were cleared to taxi. By noon we were cruising south at an altitude of forty-one thousand feet over Houston, Texas, on route to Mexico. That's when we entered a layer of cirrus clouds that quickly lowered our visibility. Our aircraft radar was not indicating any severe weather. Then air traffic control (ATC) warned us of a storm system ahead on our flight track and asked, "World 348, would you like a vector around the storm system?"

"Affirmative," I replied. As soon as I received a new heading, I maneuvered onto a slightly different path.

Wham! Without warning, severe turbulence hit the aircraft hard. Our DC-8 raced upward to an altitude of forty-three thousand feet, greatly reducing our airspeed. The automated emergency-warning system sprang to life. Its robotic voice called out, "Stall! Stall! Stall!"

After managing to level off the DC-8 above forty-three thousand feet, I responded to ATC: "We found the storm system. In fact, we're in the middle of it."

Before they could reply, we hit another pocket of bad air. Our DC-8 plummeted at an alarming rate of descent. As we plunged to an altitude of thirty-nine thousand feet, we transitioned from a stall warning to an over-speed warning.

The cockpit door had sprung open, and I could hear catering bins springing open and contents falling out and crashing to the galley floor just outside the cockpit door. I could hear Flight Attendants screaming. I had to devote my entire mental and physical being to gaining control of the DC-8, while Larry and Bill applied their expertise to areas I couldn't attend to. The DC-8 grappled against the viciousness of the storm, while its body creaked. The aircraft rolled side to side and pitched up and down.

After a terrifying period of zooming through the bank of thick clouds, we emerged into a brilliant blue sky and regained our assigned flight level of forty-one thousand feet.

"That'll wake you up," Bill commented. I said, "Nice flying, gentlemen." I then asked Bill to immediately check on the Flight Attendants to be sure no one was injured.

Larry exhaled. "Thanks," he said. "But to be honest, most of the time I kept observing what you were doing." I said, "Larry I could feel you on the control with me, it was a two-man effort to prevent an aircraft upset, Thank You."

Three hours later, after landing in Acapulco and closing out our post-flight checklist, I found the Flight Attendants near the front of the cabin. "How's everyone doing back here," I asked. "Anybody get hurt?"

Carol Papetti responded. "Shaken up," she said, "but not broken. Let me be the first to say we are glad it was you in the left seat today. You did a marvelous job, captain."

She and I walked to the aft of the long aircraft to examine the scene. Busted cans of tomato juice and other liquids had splashed about the galley. Overall though, not too bad, given the very challenging stretch of severe turbulence we had encountered. We had the cabin cleaned and had re-catered the galleys before loading our passengers for the return flight.

CHAPTER 76
1976

NEVER IN MY wildest dreams did I believe I would think fondly of the term *Mayday*. But when asked if I would be interested in doing all the flying for a television movie called *Mayday at 40,000 Feet!* I jumped at the chance. The film starred David Janssen, Don Meredith, Broderick Crawford, Lynda Day George, and many others. My job was to fly a B-727 through the frigid skies above Salt Lake City, Utah. It was an exhilarating experience, to say the least. In addition to the flying, I greatly enjoyed interacting off-set with Dandy Don Meredith. I found the former Dallas Cowboys quarterback and Monday Night Football commentator to be earnest and funny.

My professional life had been on a roll. In late February 1977, I was promoted to chief pilot of World Airways and check captain on the B-747, DC-8, and B-727. Ed Daly strived to set the pace in the industry or at least to keep up with the big boys who served as our competition. Every time he purchased another fleet of commercial jets or instituted stricter maintenance protocols, it confirmed that he was constantly trying to give us our best chance to achieve success. During that time, World Airways expanded its reach with enhanced commercial service throughout Southeast Asia, Mali, and Yemen. He purchased a fleet of DC-10-30 commercial jets to compete against the major airlines in the transcontinental market.

His expansion plans stretched World Airways' long-term debt beyond the $200 million range, and I stayed focused on doing my job well. My older son, Tim, now fourteen, was drawn to everything that had to do with flying an airplane. Brian, my younger son, was going on seven. I was careful not to influence either of my sons to pursue a piloting career. They each needed to set their own course in life.

Mr. Daly had been pushing for the deregulation of the airline industry to help level the playing field for small and mid-sized airlines. But after a two-month labor strike ended at World Airways, the larger airlines reduced their flat-rate, coast-to-coast airfares. The result was that the razor-thin profit margins of World Airways would disappear if a full-on price war were to develop.

In the face of cut-throat competition, he called a meeting with senior flight-operations personnel—me included—to make an announcement. "Gentlemen," he said, "it's time once again for World Airways to pioneer a great cause. We're going to help South Vietnamese people who fled their country during the Vietnam War. We're commencing Operation Boat People Lift. Beginning August 6, 1979, World Airways will airlift thousands of immigrant boat people who have been mired in refugee camps in Hong Kong, Singapore, Bangkok, and the Far East. It's good for them and good for us."

I asked about the destination for transporting Vietnamese refugees. He said the initial destination would be Travis Air Force Base, between San Francisco and Sacramento, California. "After the immigrants have been officially cleared," he continued, "they will be relocated throughout California, Minnesota, and Virginia. These people are literally dying to get themselves out of those godforsaken refugee camps, and they're eager to begin a new life in America."

The business of an airline company is to keep the planes flying with as many passengers as possible on each leg of every flight. I dove into my role of flying appreciative South Vietnamese refugees from several sites in the Far East first into Okinawa, Japan, and finally delivering them to Travis Air Force Base. It was grueling work, but I was thankful for it. The emotional strain of not being able to spend as much time with Ingrid and our boys was difficult. On more than one occasion, Ingrid brought the boys to Travis to see me during my brief turnaround times before flying back to Okinawa.

Ed Daly had been a boxer in his youth, and in late September 1979, I was with him when boxing champion Muhammad Ali arrived to discuss a charitable promotion. Daly was more interested in the art of the sport than the promotional deal that Ali was pitching, so the meeting went overtime. Then Ali realized he was going to miss his flight to Los Angeles for a planned evening event.

Ed said to Ali, "No problem. Warren will fly you from Oakland to Los Angeles in my Convair." I preferred to join Ali in the passenger cabin, so I called Captain Heering. I asked him to get his co-pilot and a flight attendant ready and to have the aircraft set to go when we arrived at the airport. I had a fabulous, ninety-minute trip conversing with Ali. The champ's engaging personality and his sleight-of-hand tricks were highly entertaining.

Warren, World Flight Attendant, and Muhammad Ali

Meanwhile, Ed Daly's often-risky business deals were paying off. Our new DC-10-30 fleet was becoming the workhorse of the company's aircraft fleet. In January 1980, I was conducting a training flight for a group of new DC-10 pilots. I received a radio call from the World Airways dispatch center asking me to land and taxi to a specific parking spot. After landing, I spotted Captain Ken Healy, who had hired me in 1965. He was striding toward the aircraft and, as he moved closer, I could see the somber expression on his face.

Captain Healy boarded the airplane and greeted me with a solemn handshake. "Warren," he said, "I'm very sorry to have to tell you this...."

A hollowed-out feeling wrenched in my gut. I asked, "What is it, Ken?"

He swallowed and replied, "Your father has passed away."

CHAPTER 77
Present Day

JUST BEFORE ONE o'clock in the morning, I yawned and stretched my arms and legs. I was still seated in my comfy chair in the study, and my three eldest grandchildren indicated they were not yet ready to call it quits.

"Maybe we should finish this last part of the story on another day," I suggested. Garrett, Kinnon, and Gentry shook their heads in unison. Garrett said, "Please don't leave now, Granddad, just a few more minutes."

I scratched my head and rubbed at my eyes. "I'll tell you what, we'll wrap this up in another thirty minutes." I shifted in my chair to offset a bit of numbness in my legs. "No matter where we finish off tonight," I said, "I love you all very much. Thanks for letting me share a little bit about my life. It has been wonderful, and I appreciate it very much."

CHAPTER 78
1983

U.S. PRESIDENT RONALD Reagan had been on the job for almost three years, and a renewed national optimism and financial boom spread nationwide. After having suffered through the late 1970's economic calamity, things looked promising. But World Airways had been forced to lay off one-third of its workforce to remain solvent. As airline deregulation unleashed a new wave of growth in the industry, I had been promoted to assistant vice-president of flight operations, then to vice-president of flight operations before becoming the senior vice-president of the flight operations division.

Our sons, Tim, eighteen, and Brian, now eleven, were flourishing. Tim's passion for aeronautics led him frequently to airport hangars, terminals, tarmacs, and maintenance facilities. Meanwhile, Brian's ability to befriend almost anyone was a remarkable gift. Due to my rather normal corporate lifestyle, Ingrid and I were enjoying plenty of time together. We had gone on family trips, best of all vacationing at our property in Idaho at Lolo Creek Ranch. The serene wilderness filled me with a sense of peace that I could not duplicate anywhere else. Whether we were fishing with the boys or cutting timber and clearing brush or trapping bears to relocate, I loved each moment.

On January 21, 1984, I received a telephone call from Mrs. Daly informing me that Ed had passed away earlier in the day. It was a shock, to say the least. Ingrid joined me on the couch in the living room and I shared the sad information with her.

"He was a swashbuckler and a pioneer businessman," I said quietly. "But more than that, Ed was a damn good man."

Ingrid nodded. "Yes, Mr. Daly is irreplaceable."

In the subsequent upheaval within the hierarchy of World Airways during two unpredictable years, I was promoted to the post of corporate executive vice-president in 1985. Later that year, a group of young executives formerly with Bain Capital group joined World Airways. They inserted a young CEO from Virginia to run the company. I surmised it was only a matter of time before our upstart leader would move the corporate headquarters to his former stomping grounds in Virginia.

Financially speaking, World Airways had weathered much of the storm for now, and in 1986 I began my return to flight operations. I was interviewing a large and diverse group of prospective new-hire crewmembers in Oakland, including women, minorities, and candidates from Puerto Rico.

One candidate was a dynamic firecracker of a woman, Nicole "Nikki" Manes. She was in her mid-twenties, with chestnut hair and a brazen personality. Raised primarily in Long Island, New York, Nikki's wit and excellent qualifications captured my attention. During Nikki's interview, Captain Steve Moates said, "Your FAA licensing is impressive for a pilot at such a young age. How have you managed to accomplish that so quickly?"

She had been flying regional routes and said she was bored with her current job. She had sent out more than one hundred resumes to the big airlines. She didn't lack ambition.

After we had covered her piloting background for Virginia Airlines, I said, "It sounds like you want to fly big jets. Is that correct?"

Nikki forced herself to hesitate while she gazed at me and Steve. Then she said, "I flew out here to join World Airways…today. If you gentlemen will just give me the chance to demonstrate my skill set in the flight simulator, I can assure you that it won't be a waste of your time."

I glanced at Steve. "Let's set her up for a simulator evaluation in Los Angeles. Nikki, does tomorrow evening work for you?"

The next night, after Steve and I had selected ten of the best applicants, we were at the simulator. Nikki slid into the left seat of the B-727 simulator cockpit. Steve returned from a bathroom break and was taken aback by her bravado. "Hey," he said, "hold on a minute! You're supposed to be in the right seat, not the left seat."

I wanted to see what Nikki could do. I told Steve, "She can do her stuff from the left seat. Let's get this session going."

We put her through an extensive, forty-five-minute evaluation ride. Just as several of her male counterparts had done, Nikki surpassed our demanding expectations.

After the session ended, I offered Nikki a job with World Airways. Steve and I flew back to the Oakland Airport and two weeks later, Nikki began her B-727 ground-school training. I took a great deal of pride in the hiring and training of the first female pilot to fly the B-727, DC-10, and B-747 for the company I cared so deeply about. World Airways had changed my life immeasurably and now it would for her, too.

Captain Nicole "Nikki" Manes

CHAPTER 79
1988

AT SOME POINT, I had heard a wise person remark that when times are good you should enjoy the moment and drink champagne. When things are not going well, a glass of tap water served at room temperature should suffice.

World Airways' long-term debt, resulting from the company's domestic route expansion, eventually led the CEO and top decision-makers to relocate corporate headquarters to Virginia. Luckily for me and my family, fate's positive momentum had once again redirected the path of my life in a healthy direction.

My career up to now had enabled me to fly all over the world. But the significant amount of time I spent away from our home in Dublin, California, prevented me from experiencing much of the day-to-day life of our older son, Tim. After he graduated from De La Salle High School in 1983 and matriculated at UCLA, I vowed to do things differently, in large part to support Brian's final three years at De La Salle High School. So, I stepped away from the executive side of the airline business and returned to the cockpit. This allowed me to do the work I loved while supporting Brian in his final years of high school and spending more time with Ingrid. In my new role, I was a pilot, instructor, and flight examiner. It felt wonderful to be on the correct track for my life and that of my family.

World Airways had landed a contract to transport rock stars, pop-music icons, their entourages, and their music equipment around the globe for the Amnesty International tour in 1988. The seventeen-city concert tour called attention to human rights atrocities worldwide and raised large amounts of money to help right the wrongs. World Airways had contracted with Amnesty International and Reebok to provide two DC-10s, one for the entertainers and their support people and the other for the groups' musical equipment and instruments.

Earlier that September, the Amnesty International consortium of music stars had performed in front of huge crowds in London, Paris, Budapest, Turin, and Barcelona. Now the recording artists, their bandmates and others were boarding my DC-10 at Barcelona International Airport in Spain. I stood just inside the jet's entryway with my first officer, Joe Bottero, as legendary performers climbed the boarding stairs. First-class seating had been reconfigured to accommodate one hundred thirty passengers and crew.

Joe was awestruck. "Captain Vest," he said, "that's The Boss (Bruce Springsteen) and his lady, Patti Scialfa. He must have at least thirty-five members of his group coming up the stairs behind him."

I smiled at Bruce Springsteen and said hello as his group moved down the aisle to claim their seats. Next came the renowned E Street Band saxophonist, Clarence Clemons, who was followed by drummer Max Weinberg.

Max shook hands with Joe and then me. "Hello captain, I'm Max, and I'm hoping to spend a lot of time with you guys in the cockpit. I'm interested in learning all I can about flying one of these jumbo jets!"

I said, "That's perfect because I'd like to learn a little about playing the drums."

Next up was Gordon Sumner, more widely known as Sting. At the entryway, he paused and said, "Hello, Captain Vest. Everybody I've talked to has told me you're the best. Is that right?"

Caught off-guard, I started to reply but Joe spoke on my behalf. "Yes, Sting," he said. "Warren sets the bar very high, and the rest of us are right with him. You've got nothing to worry about."

Sting's entourage followed him aboard. Next came Peter Gabriel. After we exchanged pleasantries, and after Gabriel's posse followed him down the main aisle, I told Joe, "That's my son Brian's favorite artist. He loves that man's music, *big time*."

"Look at you, Captain Vest," Joe said. "I had no idea that you even knew that was Peter Gabriel."

Immediately I was shaking hands with Tracy Chapman, who entered the airplane with a small group. Then Youssou N'Dour, the influential singer-songwriter from Senegal, entered the cabin and greeted us with a dazzling smile and a warm clasping of hands.

Lastly, the dozen or so organizers and producers from Amnesty International and Reebok worked their way down the aisle to find their seats.

After Joe and I finished our pre-flight checklist, he said, "This might be the only time in our lives that we'll get to fly rock stars all over and get to watch them perform in front of thousands of people in Costa Rica, Toronto, Montreal, Japan, and every other destination on our agenda. It's going to be a bit odd, having to lay over in all the first-class hotels along the way, especially in light of the fact that we're raising awareness for Amnesty International Human Rights Now."

"That's a good point," I said. "But if we handle our end of the bargain, we're helping the cause and that's what counts. By the way, I've heard a rumor about a special concert being squeezed into Oakland between the stops in Los Angeles and Tokyo."

A few days later, after performances in Costa Rica in front of thousands of people, I flew the DC-10 from Central America to Toronto, Canada. As we cruised at forty-one thousand feet, Max Weinberg, the E Street Band's drummer, made himself at home in the cockpit. His sincere interest in piloting was plain to see. He asked plenty of questions, including "Have you ever seen a UFO when you're up in the air this high up?"

I shrugged. "If I had, I wouldn't tell you about it."

Max laughed. "Captain Vest, if you had to list the three most important factors that make an outstanding pilot, what would they be?"

Joe began to respond, but Max politely cut him off. "For the captain, if you don't mind please?"

I had to think about this one. "Complete confidence in your abilities," I began. "Perfect preparation every time. And total trust in your cockpit crew and in-flight personnel."

"Makes sense," Max said. "It's sort of like being a member of a world-famous band. You've got to nail it every single time."

Our conversation continued for the next few hours. Max mentioned that Clarence Clemons had created a football pool so people could wager each week on the outcome of NFL games. He also was keeping people energized during the long flight with a rowdy, cash-only game of dice. Rock stars had their quirks like everybody else.

The following night in Toronto, I was standing backstage during the raucous concert at the Maple Leaf Gardens indoor arena. Some fifteen thousand screaming fans celebrated non-stop during the show. I experienced an amazing, tingling sensation throughout my head and body. It was unreal and intoxicating. The god-like feeling that swelled within me from the adulation coming from the crowd struck me like a thunderclap. I reeled slightly as I watched Bruce Springsteen take control of the audience, which kept begging him for more.

A thought skipped through my mind, then spun back and hit me again to ensure that my brain recognized its importance. I had been fortunate up to this moment, and under no circumstances would I take my life for granted.

I snapped out of my trance when The Boss began his next song. I lost myself in the sheer joy and pleasure of the night. Springsteen was belting out, "Born in the U.S.A. . . . I was born in the U. S. A.!"

During the next few weeks, I had the chance to observe and appreciate the interesting facets of the performers' personalities. The musicians on tour possessed such high-caliber talent that they reminded me of top professional athletes. The artists' ability to perform in front of their demanding fans required insane confidence and an unbelievable level of charisma.

During the two weeks of touring following the stop in Toronto, performances in Montreal, Philadelphia, Los Angeles, and Oakland were wonderful. Then there was a great concert in Tokyo. However, the scope of the show in New Delhi, at the Jawaharlal Nehru Stadium surrounded by one hundred thousand people, was breathtaking. The undulating sea of one hundred thousand humans gyrating and singing along with Tracy Chapman, Sting, Peter Gabriel, the Boss, Youssou N'Dour, and musical legend Ravi Shankar, caused me to feel as if I had somehow been teleported to another planet. The huge stadium vibrated and shifted with each change of direction of the multitude of people. I relished each new tune with them.

Brian's sixteenth birthday was coming up on October 4, so I asked to be replaced by another World Airways pilot for the remaining two weeks of the tour. Before I flew home from Athens, Greece, Peter Gabriel presented me with a customized birthday greeting for Brian. The gift was a set of autographed pictures of The

Boss and Patti, Sting, Tracy Chapman, Youssou, and Peter. It was a very thoughtful gesture.

CHAPTER 80
2002

ON A RATHER balmy morning at the World Airways headquarters building in Peachtree City, Georgia, I was meeting with CEO Hollis Harris. At the end of a senior staff meeting, he asked me to stay.

We sat kitty-corner from each other at his office desk, and I admired his strong facial features and salt-and-pepper hair. I mused once again that Hollis might have become president of the United States if he had wanted to attain that goal. He possessed a disarming southern charm and he was spectacularly intelligent. His powerful counterparts not only respected him greatly, but they also trusted him in every regard.

Hollis placed his reading glasses on the desk, then rubbed his eyes. "It has been almost thirteen months since the disaster of 9-11, Warren, and in my years as president of Delta, and head of Continental and Air Canada, I've never seen anything like it. The fallout in our industry has been worse than I anticipated. Without having you by my side since I joined World Airways in 1999, things would have been even more difficult for me. I wanted to let you know how much I appreciate everything you've done for this company."

Before I replied, I pledged silently that I would run through a wall for this man. Then I answered. "I appreciate it very much, Hollis, but you're giving me too much credit. Everybody at World, including me, knows you are the reason the company is finally profitable again. It's been a wonderful experience serving under you."

Hollis nodded but remained silent. I continued, "You know, a few years ago when the Bain people departed the scene and Jack Brown and I hired Randy Martinez to fill the crew resource manager spot, that was a good choice."

"Martinez is very sharp," Hollis said. "I could see him running the company someday soon. Sorry for interrupting you, Warren."

"No bother," I said. "When I was asked by Mr. Russell Ray, CEO and senior board member, to return to management and serve as senior vice-president of the Operations Group and acting COO, I will *never* forget how dire our situation was."

Hollis paid me another compliment. "Rare is the airline pilot who can effectively transition to managing flight ops, ground ops, and maintenance personnel."

Hollis continued. "I'm only four years older than you, Warren. Do you mind if I ask you something?"

"Sure, anything."

He said, "You've had a legendary career at World, and even more so as a pilot. Tell me, how much longer do you think you will be flying?"

He was paying me yet another compliment, and I was overwhelmed, but the question he added at the end surprised me.

"Hollis," I replied, "that's a fair question. But truth be told, I only know one way to answer it. Once a pilot begins to seriously think about retirement, it's probably time to turn in their wings. For me, retirement is not on my mind while we are working to return World back to financial stability."

Hollis cracked a smile. "You're right, Warren, and I'm sorry that I asked. How about we change the subject to business? I've had more than enough time to review our financials today." Then he stopped and rubbed his eyes again. He surprised me when he suggested we give the spreadsheets a rest. Instead, he wanted to hear more about my long history with World Airlines and the many changes I'd witnessed in the industry.

"Do I remember correctly that you certified our first female pilot, Nikki Manes, to fly the DC-10 in 1993?" he asked. "Yes, that was a huge advance for World," I said. "Nikki was a phenomenal pilot, and our ranks were becoming diverse. It wasn't a boys' club any longer."

Then I started thinking about how my professional world had overlapped with my private world. My older son, Tim, had been flying for years. On a flight in 1997, Tim and I were on flight tracks that intersected. I wasn't sure if Hollis knew this story.

"I was at forty-one thousand feet, flying an MD-11 from Mobile, Alabama, to London. Tim was flying a DC-8 westbound from Moscow to Miami, transporting a load of racehorses at twenty-eight thousand feet. We established radio contact and were able to make visual contact off the coast of Ireland."

Hollis folded his hands behind his head and closed his eyes. I wasn't sure if he was exhausted or simply losing himself in aircraft-industry lore. He said, "Didn't you and Tim happen to be in Newfoundland at the same time? I seem to recall that you met for ice cream before each of you flew off on your separate flights."

"That was October 1997," I said. "And what a treat it was. It's amazing how much technology has changed the airline industry since I began flying more than forty years ago. I still can't get over the fact that I did all of my MD-11 training in a simulator and none of it in the aircraft before I flew the MD-11 from Los Angeles to Honolulu. Then, in Hawaii, I got certified by the FAA as an MD-11 check pilot on the aircraft after my very first flight."

Hollis grinned, but he didn't open his eyes. "It's the wave of the future," he said. "and it's cheaper to train pilots in those new, high-tech sims."

My memories returned to family. "I'll never forget the Christmas season of '97 when my son Brian got antsy to have a new Volvo," I said. "He decided to order one. I met him in Sweden to pick it up, and we spent several days together. It was a special time for the two of us. Another time, during the 2001 Indonesian Hajj, Ingrid and Brian met me in Borneo and we toured the rain forests together. At the end of the Hajj, we enjoyed a vacation in Bali before returning to California. That was also a very nice time for us."

"Family." That was the only word Hollis uttered. He was drifting off into his customary, early-afternoon, Saturday nap. I quietly stood up and returned to my office.

A few minutes later, the phone on my desk rang several times. I listened to Ingrid's sad voice as she told me my mother had passed away. She would have been ninety-three in three months.

I told Ingrid how much I loved her, then broke the phone connection. I put my shaking hands up to my face and I wept like never before.

CHAPTER 81
2005

LESS THAN TWO months from my seventieth birthday, I was waiting on the ramp prior to takeoff at the airport in Kuwait. Captain Scott Gibson was serving as my first officer and we hadn't yet heard from maintenance personnel whether the MD-11's number-one engine had been secured in a non-rotating state.

Two weeks earlier, Captain James Reese and I had agreed to retire on the same day. We had put in more than eighty years of combined service to World Airways. We would soon step aside as the two most senior captains in the company, thereby paving the way for the next generation of pilots to ascend.

Back in Kuwait, Scott Gibson asked, "When you got word of this bird strike engine problem, how did you end up getting here?"

He knew the situation in Iraq and Kuwait made it impossible for us to change out a damaged engine. Flight ops had asked me to position myself to Kuwait so I could fly the MD-11 on only two engines to Frankfurt, Germany, where the damaged engine could be replaced.

"We have a very small select group of check captains trained to perform this type of engine-out ferry flight," I told Scott. "I was the only one available to immediately position from Atlanta to Kuwait."

"How many of these engine-out flights have you made during your career?" he asked.

"I've done such flights on the B-707, B-727, B-747, and the DC-8," I said. "But today will be my first one on the MD-11." I extracted my laminated pilot's license from my wallet to show Scott my airplane certifications: DC-3, DC-6, DC-7, DC-8, DC-10, CV-240, CV-340, CV-440, B-707, B-720, B-727, B-747, and MD-11. The certifications represented nearly twenty-seven thousand hours in flight.

Scott whistled. "That's more than three full years in the air. Truly amazing."

Our maintenance personnel confirmed that our number one engine was secured in a none-rotating state and we were cleared to start engines number two and three.

We obtained Air Traffic Control clearance to Frankfurt and engine start clearance.

A few moments later the tower cleared us for departure to Frankfurt, Germany. We would lift off from Kuwait with the aircraft's number one engine inoperable. I would fly the MD-11 wide-body jet airliner using only two engines.

We sped down the runway and lifted off without any unanticipated malfunctions. We climbed to our assigned flight level of twenty-eight thousand feet for the five-hour journey northwest to Germany.

Scott asked about my sons. At that time, Tim was a captain with Jet Blue. My younger son, Brian, was a successful businessman. Ingrid and I couldn't have been prouder of them.

After flying over Munich, we started our descent into Frankfurt. I approached the landing strip for the last time as a commercial airline pilot and landed the MD-11 smoothly using just two engines. I taxied to the Lufthansa maintenance facility where the damaged engine would be replaced.

In a sincere gesture of respect for my having completed my airline career, Scott remained in his seat. He waited for me to make the first move. It took me a moment to corral my wits. A fleeting image of Ingrid in her beautiful youth skipped through my mind. I recalled the fateful day in 1960 when my aircraft had engine trouble and I met my future wife for the first time *at this very airport.*

Eventually, I was ready to leave the cockpit. I would retire on March 31 and it would take a while for me to adjust to that status. I smiled before rising from the left seat and standing up in the cockpit.

I shook hands with Scott. He was beaming as he kept saying, "Congratulations!" He let me know how deeply honored he was to have worked with me on my final flight.

Before I exited the cockpit for the last time, Scott asked, "Will you be taking part in the thirty-year anniversary of the Vietnam Baby Lift?"

His question caught me off guard. "I hope so," I told him. "It's going to be a historic event."

The reunion was coming up. Ingrid had undergone emergency hip surgery and was recovering. I didn't feel that I should leave her to attend the event. But our sons convinced me that our family could take care of her. They very much wanted me to participate in the overseas portion of the Vietnam Baby Lift Reunion.

In a hurried rush, Tim shoehorned me into the passenger seat of his Cessna and flew me to the Oakland Airport. He had obtained prior clearance so he could land quickly. He taxied across the tarmac and parked his tiny Cessna beside the gigantic MD-11.

Chairman of the Board Ron Fogleman and wife Miss Jane; Warren Vest; CEO Randy Martinez and wife Jennifer; and Mr. Hollis L. Harris (ex-CEO)

I hustled onboard the jumbo jet moments before it departed for Taipei. I was cheerfully greeted by a host of my longtime friends and colleagues from World Airways. More than two dozen now-grown Vietnamese orphans who our company had saved thirty years earlier were joining us on the flight.

It was humbling and heartwarming, not only to be in the company of friends from the airline industry but also to see the smiling faces of the orphans. They had built successful lives in America after escaping the wrath of the communist Vietnamese. Many of them had earned college degrees and had gone on to become engineers, doctors, lawyers, teachers, and business owners.

During the fifteen-hour flight from Oakland to Taipei, I spent several hours visiting with my former peers, Captain Healy and Captain Keating. Both men would soon turn ninety, and I would forever be thankful that I had been able to serve with them.

Warren and Ken Healy

The three of us laughed freely as we told stories about the charitable works of the late Ed Daly. We also enjoyed recounting his negotiating tirades, which added to his bigger-than-life personality. After a night of rest in Taipei, we flew into Saigon, which had been renamed Ho Chi Minh City. The reunion's welcoming reception was glorious, featuring live music and dancing. During the evening, the orphans gave heartfelt speeches.

The following day, we cruised on the Saigon River on board a splendid wooden vessel. During

Mr. Hollis Harris

the river cruise, I spent time with my friend and retired World Airways CEO, Hollis Harris. Randy Martinez, who was part of the reunion, had succeeded Hollis as CEO.

Hollis and I reminisced about our good times working together in the corporate headquarters in Virginia and Georgia, and the multitude of vital business decisions we had made back then.

I experienced my most intense emotions when our party visited an orphanage housing the most unfortunate and despondent children in Saigon. Only then did I understand what this reunion journey was truly all about. At the orphanage I was hit with a bout of despair for the abandoned, deformed, disabled, and mentally handicapped Vietnamese children lying on their beds. I watched the stunned and incredibly thankful grown-up orphans whom our company had saved three decades earlier. They toured the facility in awestruck silence.

I stood beside the bed of a skinny, ten-year-old boy. His body was twisted, and he moaned quietly while staring at the ceiling.

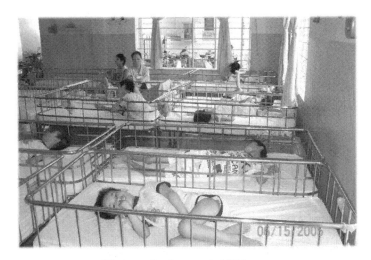

Vietnam Orphanage in 2005

**World Airways CEO Randy Martinez
Presenting a Check to the Orphanage**

An attractive, female orphan whom World Airways had rescued thirty years earlier came up to his bed. She and I gazed at the child, and she touched my shoulder. "That could have been me, Mr. Vest," she said. "Thank God for the wonderful people of World Airways. Believe me, not a single day goes by when I don't give thanks. When we get back to California, the first thing I'm going to do is kiss the ground of the U.S.A.

"My mother was Vietnamese," she continued, "but my father was a member of the U.S. military. If the North Vietnamese had gotten their hands on me, they might have drowned me in the river and killed my mother. They called babies like me *half-and-halves*. I was so lucky to get out of here alive."

I asked how it came about that she was able to escape. She had tears in her eyes as she withdrew the loop of her necklace. A Christian pendant was hanging on the delicate chain. She patted it once, then wiped her eyes. "I'm a believer in Christ," she said.

"Me too," I told her.

"Sometimes," she continued, "I think there might be *more* to all of this. There must be something different that helps us navigate through this crazy world and make it to the next day in one piece."

"Do you think it might be fate?" I asked.

She smiled. "Fate and destiny? Hmm."

We exited the orphanage and boarded the charter bus. While riding back to our hotel, my thoughts returned to Ingrid and I contemplated the next phase of our life together.

CHAPTER 82
Present Day

SIX WEEKS AFTER celebrating my eighty-third birthday, I enjoy a light breakfast with Ingrid. Then I get in the shower and turn the water temperature to hot. After that, dressed in my bathrobe and slippers, I wipe condensation off the bathroom mirror and stare at a reflection of my face.

Even though I'm now considered to be an old man, and on most days my creaking body concurs with that assessment, on this day I feel like there's an extra bounce in my step.

Thirteen years have passed since I flew my last flight for World Airways. Standing here looking at myself, it's difficult to fathom that hard, cold fact. I did my best to stave off life's ticking clock during much of my lifetime. I played sports or exercised on a regular basis; and regardless of the food or drink, I never went overboard.

In March 2014, when Captain Jeff Gandin called me to say our beloved World Airways was ceasing operations permanently, it sent me into a temporary depression. I never expected to outlive the company that changed my life forever. My working life was full of change, learning, challenge, adventure, and relationships. I have found it difficult to morph into full-time retirement. Making things even more difficult has been the inevitable deaths of some dear friends of mine.

I'm standing here musing, and suddenly Ingrid is tapping on the bathroom door. "The boys will be here soon, Honey," she says. "Time for you to get moving."

"Okay, my love. Will do."

I get back to shaving while my brain clicks through images of many of the still-living or deceased colleagues and family members I have known. My mother and father, and my brother, Lendol, now seventy-one years old, and my former classmate from back home, Paul Triplett. My Australian buddy, Peter Norrie; and Uncle Bus and Aunt Edie, who picked me up in Washington, D.C., after I returned from my unexpected, worldly adventure. Uncle Glenn and Aunt Mary in Kansas City, who gave me a place to live while I searched for a way to pursue my desired future. Uncle Glenn convinced me that taking a job bucking rivets into airplane wings would be the first step toward a career as a pilot.

I think about my buddies from the Air Force and those from many years of commercial aviation. There was my lifelong friend, Art Dickinson, from cadet training and beyond. Bill Hardenstine has been a friend and associate of both Ingrid and me for sixty years. My buddy Douglas "Pete" Peterson went on to become a congressman and U.S. Ambassador to Vietnam after being a POW near Hanoi. I recall excellent navigator Terry Gautsch and our series of fun times centered around the House of Pilots in New Jersey. There were Captains Henry Holt, Don Treichler, Jim Reese, Bob Franklin, and Andre Dressler of World Airways, and many more. It is humbling to recall all the names, faces, and great times together.

I inhale deeply and let out lengthy exhales before leaving the bathroom and walking to our bedroom to get dressed.

It's now an hour later. I kiss Ingrid goodbye and confess my love for her once again. I put on my baseball cap and stepped out the front door. It warms my heart knowing that Ingrid has stood by me for fifty-five years, through good and bad. I amble down the front walkway and climb into the front passenger seat of Tim's car. It's a beautiful, sunny day.

Tim is driving and Brian is sitting in the back seat. I thank them for setting up today's event, which is like a dream come true. "I love you guys," I say to them.

We drive northbound on Highway 680 for about thirty minutes, until Tim parks in the small lot adjacent to the modest Buchanan Field Airport in Concord, California. I see an old Piper Cub speeding down the runway and watch it veer away into the sky.

"This is for you, Dad," Brian says. Tim smiles and says, "It will be great to watch you fly again. Enjoy it, Dad."

We walked toward the entry gate. Through the chain-link fence, I see a trio of well-maintained WWII bombers on the tarmac. Fans of the vintage aircraft stop to examine their timeless features and powerful beauty.

I soak up the emotions. Out on the tarmac, I spot the impressive B-17 Flying Fortress and the equally large outline of a B-24 Liberator nearby.

I stop for a moment to catch my breath. Finally, I remember the feeling from sixty-one years earlier that comes rushing to the surface. I mentally and physically prepare myself to fly one last time.

I spot Tim and Brian standing beneath the nose cone of the historic and beautiful B-25 Mitchell Bomber. They are taking pictures of the B-25 and talking to the young pilot who will join me in the cockpit during my flight. I head in their direction.

I feel as if I'm being pulled back through the portals of time. As I draw nearer to the aircraft, I feel layers of my accumulated years peel away from my psyche. The invigorating feeling causes me to quicken my pace.

I can hear the expert voice of my Air Force B-25 flight instructor from sixty-one years in the past. He is imparting his wisdom to me as if it were only yesterday.

I reach the B-25 and my sons introduce me to the youthful pilot. He and I shake hands, and he says, "It's a pleasure to meet you, Warren, and it's a great day to fly."

"Yes, it is," I reply.

I walk around and underneath the B-25 while examining its sturdy design. Eventually, I bid adieu to Tim and Brian before ascending the narrow stairwell to join the pilot in the vintage cockpit. He is sitting in the left seat, and I take my place on the right.